PATHWAYS

SECOND EDITION

Reading, Writing, and Critical Thinking

MARI VARGO

LAURIE BLASS

NATIONAL
GEOGRAPHIC
LEARNING

Australia • Brazil • Mexico • Singapore • United Kingdom • United States

NATIONAL GEOGRAPHIC
L E A R N I N G

Pathways
Reading, Writing, and Critical Thinking 3,
Second Edition

Mari Vargo and Laurie Blass

Publisher: Andrew Robinson

Executive Editor: Sean Bermingham

Development Editor: Melissa Pang

Director of Global Marketing: Ian Martin

Product Marketing Manager: Tracy Bailie

Media Researcher: Leila Hishmeh

Senior IP Analyst: Alexandra Ricciardi

IP Project Manager: Carissa Poweleit

Senior Director of Production: Michael Burggren

Senior Production Controller: Tan Jin Hock

Manufacturing Planner: Mary Beth Hennebury

Art Director: Brenda Carmichael

Compositor: MPS North America LLC

Cover Photo: A rock moves across the Racetrack Playa in California's Death Valley National Park: © KiskaMedia/iStock/Getty Images

For product information and technology assistance, contact us at
Cengage Learning Customer & Sales Support, cengage.com/contact
For permission to use material from this text or product,
submit all requests online at **cengage.com/permissions**
Further permissions questions can be emailed to
permissionrequest@cengage.com

Student Book:
ISBN-13: 978-1-337-40779-3

Student Book with Online Workbook:
ISBN-13: 978-1-337-62512-8

National Geographic Learning
20 Channel Center Street
Boston, MA 02210
USA

National Geographic Learning, a Cengage Learning Company, has a mission to bring the world to the classroom and the classroom to life. With our English language programs, students learn about their world by experiencing it. Through our partnerships with National Geographic and TED Talks, they develop the language and skills they need to be successful global citizens and leaders.

Locate your local office at **international.cengage.com/region**

Visit National Geographic Learning online at **NGL.Cengage.com/ELT**
Visit our corporate website at **www.cengage.com**

Printed in Mexico
Quad / Graphics México.

Print Number: 03   Print Year: 2019

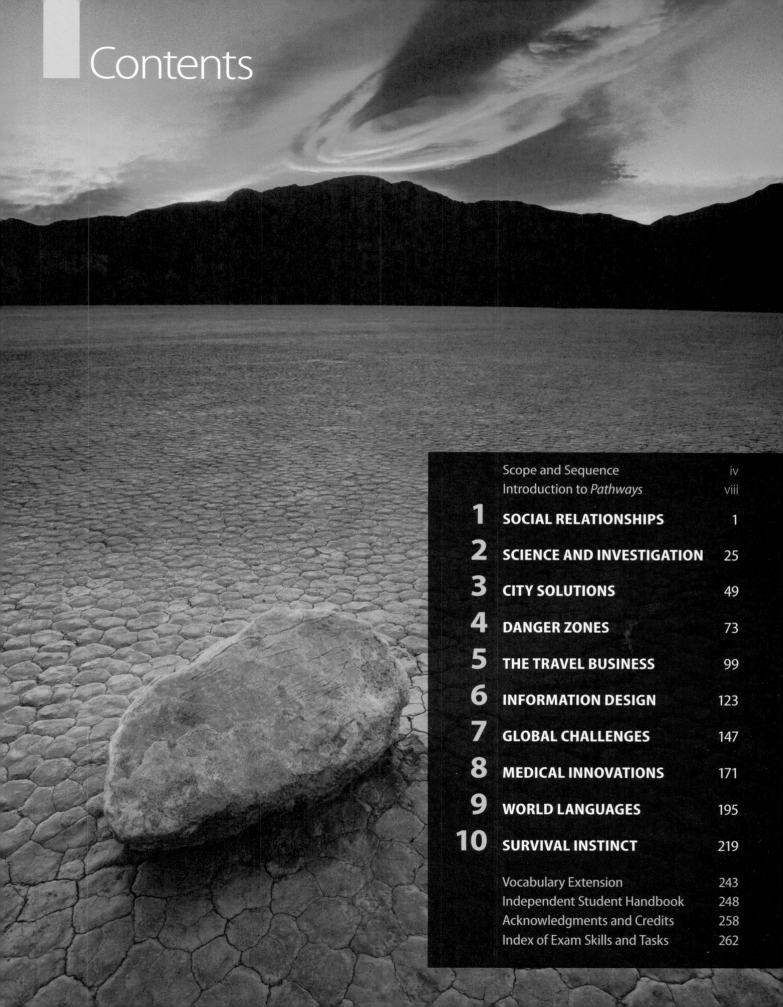

Contents

Scope and Sequence

Critical Thinking	Writing	Vocabulary Extension
Focus Analyzing Evidence Evaluating Evidence, Reflecting, Synthesizing	**Skill Focus** Writing Body Paragraphs **Language for Writing** Making Comparisons **Writing Goal** Writing two body paragraphs comparing animal and human behavior	**Word Link** *pre-*
Focus Analyzing Levels of Certainty Evaluating, Synthesizing	**Skill Focus** Writing a Summary **Language for Writing** Paraphrasing **Writing Goal** Writing two summaries	**Word Link** *-ist*
Focus Analyzing Quotes Justifying Your Opinion, Evaluating, Synthesizing	**Skill Focus** Writing Introductory and Concluding Paragraphs **Language for Writing** Using the Simple Past and the Present Perfect **Writing Goal** Writing a problem-solution essay about how a city solved a problem it faced	**Word Partners** Expressions with *income*
Focus Inferring Applying, Analyzing Evidence	**Skill Focus** Writing a Process Essay **Language for Writing** Using Parallel Structures **Writing Goal** Writing a process essay about how people can prepare for a natural hazard	**Word Forms** Changing Nouns and Adjectives to Verbs with *-en*
Focus Evaluating Arguments Synthesizing, Evaluating/ Justifying	**Skill Focus** Writing a Cause-Effect Essay **Language for Writing** Using *if* ... , *(then)* ... **Writing Goal** Writing a cause-effect essay about the positive and negative effects of tourism on a place	**Word Forms** Adjectives and Nouns ending in *-ive*

Scope and Sequence

Critical Thinking	Writing	Vocabulary Extension
Focus Evaluating Visual Data Evaluating Infographics, Applying, Synthesizing	**Skill Focus** Writing a Persuasive Essay **Language for Writing** Describing Visual Information **Writing Goal** Writing a persuasive essay and using visual data to support arguments	**Word Link** *mis-*
Focus Inferring Attitude Evaluating	**Skill Focus** Writing an Opinion Essay **Language for Writing** Using Adjective Clauses **Writing Goal** Writing an opinion essay about the best way to ensure a sustainable future	**Word Partners** Expressions with *cut*
Focus Inferring Purpose Reflecting, Applying, Synthesizing	**Skill Focus** Evaluating Information Online **Language for Writing** Introduction to Quoting and Citing Sources **Writing Goal** Writing a research-based essay about a medical innovation and its significance	**Word Partners** Antonyms
Focus Applying Ideas Synthesizing, Analyzing Arguments	**Skill Focus** Planning an Essay Using a T-Chart **Language for Writing** Presenting Counterarguments **Writing Goal** Writing a persuasive essay about whether everyone in the world should speak the same language	**Word Partners** adjective + *language*
Focus Interpreting Figurative Language Reflecting, Applying, Synthesizing	**Skill Focus** Writing a Descriptive Narrative Essay **Language for Writing** Using Past Forms for Narratives **Writing Goal** Writing a narrative essay about someone who survived a dangerous situation	**Word Forms** Adjectives ending in *-ed* and *-ing*

The Pathway to Academic Readiness

Pathways Reading, Writing, and Critical Thinking, Second Edition uses National Geographic stories, photos, video, and infographics to bring the world to the classroom. Authentic, relevant content and carefully sequenced lessons engage learners while equipping them with the skills needed for academic success. Each level of the second edition features **NEW** and **UPDATED** content.

Academic skills are clearly ▶ labeled at the beginning of each unit.

ACADEMIC SKILLS

READING   Identifying arguments and counterarguments
WRITING   Writing a persuasive essay
GRAMMAR   Describing visual information
CRITICAL THINKING   Evaluating visual data

NEW AND UPDATED ▶ reading passages incorporate a variety of text types, charts, and infographics to inform and inspire learners.

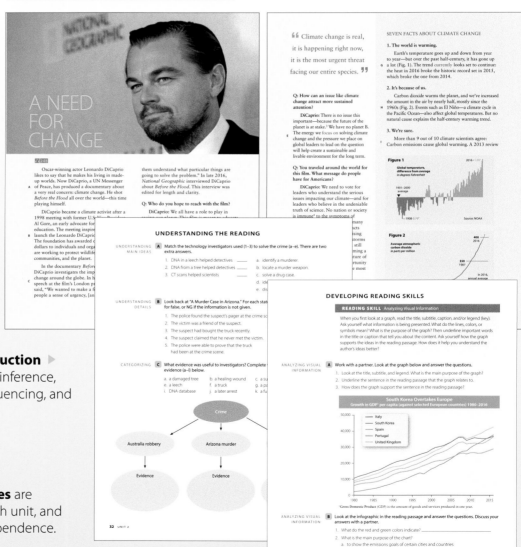

Explicit reading skill instruction ▶ includes main ideas, details, inference, prediction, note-taking, sequencing, and vocabulary development.

▼ **Critical thinking activities** are integrated throughout each unit, and help develop learner independence.

CRITICAL THINKING   A writer may **quote** an expert to support an idea presented in an article. When you read a quote from an expert, ask yourself: Which of the writer's main or supporting ideas does the quote support?

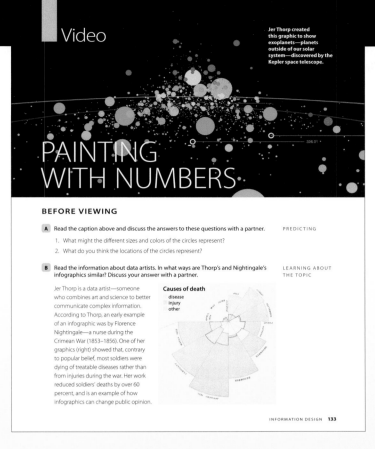

Video

Jer Thorp created this graphic to show exoplanets—planets outside of our solar system—discovered by the Kepler space telescope.

PAINTING WITH NUMBERS

BEFORE VIEWING

A Read the caption above and discuss the answers to these questions with a partner.

PREDICTING

1. What might the different sizes and colors of the circles represent?
2. What do you think the locations of the circles represent?

B Read the information about data artists. In what ways are Thorp's and Nightingale's infographics similar? Discuss your answer with a partner.

LEARNING ABOUT THE TOPIC

Jer Thorp is a data artist—someone who combines art and science to better communicate complex information. According to Thorp, an early example of an infographic was by Florence Nightingale—a nurse during the Crimean War (1853–1856). One of her graphics (right) showed that, contrary to popular belief, most soldiers were dying of treatable diseases rather than from injuries during the war. Her work reduced soldiers' deaths by over 60 percent, and is an example of how infographics can change public opinion.

Causes of death
- disease
- injury
- other

INFORMATION DESIGN **133**

◀ **NEW AND UPDATED** *Video* sections use National Geographic video clips to provide a bridge between Readings 1 and 2, and to give learners ideas and language for the unit's writing task.

◀ **NEW** An additional short reading passage provides integrated skills practice.

Reading 1

PREPARING TO READ

BUILDING VOCABULARY

A The words in blue below are used in Reading 1. Read the sentences. Then match the correct form of each word to its definition.

Good journalists aim to present the news in an **objective** manner without inserting their own opinions into their reports.

People with poor **vision** correct their eyesight by wearing glasses or contact lenses.

In order to make their products seem more effective, companies might **deliberately** include **misleading** information in their advertisements.

One **downside** to using information from the Internet is that the source may not be reliable.

Most people have strong opinions about whale hunting. Not many people are **neutral** about the issue.

When writing a report, it's important to check that the points make sense and don't contain **faulty** logic.

1. _____ (n) a disadvantage
2. _____ (adv) on purpose or intentionally
3. _____ (n) the ability to see
4. _____ (adj) containing mistakes; inaccurate
5. _____ (adj) based on facts, not personal bias
6. _____ (adj) not having an opinion about something
7. _____ (adj) making someone believe something that is not true

USING VOCABULARY

B Discuss these questions with a partner.

1. What do you think are the **downsides** to using information from the Internet?
2. What kinds of **misleading** information have you seen online?

BRAINSTORMING

C What are some benefits of infographics for people working in business, education, or journalism? Discuss with a partner.

PREDICTING

D Skim the first sentence of each paragraph in the reading passage. What do you think the passage is about? Check your idea as you read.

a. the purposes of different types of infographics
b. the history of data visualization
c. the pros and cons of using infographics

126 UNIT 6

▲ **Key academic and thematic vocabulary** is practiced, and expanded throughout each unit.

VOCABULARY EXTENSION UNIT 1

WORD LINK *pre-*

Words that begin with the prefix *pre-* mean "before in time." For example, *previously* means "before the time period that you are talking about." *Pre-* can be added to some common root words. For example, *preview* means "to see a part of something before watching the whole thing."

Complete each sentence with the words below. One word is extra.

| predict | prepare | preschool | prevent | preview | previous |

1. It is a good idea to _____ some slides before giving a presentation.
2. Scientists are developing apps that can _____ a person's behavior better than a human can. For example, the app can tell if a customer will buy a product again.
3. For many entry-level jobs, no _____ experience is required.
4. To _____ conflict in a workplace, try to avoid aggressive behavior with your co-workers.
5. Movie companies often upload a short video online to give people a _____ of an upcoming movie and get them excited about it.

VOCABULARY EXTENSION UNIT 2

WORD LINK *-ist*

Some nouns that end in *-ist* can refer to someone who works in a specific academic or professional field. An *archaeologist*, for example, works in the field of archaeology. In general, for words ending in a vowel or *-y*, drop the vowel or *-y* and add *-ist*.

Complete each sentence with the correct noun form of the underlined word.

1. Someone who writes <u>novels</u> is a _____ .
2. Someone who produces <u>art</u> is an _____ .
3. Someone who looks at how the <u>economy</u> works is an _____ .
4. Someone who provides <u>therapy</u> to other people is a _____ .
5. Someone who plays the <u>piano</u> as a job is a _____ .

VOCABULARY EXTENSION **243**

▲ **NEW Vocabulary extension activities** cover word forms, word webs, collocations, affixes, and more, to boost learners' reading and writing fluency.

Writing Skills Practice

Pathways' approach to writing guides students through the writing process and develops learners' confidence in planning, drafting, revising, and editing.

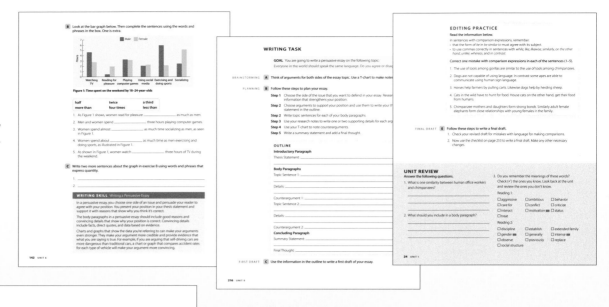

Writing Goals and *Language for Writing* ▶ sections provide the focus and scaffolding needed for learners to become successful writers.

WRITING TASK

GOAL You are going to write a persuasive essay on the following topic: Everyone in the world should speak the same language. Do you agree or disa...

LANGUAGE FOR WRITING Presenting Counterarguments

Arguments in a persuasive essay are more convincing and balanced when write... present and then refute the counterarguments—the arguments on the other si... of the issue. Writers introduce counterarguments using **concession words and phrases** such as *while*, *even though*, and *although*.

COUNTERARGUMENT

***While** flying around the world to record speakers of disappearing languages may... expensive, protecting the valuable knowledge these languages contain is worth it.*

WRITER'S ARGUMENT

In addition, writers often use modals such as *may*, *might*, and *could* when presenting counterarguments to show that these arguments are weaker—less likely or certain—than their own arguments. Writers sometimes also present the... own arguments with modals such as *must*, *have to*, and *should* to show that their arguments are stronger.

WEAKER

*While saving endangered languages **may** preserve some cultural or scientific information, we **must not** discourage children from learning the dominant language of their region.*

STRONGER

UPDATED Revising ▶ **Practice** sections incorporate realistic model paragraphs and help learners refine their writing.

▼ An **online workbook**, powered by MyELT, includes video clips and automatically graded activities for learners to practice the skills taught in the Student Books.

NEW Guided online writing ▶ **practice** provides reinforcement and consolidation of language skills, helping learners to become stronger and more confident writers.

SOCIAL RELATIONSHIPS 1

Polar bear cubs stay with their mothers for more than two years.

THINK AND DISCUSS

1 Aside from humans, what other animals live in social groups?
2 What similarities do you think there are between human relationships and animal relationships?

EXPLORE THE THEME

A Read the information on these pages and answer the questions.

1. What are some examples of nonhuman primates?

2. What similarities have researchers discovered between humans and other primates?

B Match the words in blue to their definitions.

_____ (v) to behave toward someone in a particular way

_____ (v) to communicate with someone or something

_____ (v) to look after someone (usually a young, sick, or old person)

Families of wild macaques often bathe in the hot springs in Yamanouchi, Japan.

SOCIAL ANIMALS

Researchers have discovered that humans share certain behavioral characteristics with other primates—the group of mammals that includes humans, monkeys, and apes.

Basic Communication

Primatologists—scientists who study primates—have found that some apes are capable of basic communication using human sign language. Researchers have also observed apes inventing and using tools to get food and complete other tasks.

Social Behavior

Both humans and other primates tend to live in social groups, and they share some characteristics in terms of their social behavior. Researchers today are looking at the similarities and differences in how humans and animals interact within their own social groups, for example, how they treat each other and care for their young.

Reading 1

PREPARING TO READ

BUILDING
VOCABULARY

A The words in **blue** below are used in Reading 1. Read the paragraph. Then match the correct form of each word to its definition.

Most workplaces are positive environments where people work well together. However, an **aggressive** employee in an office can easily lead to workplace stress—by treating coworkers unfairly, **criticizing** them, or taking credit for their work. Employees who experience workplace **conflict** on a regular basis can lose **motivation** to do good work. Why do some employees not cooperate with their coworkers? It may be that the employee is **ambitious** and thinks that aggressive **behavior** will help them get ahead. Or the employee is afraid of losing **status** in the company and thinks that aggressive behavior will help them stay on top.

1. _____ (n) a serious disagreement

2. _____ (n) the way someone acts

3. _____ (adj) acting in a forceful or competitive way

4. _____ (n) a feeling of being excited to do something

5. _____ (v) to speak badly of someone or something

6. _____ (adj) wanting to be successful

7. _____ (n) an individual's position within a group

USING
VOCABULARY

B Discuss these questions with a partner.

1. How **ambitious** are you? Would you rather be a president of a company, or a low-level or mid-level employee without a lot of responsibilities? Why?

2. How would you react to an **aggressive** coworker? Give an example.

BRAINSTORMING

C Discuss your answers to these questions in groups.

1. In what ways do you think employees cooperate in the workplace? Give two examples.

2. In what ways do you think primates cooperate in the wild? Give two examples.

PREDICTING

D Read the title, headings, and captions in the reading passage. How do you think human behavior in the office is similar to primate behavior in the jungle? Write three ideas. Then check your ideas as you read.

_____

_____

_____

THE APE
IN THE OFFICE

🎧 1.01

A   Does the "office jungle" mirror behavior in the real jungle? New research shows people in offices may use conflict and cooperation in similar ways to primates in the jungle.

B   Animal behavior specialist Richard Conniff is the author of *The Ape in the Corner Office*. In his book, Conniff examines corporate behavior through the eyes of a primatologist. He suggests cooperation is the key to success for both humans and other primates. He sees similarities in the ways they use social networks and hierarchies[1] to gain status. He also points out that while conflict can be effective at times, both humans and apes usually prefer to cooperate.

[1] **Hierarchies** are groups or situations that are organized from higher to lower by rank, social status, or function.

COOPERATION VERSUS CONFLICT

C

People often think that the animal world is full of conflict. However, conflict and aggression actually play a smaller role in the wild than cooperation. In fact, according to Conniff, both humans and other primates are social creatures, and both groups normally try to avoid conflict. Chimpanzees, for example, typically spend their days caring for their young and traveling together in small groups. Conniff points out that chimps spend about 5 percent of the day being aggressive, but 15 to 20 percent of the day grooming[2] each other. For humans and other primates, conflict is rare and does not last long. For both species, cooperation is a more effective way to succeed and survive.

THE VALUE OF NETWORKING

D

Research also shows that people and other primates use similar social networking strategies to get ahead in life. They create tight social bonds by sharing resources, doing each other favors, building teams, and making friends. Employees with ambitious career goals, for example, often rely on powerful people in their office to help them get better jobs. In a similar way, chimps work to strengthen relationships with other chimps.

E

Frans de Waal, a primatologist at Emory University in Atlanta, Georgia, claims that for chimps, "you can never reach a high position in their world if you don't have friends who help you." In fact, research shows that chimps often create bonds to strengthen their status, or importance, in the community. They do favors for one another and share resources. They sometimes also use their cunning[3] to get ahead. "In chimps a common strategy is to break up alliances that can be used against them," de Waal explains. "They see a main rival sitting with someone else and they try to break up [that meeting]."

▼ Aggressive behavior may bring results, but also leads to isolation for the aggressor.

[2] Grooming is the activity of animals cleaning each other.
[3] Cunning is the ability to achieve things in a clever way, often by deceiving other people.

Chest-pounding is a sign of aggression among gorillas.

THE IMPORTANCE OF HIERARCHIES

F Groups of coworkers and primate groups have similar social rules. In both cases, the groups organize themselves into hierarchies, and individual members know their roles. Individuals in both human and ape groups have a particular position in relation to other group members. This decides their behavior in the group. For example, young people may speak softly or avoid eye contact when they talk to people with higher status. Similarly, Conniff explains that when chimpanzees approach a powerful or senior member, they try to make themselves look as small as they can.

THE LIMITS OF AGGRESSION

Although cooperation is more common in groups, both humans and other primates sometimes use conflict in order to gain status. Aggressive behaviors get attention, and they show an individual's power in the group. People sometimes shout or intimidate others to make a point or win an argument. Apes show aggression by pounding their chests, screeching, or hitting trees. However, G Conniff notes that conflict does not gain long-term success for either species. When bosses criticize their employees, treat them unfairly, or make their working lives difficult, employees become stressed, lose motivation, and quit their jobs. When apes are aggressive, they chase other apes away. In both cases, aggressive individuals can become isolated, and neither humans nor apes want to be alone.

In his book, Conniff makes the case that interacting in a kind and polite way is more beneficial for both humans and primates. "The truth is we are completely dependent on other people emotionally as well as for our physical needs," H Conniff concludes. "We function as part of a group rather than as individuals." Employees who cooperate in the office and primates who cooperate in the wild find themselves happier, more effective, and more likely to survive.

UNDERSTANDING THE READING

A According to the reading passage, what were the two main reasons Conniff wrote *The Ape in the Corner Office*? Check (✓) the most suitable answers.

☐ 1. to explain how apes and humans behave similarly

☐ 2. to show how humans have learned from animal behavior

☐ 3. to argue that animals cooperate better than humans do

☐ 4. to show how humans and other primates value cooperation

B Complete the summary below. Write no more than one word in each space.

People in offices and primates in the wild both prefer to [1] _____
with one another and avoid [2] _____. They also use social
[3] _____ skills to be successful. Both groups organize themselves into
[4] _____, which affect how they behave in a group. While uncommon,
both office workers and primates sometimes use [5] _____ behavior to
assert themselves.

C Complete the Venn diagram with examples (a–j) from the reading passage describing human and other primate behavior.

a. speak softly or avoid eye contact
b. share resources
c. do favors
d. build teams
e. groom one another

f. travel together in groups
g. do well in groups
h. pound chests, screech, or hit trees
i. rely on powerful people to get better jobs
j. reduce body size to look smaller

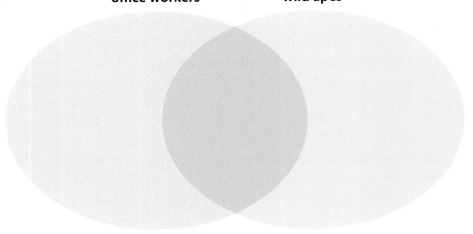

office workers   wild apes

CRITICAL THINKING When a writer is making a claim or an argument, it is important to **analyze the evidence** (examples, statistics, research, etc.) that they provide. As you read, think about and evaluate the evidence mentioned. Does this evidence clearly support the writer's main ideas?

D What evidence does the writer use in the passage to support their main idea in each section? Complete the chart with the key points of evidence.

CRITICAL THINKING: ANALYZING EVIDENCE

Section	Evidence
Cooperation versus Conflict	Statistics:
The Value of Networking	An expert / Research:
The Importance of Hierarchies	An example:
The Limits of Aggression	An example:

E Work in groups. Look at the evidence in exercise D. Based on the evidence provided, which section do you think is the least convincing? Why?

CRITICAL THINKING: EVALUATING EVIDENCE

F Find and underline the following words in the reading. Use context to identify their meanings. Then circle the correct options to complete the definitions.

INFERRING MEANING

bonds (paragraph D)	intimidate (paragraph G)
rival (paragraph E)	beneficial (paragraph H)

1. If an interaction is *beneficial*, it is **useless** / **useful**.

2. A *rival* is someone you are **cooperating** / **competing** with.

3. If you *intimidate* people, you make them feel **frightened** / **happy** enough to do what you want them to do.

4. If you have strong *bonds* with someone, you feel very **connected to** / **distant from** them.

G Work with a partner. Can you think of two examples from your own experience that either support or contradict the ideas expressed in the reading?

CRITICAL THINKING: REFLECTING

_____

_____

DEVELOPING READING SKILLS

READING SKILL Identifying Main and Supporting Ideas

The main idea of a paragraph is the most important idea, or the idea that the paragraph is about. It is often, but not always, stated in the first sentence. Supporting ideas help to explain the main idea. They answer questions about the main idea, such as how, why, what, and when. As you read, it is helpful to identify the main ideas of paragraphs in a passage, and distinguish them from supporting ideas.

Which of these sentences best expresses the main idea of paragraph C of Reading 1?

a. Both primates and humans tend to spend more time being cooperative than they do fighting with one another.

b. Chimpanzees typically spend their days traveling together and taking care of one another.

Sentence **a** best expresses the main idea of the paragraph. Sentence **b** expresses a supporting idea: It helps to explain the main idea by providing an example.

IDENTIFYING MAIN AND SUPPORTING IDEAS

A Read the following paragraph about gorilla behavior. Is each sentence (1–4) a main idea or a supporting idea? Write **M** for Main Idea or **S** for Supporting Idea. One is extra.

Scientists have found that male gorillas in the forests of northern Congo splash water to help them find a mate. Richard Parnell, a primate researcher at the University of Stirling, observed that male gorillas intimidate other males and try to get the attention of females by splashing water with their hands. In one type of splashing behavior, for example, male gorillas raise one or both arms and hit the surface of the water with their palms open. Using water in this way, Parnell says, shows that gorillas are "adaptable, innovative, and intelligent creatures."

_____ 1. Male gorillas sometimes hit the water with their palms open.

_____ 2. Parnell says that splashing proves that gorillas are capable creatures.

_____ 3. Splashing water helps scare off other males.

_____ 4. Larger male gorillas are usually more successful at finding mates.

_____ 5. A study shows that male gorillas splash water to attract female gorillas.

IDENTIFYING MAIN AND SUPPORTING IDEAS

B Look at your answers to exercise A. How do you know which sentences are supporting ideas? What questions (why, how, where, what) do they answer about the main idea? Discuss with a partner.

APPLYING

C Look back at paragraph G of Reading 1. Underline a main idea of the paragraph and two ideas that support it.

Video

ELEPHANT ORPHANS

A shelter in Kenya cares for young elephants that have lost their parents.

BEFORE VIEWING

A Read the photo caption. What kind of care do you think the elephant orphans need? Discuss with a partner.

PREDICTING

B Read the information about the illegal ivory trade and answer the questions. Then discuss them with a partner.

LEARNING ABOUT THE TOPIC

One of the biggest dangers facing African elephants is hunting by poachers—people who illegally catch or kill animals for profit. Poachers kill elephants so they can remove and sell their valuable ivory tusks. Ivory is usually made into jewelry and art objects. Although the ivory trade is banned in most countries, ivory is often smuggled[1] in and sold illegally. Between 2010 and 2012, poachers killed over 100,000 African elephants. In Central Africa, the elephant population has decreased by 64 percent in a decade. Poachers have shortened these animals' life spans and disrupted their close communities.

[1]**smuggled:** brought into or out of another country or area illegally

1. Why do you think people continue to buy objects made of ivory?

   _____

2. What do you think could be done to stop the illegal ivory trade?

   _____

   _____

C The words in **bold** are used in the video. Read the paragraph. Then match the correct form of each word to its definition.

The David Sheldrick Wildlife Trust in Nairobi, Kenya, takes care of orphan elephants. Many of these elephants are orphans because poachers **slaughtered** their mothers. **Caretakers** at the Trust stay with the orphans 24 hours a day, in order to provide them with plenty of **maternal** interaction. The organization's goal is the **reintroduction** of the elephants back into the wild.

1. _____ (adj) like a mother

2. _____ (v) to kill in large numbers

3. _____ (n) a person responsible for looking after someone or something

4. _____ (n) the act of putting something back into an environment where it once was

WHILE VIEWING

A ▶ Watch the video. What is one of the biggest challenges that the David Sheldrick Wildlife Trust faced in keeping the baby elephants alive? Circle the best answer.

a. getting them to trust humans

b. keeping them warm

c. learning what to feed them

B ▶ Watch the video again. Write answers to the following questions.

1. According to the video, what are two things baby elephants need?

_____

2. What is one way caretakers try to copy an elephant's relationship with its mother?

_____

3. What are three ways human and elephant babies are similar?

_____

_____

AFTER VIEWING

A Discuss these questions with a partner.

1. At the end of the video, the narrator says, "These orphans are all safe here—for the time being." Why do you think the narrator uses the phrase "for the time being"?

2. How effective do you think elephant orphanages are in addressing the issue of poaching? Why?

B Write one behavior that both primates and elephants have in common with humans. Use information from the video and Explore the Theme.

_____

Reading 2

PREPARING TO READ

A The words and phrases in blue below are used in Reading 2. Read the sentences. Then match the correct form of each word or phrase to its definition.

BUILDING
VOCABULARY

> Researchers have **observed** that children **generally** sleep better when parents **establish** a regular bedtime routine.
>
> **Previously**, it was common for **extended families** to live together in one home. But today, fewer people live with their grandparents or other relatives.
>
> Coyotes and wolves have similar **social structures**—both live in family groups.
>
> It's normal for children, regardless of **gender**, to have an **intense** feeling of fear when they are separated from their parents. These strong feelings often go away with time.
>
> One way to **discipline** children is to send them to their rooms alone.
>
> When animals shed their fur, new fur grows to **replace** the fur that is lost.

1. _____ (adv) usually

2. _____ (adj) very great or extreme

3. _____ (n) a group that includes uncles, cousins, grandparents, etc.

4. _____ (n) the way a group of people or animals is organized

5. _____ (n) the characteristics of being male or female

6. _____ (v) to create or start something that will last a long time

7. _____ (v) to train someone to follow rules or codes of behavior

8. _____ (v) to notice something after looking closely

9. _____ (v) to have something new or different instead of the original

10. _____ (adv) before the time period that you are talking about

B Discuss these questions with a partner.

USING
VOCABULARY

1. What are two ways in which **establishing** a routine can make your life easier?

2. What are some benefits of living in an **extended family**? What are some drawbacks?

C Read the title and the subheadings in the reading passage. What links the three stories together? Check your idea as you read.

PREDICTING

a. male and female roles in animal societies
b. scientific research of primates in Africa
c. animal societies in which females have power

GENDER IN THE WILD

🎧 1.02

A How does gender impact family relationships in the wild? Recent studies show how gender influences the social structure of elephants, geladas, and chimps.

Studies Show Gender Effect in Elephant Societies

B Young elephants grow up in extended matriarchal[1] families. Elephant mothers, aunts, grandmothers, and female friends cooperate to raise babies in large, carefully organized groups. This system helps protect young orphan elephants when hunters or farmers kill their mothers. When a young elephant is orphaned, other females take over the dead mother's role. The strong bonds between females continue throughout their lives, which can be as long as 70 years. In contrast, young male elephants stay close to their female family members until they are 14. Then they generally leave their mothers and form other groups with male elephants.

C Previously, male elephants were perceived to be less social than females. However, a recent study at Etosha National Park in Namibia shows that males often form intense, long-lasting friendships with other males. During

---

[1] In a **matriarchal** family or group, the rulers are female and power is passed from mother to daughter.

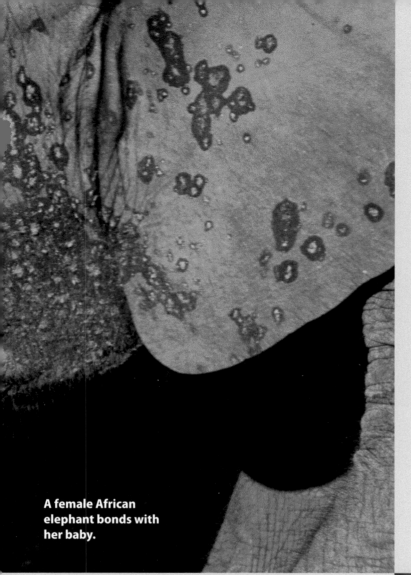

A female African elephant bonds with her baby.

Gelada Study Reveals Female Primates with Power

Geladas are primates that live in the remote highlands of Ethiopia. Males are larger than females, but females have the real power in family groups. Wildlife biologist Chadden Hunter studies geladas in Simen Mountains National Park in Ethiopia. Hunter has observed that typical family units have between

D two and eight adult females, their offspring, and a primary male, which researchers call the family male. Gelada males have little say in what the family does from day to day. The females decide where and how long to graze[3] for food, when to move, and where to sleep. They also choose which male will be their mate and when it is time to replace that mate.

Young bachelor[4] males live in separate groups. They spend most of their time observing family groups and looking for

E opportunities to challenge the family males. When a young bachelor comes too close to a family, the family male chases him away.

[3] When animals **graze**, they eat the grass or other plants that are growing in a particular place.
[4] A **bachelor** is a single male without a female partner or children.

the study, Stanford University behavioral psychologist Caitlin O'Connell-Rodwell found that each member knew his status, and that the group followed a strict social hierarchy. Older males act as teachers and mediators[2] for younger ones, controlling or disciplining them when conflict occurs. These strict rules of behavior are helpful when food and drink are scarce. O'Connell-Rodwell observed that "in dry years, the strict pecking order they establish benefits all of them." For example, the young bulls know they must get in line behind the more senior elephants. In this way, everyone gets a turn to eat and drink, conflict is avoided, and peace is maintained.

[2] A **mediator** is someone who helps two people or groups solve an issue or a problem.

In gelada societies, females are the real decision-makers.

To replace a family male, the females invite a bachelor into the family. Females typically do this when a family male becomes weak or does not give enough attention to them or their offspring. Hunter explains, "That's especially true in families where there are six or seven females; it's a lot of work to keep them all happy."

F
Hunter has observed that no family male lasts more than four years, and many are replaced before three. However, replaced males do not leave their families. Rather, they stay on in a kind of grandfather role. "That way, they can protect their children," he says, "and they're very aggressive about that." Hunter's study has generated new interest in geladas, and it will challenge primatologists to learn more about their gender behavior.

Researchers Discover Gender-Driven Play in Chimps

G
Just as human children often choose different toys, some monkeys in captivity have demonstrated gender-driven toy preferences. For example, young female vervet and rhesus monkeys often play with dolls in captivity, while young males prefer toys such as trucks. Now, for the first time, a study in Kibale National Park in Uganda shows that the same is true for chimps in the wild.

Richard Wrangham, a primatologist at Harvard University, has been studying the play behavior of male and female chimps. His team observed that the way a community of young Kanyawara female chimps played with sticks mimicked caretaking behaviors. The young females took sticks to their nests and cared for them like mother chimps with their babies. The
H chimps appeared to be using the sticks as dolls, as if they were practicing for motherhood. This play preference, which was very rarely seen in males, was observed in young female chimps more than a hundred times during 14 years of study. In contrast, young males did not normally play with objects. Instead, they preferred active play—climbing, jumping, and chasing each other through trees.

I
Stick play may have evolved to prepare females for motherhood. It may have given them an advantage by providing skills and knowledge that contributed to their survival. It is also possible that stick play is just an expression of the imagination—an ability found in chimps and humans but few other animals.

UNDERSTANDING THE READING

A Choose the sentence that best expresses the main idea of each section in the passage.

UNDERSTANDING MAIN IDEAS

1. Studies Show Gender Effect in Elephant Societies

   a. Both male and female elephants have an excellent memory and are able to remember elephants they meet.

   b. Female elephants are in charge of raising families, while males form hierarchical groups with other males.

2. Gelada Study Reveals Female Primates with Power

   a. Female geladas control family groups in gelada society.

   b. There is a strict hierarchy within female geladas in a single family.

3. Researchers Discover Gender-Driven Play in Chimps

   a. The types of play that young chimps prefer seem to be related to gender.

   b. Young chimps learn their social skills by playing with their mothers.

B Complete the main ideas (M) and supporting ideas (S) from "Gelada Study Reveals Female Primates with Power." Write no more than three words in each space.

IDENTIFYING MAIN AND SUPPORTING IDEAS

Paragraph D

   M: Female geladas have _____ in family groups.

     S1: Family groups have a large number of geladas.

     S2: Female geladas decide what the family does _____.

     S3: Female geladas choose their _____.

Paragraph E

   M: Nonfamily male geladas live in _____.

     S1: Bachelor males wait for a chance to challenge the _____.

     S2: Female geladas _____ bachelor males when they want to.

Paragraph F

   M: Most family males are _____ after a few years.

     S: The old family males _____ in the family group.

C Complete each sentence with details from the reading passage. Write no more than three words in each space.

UNDERSTANDING DETAILS

Studies Show Gender Effect in Elephant Societies

1. In male elephant groups, each member knows his _____.

2. _____ discipline young male elephants when they fight.

Gelada Study Reveals Female Primates with Power

3. In a typical gelada family, there is one _____.

4. When the family male is replaced, he usually takes on a _____ role.

Researchers Discover Gender-Driven Play in Chimps

5. Young females play with sticks, while young males tend to prefer _____.

6. Playing with sticks may prepare young female chimps for _____.

D What evidence does the author use in "Researchers Discover Gender-Driven Play in Chimps"? Complete the statements below. Then discuss your ideas with a partner.

1. The article describes a _____ in Kibale National Park as evidence for gender-driven play in chimps.

2. The expert who did the chimp study is Richard Wrangham, a _____ from Harvard University.

3. Wrangham's team observed that female chimps' stick play was similar to _____ behaviors.

4. Wrangham's study lasted _____ years. During this time, his team observed the same behavior more than _____ times.

E Discuss these questions with a partner.

1. Do you think the supporting evidence in exercise D is convincing? Why or why not?

2. Compare the three reports in the passage. Which one do you think provides the most convincing supporting evidence? Why?

F Find and underline these words and phrases in the passage. Use context to identify their meanings. Then complete the sentences with a suitable form of the words and phrases.

pecking order (paragraph C)	in captivity (paragraph G)
offspring (paragraph D)	mimicked (paragraph H)

1. Hyenas live in groups with a strict _____. One female has the most power and makes all of the decisions for the group.

2. Researchers saw that a baby chimp _____ her mother's behavior.

3. A mother emperor penguin protects her _____ from the Antarctic cold by keeping it under a warm layer of feathered skin.

4. It is difficult to study animals in the wild, but it is easy to study animals _____.

G Compare the animal species you learned about in this unit. Check (✓) the column(s) that apply to each species. Discuss the reasons for your answers with a partner.

Species	Females Control the Group	Hierarchy Is Important	Forming Strong Bonds Is Important
chimpanzees			
elephants			
geladas			

Writing

EXPLORING WRITTEN ENGLISH

A Read the sentences below. Write **S** for sentences that show similarities. Write **D** for sentences that show differences.

NOTICING

1. _____ As both humans and other primates tend to live in social groups, they may share some characteristics in terms of their social behavior.

2. _____ Young people may speak softly or avoid eye contact when they are talking to people with higher status. Similarly, when chimpanzees approach a powerful or senior member, they try to make themselves look smaller.

3. _____ A male gorilla usually has the power in a gorilla family group. In contrast, females make the decisions in a gelada family group.

4. _____ Human boys and girls often choose different toys. Likewise, young chimps in captivity have shown gender-driven toy preferences.

5. _____ Unlike young female chimps, young males did not normally play with objects.

LANGUAGE FOR WRITING Making Comparisons

Use these expressions to show similarities.

> Office workers **are similar** to primates. **Both** use conflict and cooperation in groups.
>
> Humans generally live in harmony. **Likewise / Similarly**, chimpanzees try to avoid conflict.
>
> **Like** humans, chimpanzees may limit aggression to avoid isolation.

Use these expressions to show differences.

> **While** aggression is part of normal primate behavior, it plays a limited role in the wild.
>
> The strong bonds among female elephants continue throughout their lives. **In contrast**, young male elephants stay close to their female family members only until they are 14.
>
> Elephant families are matriarchal. **On the other hand**, males traditionally have the power in gorilla groups.
>
> Young male elephants live with their female family members, **whereas** older males form their own groups.
>
> **Unlike** young male chimps, who prefer active play, young female chimps have a preference for playing with sticks.

Note:

• The form of *be* in *be similar to* must agree with its subject.

• Use *likewise* and *similarly* at the beginning of sentences, followed by a comma.

• *In contrast* and *on the other hand* can appear at the beginning of sentences, followed by a comma. They can also appear after the subject. Note the use of commas in this case: *Males, on the other hand, traditionally have the power in many human cultures.*

B Underline the words and phrases in exercise A that show similarities and differences.

C Complete the sentences with suitable words or phrases for making comparisons. Add commas if necessary.

1. Female geladas hold the power in the family. _____ males have little say about what goes on in the family.

2. Social networking is important in the human workplace. _____ chimpanzees form strong bonds within their groups.

3. Male geladas are big and have bushy manes _____ female geladas are small and less distinctive-looking.

4. Young male chimps prefer active play. Young female chimps _____ prefer less active play.

5. Humans have invented tools to help them survive. _____ chimpanzees make and use tools for specific purposes.

D Use the expressions in the Language for Writing box to write three sentences comparing elephants, chimpanzees, and geladas. Use the information from the chart in exercise G in Understanding the Reading 2.

_____

_____

_____

_____

WRITING SKILL Writing Body Paragraphs

An essay is a piece of writing that presents information and ideas on a topic. It typically has the following structure:

Introductory paragraph ⟶ Body paragraphs ⟶ Concluding paragraph

You will learn more about the introductory and concluding paragraphs in Unit 3. An essay has two or more **body paragraphs**. Each one expresses one main idea. A good body paragraph includes a topic sentence that presents the paragraph's main idea. It also includes supporting ideas that develop the main idea. Explanations, details, and examples give further information about the supporting ideas.

In a comparison essay, one way to organize body paragraphs is the point-by-point method. With this method, you discuss one **point of comparison** in each paragraph. For example, in an essay comparing wolves and dogs:

Body paragraph 1   the animals' relationships with humans

Body paragraph 2   the social structures of both animals

Below are typical ways to organize body paragraphs for a comparison essay:

Body paragraph 1		**Body paragaph 2**
a similarity	⟶	another similarity
a difference	⟶	another difference
a similarity	⟶	a difference

E Read the body paragraph below. Answer the questions and then discuss your answers with a partner.

One way that dogs and wolves differ is in their relationships with humans. Dogs are generally friendly and helpful around humans. This is probably because they have been living closely with humans for thousands of years. No one knows exactly why early wolves (ancestors of dogs) approached humans and began living with them, but these tamer individuals gradually evolved into the dogs we know today. Over time, dogs and humans developed a mutually beneficial relationship: humans sheltered and fed dogs, and dogs did jobs for humans. For example, dogs helped early humans hunt. Wolves, on the other hand, are shy and fearful of humans. One reason for this is that wolves are generally afraid of anything that is unfamiliar. This tendency most likely evolved as a survival strategy. Anything unfamiliar in a wolf's environment is a potential danger, so this fear helps it avoid threats to its existence. As a result, wolves are less likely to interact with humans.

1. Does the body paragraph focus mainly on a similarity or a difference?

   _____

2. Read the following thesis statement. Which of the two points of comparison does the body paragraph explain? Underline it.

   *While wolves and dogs are similar in some ways, the two animals are different in terms of **their relationships with humans** and **their social structures**.*

3. In the paragraph above, underline and label:
   a. the topic sentence
   b. a supporting idea about dogs
   c. a supporting idea about wolves
   d. an example that shows dogs' relationship with humans
   e. an explanation for wolves' behavior

The ancestors of the Mexican wolf were likely the first wolves to arrive in North America.

WRITING TASK

GOAL You are going to write two body paragraphs on the following topic:

Think about an animal in this unit or another animal that is similar to humans in some way. What is one way its behavior is similar to and different from human behavior?

BRAINSTORMING **A** Choose an animal that is similar to humans in some way. Write notes about the animal's behavior. For example, what is its social hierarchy like? How are gender roles different?

PLANNING **B** Follow these steps to make notes for your body paragraphs.

Step 1 From your notes, choose two points of comparison to write about.

Step 2 Complete the first thesis statement if both your points of comparison are on similarities or both are on differences. Complete the second thesis statement if they are one of each.

Step 3 Write a topic sentence for each body paragraph.

Step 4 Add supporting ideas and details (examples, explanations, etc.) for each point.

OUTLINE

Thesis Statement

1. While _____ and _____ are similar / different in some ways, the two are different / similar in terms of their _____ and _____ .

2. _____ and _____ are similar in some ways but different in others. They both _____ , but they differ in terms of _____ .

Body Paragraph 1

Topic Sentence: _____

_____

Supporting Ideas / Details: _____

_____

Body Paragraph 2

Topic Sentence: _____

_____

Supporting Ideas / Details: _____

_____

FIRST DRAFT **C** Use the information in your outline to write a first draft of your body paragraphs.

REVISING PRACTICE

The drafts below are the second body paragraph for the thesis statement in exercise E on page 21.

What did the writer do in Draft 2 to improve the paragraph? Match the changes (a–d) to the highlighted parts.

a. added a supporting detail
c. added a topic sentence
b. corrected language for making comparisons
d. deleted unrelated information

Draft 1

Wolves in the wild live in social groups called "packs." A wolf pack is made up of a male and female "alpha" pair—the leaders of the pack—and the alpha pair's offspring and extended family. Most wolves live in the United States, Canada, and Russia. Wolves live this way mainly because they have to hunt for their food, and packs hunt more successfully than individuals. Their clear hierarchy helps them cooperate in hunts and avoid fighting over food within the group. Unlike wolves need to live in packs, dogs do not. This is because, unlike wolves, dogs do not need to hunt to survive. Dogs in the wild search for food scraps left by humans or other animals on their own. Domestic dogs are fed by their human owners. Even when two or more dogs live together in a house, there is no alpha in the group. The dogs deal with conflict on a case-by-case basis, and any member of the group can breed.

Draft 2

Another way that wolves and dogs differ is in their social structures. Wolves in the wild live in social groups called "packs." A wolf pack is made up of a male and female "alpha" pair—the leaders of the pack—and the alpha pair's offspring and extended family. Wolves live this way mainly because they have to hunt for their food, and packs hunt more successfully than individuals. Their clear hierarchy helps them cooperate in hunts and avoid fighting over food within the group. The alphas eat first, make all the decisions for the pack, and are the only ones in the pack that breed. While wolves need to live in packs, dogs do not. This is because, unlike wolves, dogs do not need to hunt to survive. Dogs in the wild search for food scraps left by humans or other animals on their own. Domestic dogs are fed by their human owners. Even when two or more dogs live together in a house, there is no alpha in the group. The dogs deal with conflict on a case-by-case basis, and any member of the group can breed.

☐
☐
☐
☐

D Now use the questions below to revise your paragraphs.   REVISED DRAFT

☐ Does your thesis statement state your points of comparison?

☐ Do your body paragraphs relate to the thesis statement?

☐ Do both body paragraphs have clear topic sentences?

☐ Do your supporting ideas and details relate to the main idea of each body paragraph?

EDITING PRACTICE

Read the information below.

In sentences with comparison expressions, remember:
- that the form of *be* in *be similar to* must agree with its subject.
- to use commas correctly in sentences with *while, like, likewise, similarly, on the other hand, unlike, whereas,* and *in contrast*.

Correct one mistake with comparison expressions in each of the sentences (1–5).

1. The use of tools among gorillas are similar to the use of tools among chimpanzees.

2. Dogs are not capable of using language. In contrast some apes are able to communicate using human sign language.

3. Horses help farmers by pulling carts. Likewise dogs help by herding sheep.

4. Cats in the wild have to hunt for food. House cats on the other hand, get their food from humans.

5. Chimpanzee mothers and daughters form strong bonds. Similarly adult female elephants form close relationships with young females in the family.

FINAL DRAFT   **E**   **Follow these steps to write a final draft.**

1. Check your revised draft for mistakes with language for making comparisons.

2. Now use the checklist on page 253 to write a final draft. Make any other necessary changes.

UNIT REVIEW

Answer the following questions.

1. What is one similarity between human office workers and chimpanzees?

_____

_____

_____

2. What should you include in a body paragraph?

_____

_____

_____

3. Do you remember the meanings of these words? Check (✓) the ones you know. Look back at the unit and review the ones you don't know.

Reading 1:

☐ aggressive   ☐ ambitious   ☐ behavior

☐ care for   ☐ conflict   ☐ criticize

☐ interact   ☐ motivation AWL   ☐ status

☐ treat

Reading 2:

☐ discipline   ☐ establish   ☐ extended family

☐ gender AWL   ☐ generally   ☐ intense AWL

☐ observe   ☐ previously   ☐ replace

☐ social structure

SCIENCE AND INVESTIGATION 2

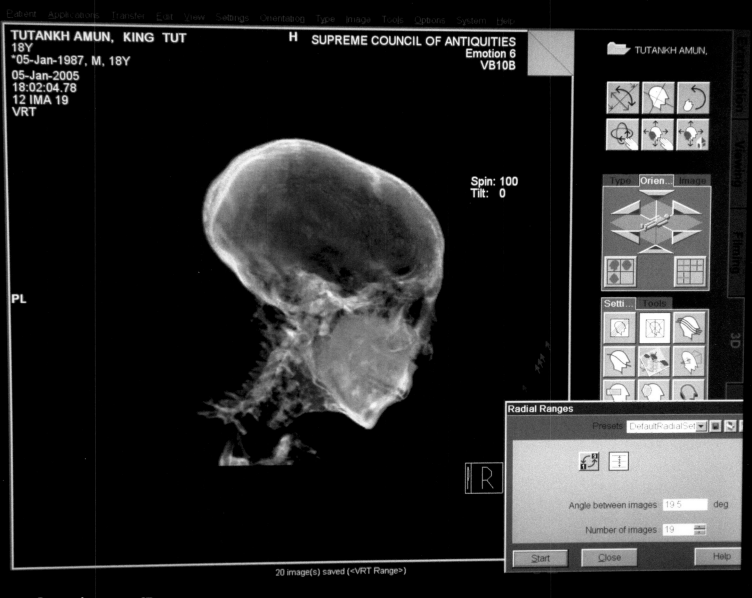

Patient Applications Transfer Edit View Settings Orientation Type Image Tools Options System Help

TUTANKH AMUN, KING TUT
18Y
*05-Jan-1987, M, 18Y

05-Jan-2005
18:02:04.78
12 IMA 19
VRT

H   SUPREME COUNCIL OF ANTIQUITIES
Emotion 6
VB10B

Spin: 100
Tilt: 0

PL

Radial Ranges

Presets DefaultRadialSet

Angle between images   19 5   deg

Number of images   19

Start   Close   Help

20 image(s) saved (<VRT Range>)

**Researchers use a CT scanner
to look inside the body of
Tutankhamun.**

ACADEMIC SKILLS

READING   Identifying a sequence of events
WRITING   Writing a summary
GRAMMAR   Paraphrasing
CRITICAL THINKING   Analyzing levels of certainty

THINK AND DISCUSS

1   In what ways can technology help
investigators solve crimes?

2   Do you know of any crimes that were solved
using technology?

A Look at the information on these pages and discuss the questions.

1. What can DNA phenotyping tell us about a person?

2. What *can't* DNA phenotyping tell us about a person?

B Match the correct form of the words in blue to their definitions.

_____ (n) a person who the police think may be guilty of a crime

_____ (v) to carry out (usually something illegal or bad)

_____ (v) to find out something by researching or calculation

PUTTING A FACE TO A CASE

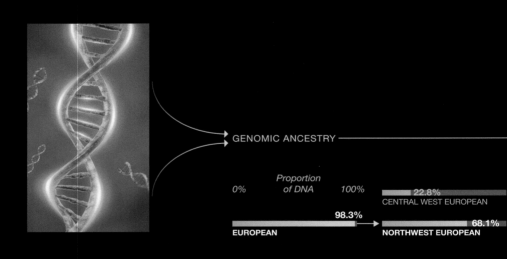

GENOMIC ANCESTRY

	Proportion of DNA		
0%		100%	22.8%
			CENTRAL WEST EUROPEAN
	98.3%		
			68.1%
EUROPEAN			NORTHWEST EUROPEAN

1. A DNA sample is first scanned.

2. A computer makes predictions about a person's traits, such as ancestry, eye color, or skin color.

DNA—a tiny molecule found in almost every part of a person's body—contains a code that gives the body instructions for the growth of cells. Except for the DNA of identical twins, every person's DNA is unique. Because each person's DNA is distinctive, it is a valuable tool for identification. For several years, police have used DNA to identify victims of crimes—and to **determine** who may have **committed** them.

Scientists have also developed a new technique called DNA phenotyping. This technique can determine a person's eye color, their natural hair color, the possible shapes of their facial features, and their geographic ancestry. With this information, technicians can create a picture or a 3-D model of what a person might look like. However, DNA phenotyping cannot determine a person's age, weight, or whether they have a beard or dyed hair. Because this technique can only provide clues about a person's appearance, it cannot necessarily be used to positively identify criminals. However, it can help police rule out **suspects**.

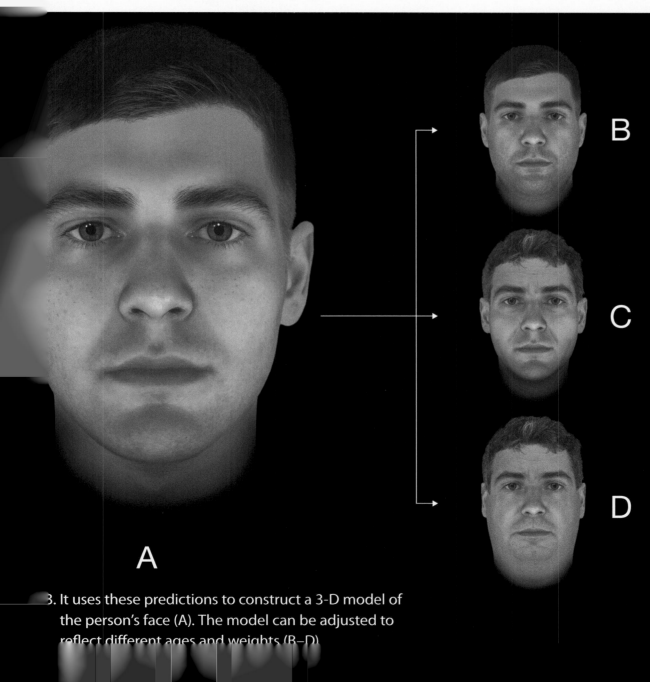

3. It uses these predictions to construct a 3-D model of the person's face (A). The model can be adjusted to reflect different ages and weights (B–D).

Reading 1

PREPARING TO READ

BUILDING
VOCABULARY **A** The words in blue below are used in Reading 1. Read the paragraphs. Then match each word to its definition.

CT Scanning

A CT scanner is a medical imaging device that can take 3-D images of the inside of almost any object. With it, a doctor can **examine** the inside of a patient's body without cutting the patient open. This technology can **reveal** conditions that aren't easily known, such as tumors, infections, and internal bleeding. CT scanners can also help police to find evidence, and scientists to solve **mysteries** about the past.

Fingerprinting

Every person on Earth has a different fingerprint pattern. Even if you cut or burn your fingers, the same fingerprint pattern will grow back when the injury **heals**. Fingerprint **analysis** can help police **detectives** solve crimes. For example, fingerprints collected at a crime scene can help **prove** that a particular person has been to that location.

1. _____ (v) gets better; becomes healthy

2. _____ (v) to uncover something that is hidden

3. _____ (n) things that are impossible to explain or understand

4. _____ (n) people whose job is to solve crimes

5. _____ (v) to look closely at something

6. _____ (n) the process of studying something carefully

7. _____ (v) to show that something is true or accurate

USING
VOCABULARY **B** Discuss these questions with a partner.

1. What skills do you think police **detectives** need to have? Why?

2. Would you be good at investigating a crime or **mystery**? Why or why not?

PREDICTING **C** Skim the first paragraph and the subheadings in the reading passage. What kinds of crime cases will you read about? How might technology be useful for these types of investigations? Discuss with a partner. Then check your ideas as you read the passage.

_____

_____

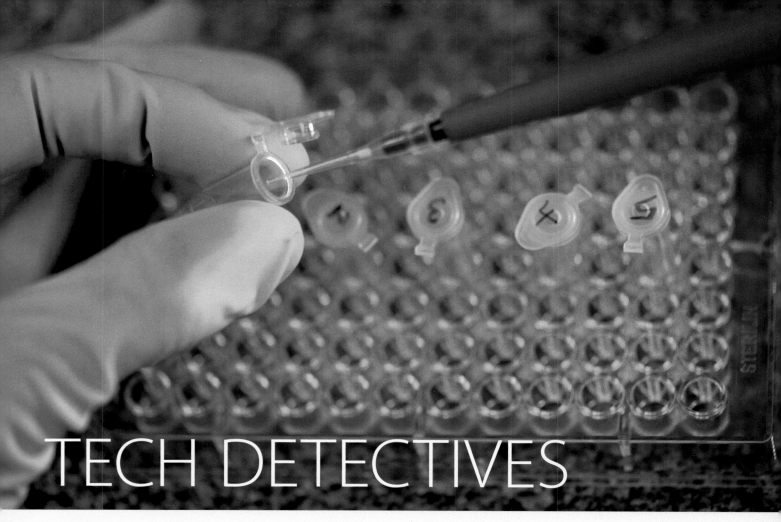

TECH DETECTIVES

🎧 1.03

A Police detectives have always made use of the latest technologies to solve crimes. As three cases show, modern technology can help scientists and detectives understand and solve mysteries both from the present and from the past.

A ROBBERY[1] CASE IN AUSTRALIA

B When most people think of leeches, they imagine disgusting blood-sucking worms that they would prefer to avoid. However, leeches can actually be useful. In fact, in 2009, detectives in Australia were able to use a leech to solve an eight-year-old robbery case. In 2001, two men robbed a 71-year-old woman in her home in the woods in Tasmania, stealing several hundred dollars. The men escaped, but soon after, detectives investigating the crime scene found a leech filled with blood. The detectives thought that the leech could have attached itself to one of the robbers in the woods. It might have sucked the robber's blood while he was traveling through the woods, and then fallen off during the robbery. The detectives extracted some DNA from the blood in the leech and kept it in their database.[2]

C Eight years later, police arrested a suspect on an unrelated drug charge. As part of his examination, his DNA was analyzed and it matched that taken from the leech. This proved that the suspect was at the scene of the crime. After the police questioned him, the suspect eventually admitted to committing the 2001 robbery.

[1] A **robbery** is the crime of stealing money or property, often using force.

[2] A **database** is a collection of data or information that is stored in a computer.

Palo verde flowers

A MURDER CASE IN ARIZONA

The first conviction[3] based on plant DNA evidence occurred in the state of Arizona, in the United States. When a murder was committed in 1992 in the state capital, Phoenix, police found a pager[4] at the scene of the crime that led them to a suspect. The suspect admitted to giving the victim a ride in his truck, but denied any wrongdoing. In fact, he claimed that she had actually robbed him, which is why his pager was found at the crime scene. Forensic[5] investigators examined his truck and found seed pods, which were later identified as the fruits of the palo verde tree. And indeed, a palo verde tree at the scene of the crime looked like a truck might have hit it.

However, this evidence alone was not enough. An investigator wondered if it was possible to link the exact tree at the crime scene with the seed pods found on the truck. A geneticist at the University of Arizona in Tucson showed that it was. Individual plants—in this case, palo verde trees—have unique patterns of DNA. Through DNA analysis of the seed pods, the geneticist determined that its DNA matched the one on the truck. This proved that the truck had definitely been to the crime scene and had collided with one specific tree— thus contradicting the suspect's story. With this information, it was possible to convict the suspect of the crime.

A BODY IN THE MOUNTAINS

Europe's oldest mummy,[6] now known as the Iceman, was discovered by hikers in the frozen ice of the Italian Alps in 1991. Scientists believe he lived about 5,300 years ago in an area north of what is now Bolzano, Italy. Wounds on the Iceman's body clearly show that he died a violent death. But CT imaging technology has helped scientists piece together even more clues about the life and death of this ancient Neolithic[7] human.

CT imaging identified an arrowhead buried in the Iceman's left shoulder, indicating that he was shot from behind. Scientists also discovered a wound on one of his hands. This told them that he had likely been in a fight and that his enemies later chased after and killed him. While this may be true, close analysis of this hand injury shows that the wound was already beginning to heal at the time of his death. So it is unlikely he injured his hand in his final days. Moreover, a later study of the CT images revealed that the Iceman had a full stomach at the time he was killed. This meant that he ate a big meal immediately before his death—not something a person would do if enemies were chasing him. Scientists guessed that the Iceman might have been resting after a meal when enemies attacked him from behind.

Perhaps the most likely explanation is that the Iceman was fleeing an earlier battle, but thought he was safe at the moment of his murder. Scientists continue to analyze the Iceman using the latest technology to find more clues to history's oldest murder mystery.

[3] If someone has a **conviction**, they are found guilty of a crime in a court of law.

[4] A **pager** is an electronic device that is used for contacting someone.

[5] A **forensic** investigation involves the use of scientific methods and techniques to solve crimes.

[6] A **mummy** is a dead body that was preserved long ago, usually by being rubbed with special oils and wrapped in cloth.

[7] If something is **Neolithic**, it is from the last part of the Stone Age.

An artist's view of the Iceman's final moments: An arrowhead discovered in the Iceman's left shoulder indicates that he was shot from behind and was probably unaware of his killers.

UNDERSTANDING THE READING

UNDERSTANDING MAIN IDEAS **A** Match the technology investigators used (1–3) to solve the crime (a–e). There are two extra answers.

1. DNA in a leech helped detectives _____
2. DNA from a tree helped detectives _____
3. CT scans helped scientists _____

a. identify a murderer.
b. locate a murder weapon.
c. solve a drug case.
d. identify a thief.
e. discover how a man was murdered.

UNDERSTANDING DETAILS **B** Look back at "A Murder Case in Arizona." For each statement below, circle T for true, F for false, or NG if the information is not given.

1. The police found the suspect's pager at the crime scene. **T F NG**
2. The victim was a friend of the suspect. **T F NG**
3. The suspect had bought the truck recently. **T F NG**
4. The suspect claimed that he never met the victim. **T F NG**
5. The police were able to prove that the truck **T F NG**
   had been at the crime scene.

CATEGORIZING **C** What evidence was useful to investigators? Complete the diagram with the pieces of evidence (a–l) below.

a. a damaged tree
b. a healing wound
c. a suspect's blood
d. an arrowhead
e. a leech
f. a truck
g. a pager
h. seed pods
i. DNA database
j. a later arrest
k. a full stomach
l. tree DNA

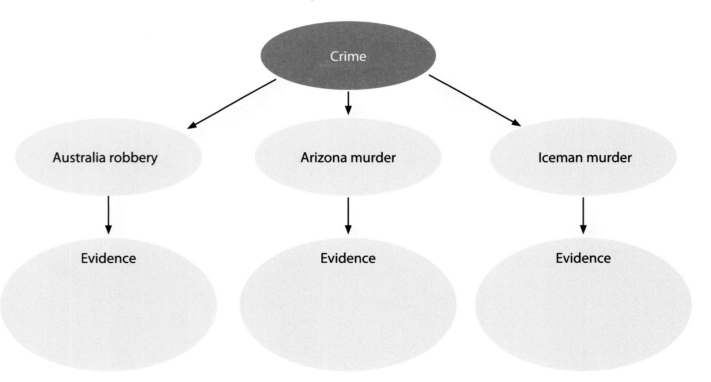

D Read these sentences from "A Body in the Mountains." How certain is the writer about each underlined piece of information? Rate them (3 = very certain; 2 = mostly certain; 1 = not certain). Then share the reasons for your answers with a partner.

CRITICAL THINKING:
ANALYZING
CERTAINTY

1. _____   Scientists believe <u>he lived about 5,300 years ago in an area north of what is now Bolzano, Italy</u>.

2. _____   Wounds on the Iceman's body clearly show that <u>he died a violent death</u>.

3. _____   Close analysis of this hand injury shows that <u>the wound was already beginning to heal at the time of his death</u>.

4. _____   So it is unlikely <u>he injured his hand in his final days</u>.

5. _____   This meant that <u>he ate a big meal immediately before his death</u> …

6. _____   Scientists guessed that <u>the Iceman might have been resting after a meal when enemies attacked him from behind</u>.

7. _____   Perhaps the most likely explanation is that <u>the Iceman was fleeing an earlier battle, but thought he was safe at the moment of his murder</u>.

E Look at "A Robbery Case in Australia" and "A Murder Case in Arizona." In each section, find a piece of information that is more certain and one that is less certain. Share your ideas with a partner.

CRITICAL THINKING:
ANALYZING
CERTAINTY

_____

_____

_____

_____

F Based on the evidence in the reading passage and your own ideas, what do you think happened to the Iceman, e.g., who he was with, why he was killed, why his body was left there? Make some notes below. Then discuss with a partner.

CRITICAL THINKING:
EVALUATING

_____

_____

_____

DEVELOPING READING SKILLS

READING SKILL Identifying a Sequence of Events

When you are trying to understand an article about a crime or a mystery, look for certain words and phrases in the story to help you understand the sequence, or order, of events.

Time markers such as days, months, years, and times of day:
on Monday	*in March*	*in 1991*	*at 5:30*

Words that indicate that one event happened **before** another event:
before	*earlier*	*(one year) ago*	*already*

Words that indicate that one event happened **after** another event:
later	*after*	*now*	*once*

Words and phrases that indicate that two events occurred **at the same time**:
at the time of	*at that moment*	*at the same time*	*while*

Words and phrases that indicate that something happened **much earlier**:
a long time ago	*for some time*	*in ancient (times)*	*in prehistoric (times)*

ANALYZING   **A**   Scan the section "A Robbery Case in Australia." Underline words and phrases that indicate when events happened.

IDENTIFYING
A SEQUENCE   **B**   Now use information from "A Robbery Case in Australia" to complete the timeline below.

a. Police arrested a suspect on a drug charge.

b. The suspect admitted that he committed the robbery.

c. Police analyzed the drug charge suspect's DNA.

d. Two men entered a house to rob the woman who lived there.

e. The leech fell off of the robber.

f. Detectives found a leech filled with blood in the house.

g. Detectives took blood out of the leech.

h. Detectives matched the DNA from the leech with the DNA of the suspect.

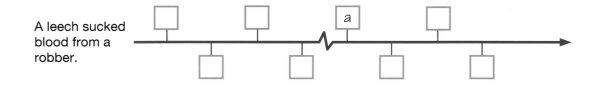

A leech sucked blood from a robber.

Video

The Iceman's body was found at this spot in the Ötzal Alps.

SECRETS IN THE ICE

BEFORE VIEWING

A Read the information about the Iceman and answer the questions below.

LEARNING ABOUT
THE TOPIC

- The Iceman was wearing a coat, a belt, leggings, and shoes, all made of leather. The shoes were waterproof and designed to help the wearer walk in snow. He was carrying tools, weapons, and two baskets of medicinal plants.

- Scientists believe that the Iceman was about 46 years old and five feet two inches (about 1.58 meters) tall. He had medium-length wavy dark hair and brown eyes.

- He had 61 tattoos, mostly consisting of parallel lines. These are the oldest tattoos ever found, and prove that tattooing has existed much longer than previously thought.

- Researchers have found 19 living relatives of the Iceman in Austria. These people and the Iceman likely share an ancestor who lived 10,000 to 12,000 years ago.

1. What information about the Iceman do you think was easily visible? What information do you think was gained using technology?

   _____

   _____

2. What three things about the Iceman do you still want to know?

   _____

   _____

B The words in **bold** below are used in the video. Read the sentences. Then match the correct form of each word to its definition.

> Because the Iceman was frozen, he was perfectly **preserved**.
>
> Studying the Iceman can give us **insights** into life 5,000 years ago. For example, we can learn about the clothes people wore in the ancient past.
>
> Studying the contents of the Iceman's stomach may tell us a lot about how **nutrition** affected his health.
>
> An analysis of his **genes** shows that he and 19 people in Austria share an ancestor.

1. _____ (n) the right diet for healthy growth
2. _____ (v) to keep in a good state
3. _____ (n) an accurate understanding of something
4. _____ (n) a part of DNA that contains the information for the physical characteristics of a person, animal, or plant

WHILE VIEWING

UNDERSTANDING
MAIN IDEAS

A ▶ Watch the video. According to Albert Zink, what makes the Iceman so special? Check (✓) the correct answers.

☐ 1. He can help us improve DNA technology.
☐ 2. He is the oldest mummy in Europe.
☐ 3. He is perfectly preserved.
☐ 4. He helps us understand how people lived in those places.
☐ 5. He gives us information about diseases.
☐ 6. He carried tools that were technologically advanced for his time.

UNDERSTANDING
DETAILS

B ▶ Watch the video again. What does Albert Zink still hope to discover about the Iceman? Note two things.

_____

_____

AFTER VIEWING

REACTING TO
THE VIDEO

A Do you think it is right to use the Iceman's body for scientific research? Why or why not? Discuss with a partner.

I think we should use the Iceman's body for scientific research because …
I think we should leave the Iceman's body untouched as …

CRITICAL THINKING:
SYNTHESIZING

B Look back at your answers to exercise F in Understanding the Reading 1. Based on information in the video, are you more certain or less certain than before about how the Iceman died? Why? Discuss with a partner.

Reading 2

PREPARING TO READ

The words and phrases in blue below are used in Reading 2. Complete the sentences with the correct form of each word or phrase.

BUILDING VOCABULARY

> Your **identity** is who you are.
>
> If you **obtain** something, you get it.
>
> You can use *moreover* to mean "in addition."
>
> If something is **unclear**, it is not definite or easy to understand.
>
> If you **mention** something, you say something about it.
>
> If you **suffer from** something, you are badly affected by it.
>
> If you **carry out** a job or a task, you do it or finish it.
>
> A **sample** of something is a small amount that shows characteristics of the whole thing.
>
> An **archaeologist** is a person who finds and examines objects from the past.
>
> A **combination** of two or more things is the result of putting those things together.

1. Due to the lack of evidence, the cause of the victim's death is still _____.

2. In his article, the author _____ that he is a(n) _____ and a scholar of ancient history.

3. The _____ of an old wound and a full stomach indicated that the Iceman probably was not in a fight when he was killed.

4. Some researchers think that the Iceman _____ heart disease. This may give us clues about what life was like in ancient times. _____, it may help us understand new ways to help people avoid the disease.

5. Researchers _____ CT scans of the Iceman's body. They also used DNA analysis to _____ information about his mysterious death.

6. The blood in a leech at a crime scene matched a DNA _____ taken from one of the robbers, so police were able to determine his _____.

B Discuss these questions with a partner.

USING VOCABULARY

1. What questions about the past do you think **archaeologists** are trying to answer?

2. Why might it be challenging to **obtain** clues or evidence in their research?

C Read the title and the headings in the reading passage. Which two mysteries do you think the passage investigates? Check your answers as you read.

PREDICTING

☐ 1. how a pharaoh's tomb was robbed

☐ 2. what caused a pharaoh's death

☐ 3. who a pharaoh's family members were

KING TUT'S FAMILY SECRETS

by Zahi Hawass

🎧 1.04

A As an archaeologist and scholar of ancient Egyptian history, I believe that we should honor the ancient dead and let them rest in peace. On the other hand, there are some secrets of the ancient Egyptian pharaohs that we can learn only by studying their mummies. Let me use the example of King Tutankhamun to illustrate what I mean.

UNLOCKING A MYSTERY

B When Tutankhamun died about 3,000 years ago, he was secretly buried in a small tomb near what is now the city of Luxor. When archaeologists rediscovered the tomb in 1922, the king's treasures—more than 5,000 artifacts[1]—were still inside. Among the artifacts was the pharaoh's solid gold coffin and a gold mask. There were also 130 staffs, or walking sticks. Mysteriously, an examination of Tutankhamun's mummy revealed a hole in the back of his skull. Also, there were two mummified fetuses[2] in the tomb.

C These mummies and artifacts were an extremely important archaeological discovery, but they did not answer many questions about the young pharaoh and his family. Who were his mother and father? Were the two fetuses his unborn children? Could the hole in Tut's head be related to his cause of death? To solve these mysteries required further study and the use of CT scans and DNA analysis.

ANALYZING TUT

D In 2005, my colleagues and I carried out CT scans of Tutankhamun's mummy. We showed

---

[1] An **artifact** is a culturally or historically significant object that is made by a human being.

[2] A **fetus** is an unborn animal or human being in its later stages of development.

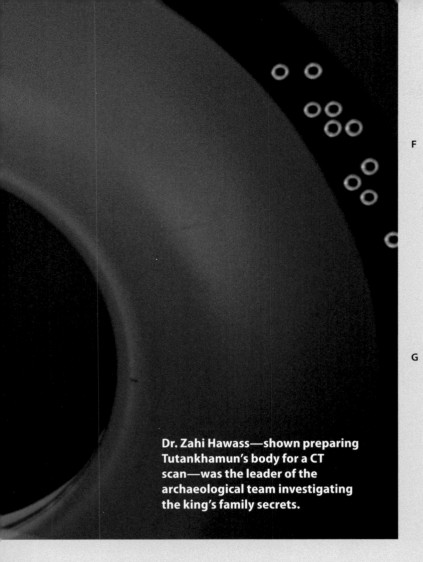

Dr. Zahi Hawass—shown preparing Tutankhamun's body for a CT scan—was the leader of the archaeological team investigating the king's family secrets.

Our team also tested Tutankhamun's mummy for evidence of infectious diseases. We found DNA from a parasite[4] called *Plasmodium falciparum*, which meant that Tutankhamun suffered from malaria. Did

F malaria kill the king? Perhaps. My opinion, however, is that Tutankhamun's health was endangered the moment he was born. To explain what I mean, let me describe our study of Tutankhamun's royal family.

TRACING TUT'S FAMILY TREE

Our team obtained and analyzed DNA samples from Tutankhamun and 10 other mummies we believed were members of his royal family. We knew the identities of three

G members of his family—Amenhotep III as well as Yuya and Tuyu, who were the parents of Amenhotep III's wife. The other seven mummies were unknown. They comprised an adult male, four adult females, and the two fetuses in Tutankhamun's tomb.

We first worked to solve the mystery of Tutankhamun's father. Many scholars believed his father was the pharaoh Akhenaten, but the archaeological evidence was unclear. Through a combination of CT scans and a comparison of DNA, our team was able to

H confirm Amenhotep III and Tiye—one of the unidentified female mummies—as the grandparents of Tutankhamun. Moreover, our study revealed that the unidentified male adult mummy was almost certainly Akhenaten, a son of Amenhotep III and Tiye. This supported the theory that Akhenaten was Tutankhamun's father.

What about Tutankhamun's mother? We discovered that the DNA of one of the unidentified female mummies matched that of the young king. To our surprise, her DNA

I proved that, like Akhenaten, she was a child of Amenhotep III and Tiye. This meant that Akhenaten and his wife were brother and sister—and Tutankhamun was their son.

that the hole in Tutankhamun's skull was made during the mummification process. Our study also showed that Tutankhamun died when he was only 19, soon after fracturing his left leg. However, the CT scans alone could not solve the mystery of how the king died, or why he died so young.

In 2008, my colleagues and I decided to analyze samples of Tutankhamun's DNA. Early in the study, our team made some new discoveries: Tutankhamun's left foot was clubbed,[3] and one toe was missing a bone. A condition known as

E necrosis (tissue death) had destroyed some bones in the foot. The discovery explained why there were so many staffs in Tutankhamun's tomb. Some scholars had argued that the staffs were symbols of power. Our DNA study showed that the king needed the staffs to walk.

[3] When a foot is **clubbed**, it is deformed so that the foot is twisted inward and most of the person's weight rests on the heel.

[4] A **parasite** is a small animal or plant that lives on or inside a larger animal or plant.

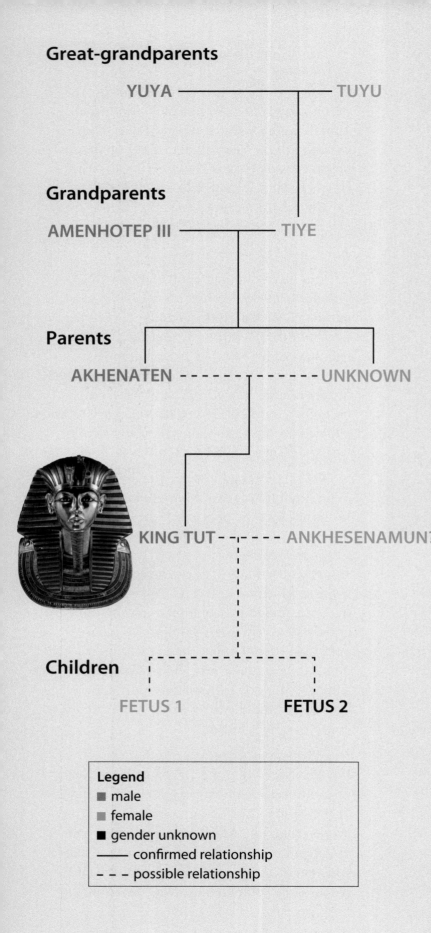

Great-grandparents

YUYA ————— TUYU

Grandparents

AMENHOTEP III ————— TIYE

Parents

AKHENATEN - - - - - - - - - - UNKNOWN

KING TUT - - - - - - ANKHESENAMUN?

Children

FETUS 1   FETUS 2

Legend
■ male
■ female
■ gender unknown
—— confirmed relationship
- - - possible relationship

J

While the data are still incomplete, our study also suggests that one of the mummified fetuses is Tutankhamun's daughter and that the other may also be his child. We have only partial data from the two other unidentified female mummies. One of these may be the mother of the infant mummies and Tutankhamun's wife—possibly a woman named Ankhesenamun. We know from history that she was the daughter of Akhenaten and his wife, Nefertiti, and therefore probably was Tutankhamun's half-sister.

HOW DID TUT DIE?

As I mentioned earlier, I believe that Tutankhamun's health was compromised[5] from birth. As our study showed, his mother and father were brother and sister. Such a relationship was common in royal families in ancient Egypt, as it offered political advantages. However,

K married siblings can pass on harmful genes. Tutankhamun's clubbed foot and bone disease may therefore have been because he had a genetic predisposition.[6] These problems, together with an attack of severe malaria or a broken leg, may have combined to cause the king's premature[7] death.

HONORING THE KING

After Tutankhamun's death, a new dynasty[8] came to power. The rulers of this new dynasty tried to erase all records of

L Tutankhamun and his royal family from history. Through ongoing DNA research, our team seeks to honor the members of Tutankhamun's family and keep their memories alive.

---

[5] If someone's health is **compromised**, it is weakened.
[6] If you have a **genetic predisposition** to a disease, your DNA makes you more likely to get that disease.
[7] Something that is **premature** happens earlier than people expect.
[8] A **dynasty** is a series of rulers of a country who all belong to the same family.

UNDERSTANDING THE READING

A Write a paragraph letter for each of these main ideas from the reading passage.

UNDERSTANDING MAIN IDEAS

1. _____ Hawass and his team studied Tut's DNA and found out that he had a bone disease.
2. _____ Tut's health may have been weakened because his parents were siblings.
3. _____ Hawass decided to use technology to answer questions about Tut's life and death.
4. _____ Hawass and his team used DNA samples to determine Tut's father.
5. _____ CT scans provided some information about Tut's body, but didn't show how he died.
6. _____ Hawass's analysis of Tut's DNA revealed that he had suffered from malaria.

B For each statement below, circle T for true, F for false, or NG if the information is not given.

UNDERSTANDING DETAILS

1. Researchers think the fetuses may have been Tutankhamun's children.   **T F NG**
2. Tuyu was Tutankhamun's wife.   **T F NG**
3. Analysis of Tutankhamun's mummy revealed that he was tall.   **T F NG**
4. Problems with Tutankhamun's bones and foot may have been genetic health problems.   **T F NG**
5. Tutankhamun's son became pharaoh after he died.   **T F NG**

C Put these events (a–g) in the order that they occurred.

SEQUENCING

a. Tutankhamun's tomb was rediscovered.
b. Archaeologists found a hole in Tutankhamun's skull.
c. Hawass and his team made CT scans of Tutankhamun's mummy.
d. Hawass and his team determined the identity of Tutankhamun's father.
e. Hawass and his team decided to study DNA from Tutankhamun's mummy.
f. Hawass and his team studied DNA from one of the female mummies in the tomb.
g. Hawass and his team discovered that Tutankhamun had a clubfoot and bone disease.

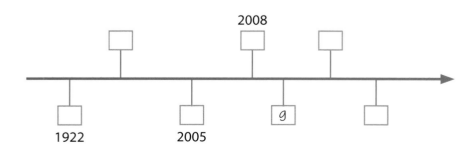

2008

1922   2005   g

D Find and underline these **bold** words in the reading passage. Use context to identify their meanings. Then write the part of speech and your own definition for each word.

1. **honor** (paragraph A)   Part of speech: _____

   Meaning: _____

2. **partial** (paragraph J)   Part of speech: _____

   Meaning: _____

3. **infant** (paragraph J)   Part of speech: _____

   Meaning: _____

4. **siblings** (paragraph K)   Part of speech: _____

   Meaning: _____

E Look back at the section "Tracing Tut's Family Tree." Find an example of information that is more certain and one that is less certain. Share the reasons for your answers with a partner.

_____

_____

F Work with a partner. Answer the questions below.

1. Based on the information in the text, check (✔) which health issues Hawass thinks may have contributed to Tut's death.

   ☐ 1. a head injury   ☐ 4. necrosis

   ☐ 2. a broken leg   ☐ 5. genetic predispositions

   ☐ 3. malaria   ☐ 6. a clubbed foot

2. Did Hawass and his team solve the mystery of Tut's death? Discuss with a partner.

G Compare Hawass's team's examination of Tutankhamun to scientists' examination of the Iceman. What are some of the similarities and differences? Note your ideas in the diagram. Then share them with a partner.

Examination of Tutankhamun   **Examination of the Iceman**

Writing

EXPLORING WRITTEN ENGLISH

A Read the two paragraphs. What did the writer do to paraphrase the original? Match the changes (a–c) to the highlighted parts.

NOTICING

a. combined two ideas together

b. used a different word with the same meaning

c. used a different part of speech for an idea

Original:

Our team also tested Tutankhamun's mummy for evidence of infectious diseases. We found DNA from a parasite called *Plasmodium falciparum*, which meant that Tutankhamun suffered from malaria. Did malaria kill the king? Perhaps. My opinion, however, is that Tutankhamun's health was endangered the moment he was born. To explain what I mean, let me describe our study of Tutankhamun's royal family.

Paraphrased version:

When Hawass's team examined Tutankhamun's remains for infectious diseases, they discovered from DNA analysis that the king had suffered from malaria. It is therefore possible that Tutankhamun's death was caused by this disease. However, in Hawass's view, Tutankhamun's health was in danger ever since his birth. Hawass describes his team's investigation of the king's royal family to support his opinion.

LANGUAGE FOR WRITING Paraphrasing

When you write a summary, it is important to paraphrase the original; that is, to use your own words to express the same information. Here are three techniques:

1. **Combine ideas.** Use words and phrases such as *and*, *because*, *while*, and *as soon as* to connect ideas. For example, the ideas in the first two sentences in the original paragraph above are combined into one sentence using *When . . . , they . . . .*

2. **Use synonyms.** For example, *investigation* instead of *study* was used in the paraphrased version. It is important to make sure that the synonym matches the context of your sentence. *Learning* is a synonym for *study*, but *investigation* works better in the context of the sentence.

3. **Use different parts of speech.** For instance, the paraphrased example above uses the noun *birth* instead of the adjective *born* to express the same meaning. If the original piece is written in the first person (*I*, *my team*, etc.), you will also need to change the point of view to third person (*He*, *Hawass's team*, etc.).

B Read the sentences and choose the best synonym for each underlined word.

1. After the police questioned him, the suspect eventually admitted to committing the 2001 robbery.

   a. allowed   b. confessed   c. welcomed

2. Scientists guessed that the Iceman might have been resting after a meal when enemies attacked him from behind.

   a. criticized   b. infected   c. assaulted

3. And indeed, a palo verde tree at the scene of the crime looked like a truck might have hit it.

   a. crashed into   b. slapped   c. punched

4. These mummies and artifacts were an extremely important archaeological discovery, but they did not answer many questions about the young pharaoh and his family.

   a. innovation   b. find   c. invention

5. The other seven mummies were unknown.

   a. foreign   b. strange   c. unidentified

6. Such a relationship was common in royal families in ancient Egypt, as it offered political advantages.

   a. improvements   b. benefits   c. pros

C Complete the paraphrased sentences below. Use a different part of speech for the boxed words, and paraphrase the underlined words using suitable synonyms.

1. When most people think of leeches, they imagine disgusting blood-sucking worms that they would prefer to avoid. However, leeches can actually be useful.

   Paraphrase: While most people's _____ is to avoid leeches, they can actually be _____ to us.

2. The suspect admitted to giving the victim a ride in his truck, but denied any wrongdoing.

   Paraphrase: The suspect admitted that the victim had _____ in his _____ , but denied responsibility for the crime.

3. Scientists also discovered a wound on one of his hands. This told them that he had likely been in a fight and that his enemies later chased after and killed him.

   Paraphrase: In addition, the _____ of an injury on one of his hands led scientists to believe that he had been in a fight before he was _____ .

WRITING SKILL Writing a Summary

A summary is a short, paraphrased version of an original passage. Paraphrasing is a useful method when writing a summary because you need to report in your own words the most important information in the original passage. Follow these steps to write a summary.

1. Read the passage once. As you read, underline the important facts. Then, without looking at the passage, write notes.

2. Reread the passage, comparing your notes against it to check your understanding. Edit any incorrect notes.

3. Use your notes to write a summary.
   - In a long text, look for sections of an article that discuss the same general idea.
   - Create a topic sentence that expresses the main idea of the section(s) that you are summarizing.
   - Paraphrase important supporting ideas from the original passage.

4. Compare your summary with the original. Make sure that your summary expresses the same meaning as the original, and that the ideas are presented in the same general order. If you use synonyms, check that they are suitable for the context.

5. Check your sentence structures and word choices. If your summary is very similar to the original, combine more ideas and paraphrase using synonyms or different parts of speech.

D Look back at "Researchers Discover Gender-Driven Play in Chimps" in Unit 1, Reading 2. Order the sentences (1–7) to make a summary.

__1__ a. Young primates in captivity often pick out toys based on their gender.

_____ b. Playing with sticks might also just be a way for the chimps to express their imaginations.

_____ c. Young male chimps, on the other hand, play energetically, chasing each other and climbing.

_____ d. Richard Wrangham, a Harvard University primatologist, has recently discovered that Kanyawara chimps in the wild do this, too.

__4__ e. Young female chimps play with sticks and take care of them like dolls or babies.

_____ f. Researchers believe that playing with sticks might have helped female chimps develop mothering skills, which helped their species survive.

_____ g. Young female monkeys choose dolls and young males choose trucks to play with.

WRITING TASK

> **GOAL** You are going to write summaries of two sections of Reading 1 in this unit.

BRAINSTORMING **A** Choose two of the sections of Reading 1 below. Without looking back, note down the main ideas of the sections and other important information that you can remember. Then compare the sections with your notes and make any corrections.

- A Robbery Case in Australia
- A Murder Case in Arizona
- A Body in the Mountains

PLANNING **B** Follow these steps to make notes for your summaries.

Step 1 Write a topic sentence that expresses the main idea of each section you are going to summarize.

Step 2 For each section, list important ideas that support each topic sentence.

OUTLINE

Summary 1

Topic Sentence: _____

_____

Important Ideas: _____

_____

_____

_____

_____

Summary 2

Topic Sentence: _____

_____

Important Ideas: _____

_____

_____

_____

_____

FIRST DRAFT **C** Use the information in your outline to write a first draft of your summaries. Write a paragraph for each one.

REVISING PRACTICE

The drafts below are based on a section of Unit 1, Reading 2.

What did the writer do in Draft 2 to improve the paragraph? Match the changes (a–d) to the highlighted parts.

a. added a topic sentence
b. added a relevant example
c. used a better synonym
d. paraphrased by combining ideas

Draft 1

In elephant groups, females develop lifelong relationships with one another, and help to raise each other's babies. Male elephants also have strong relationships with one another. In male groups, there is a firm hierarchy. Older males act as teachers for younger elephants. They control them when conflict occurs. This organization helps continue the peace when food and water are limited because the young males know that the older ones eat and drink first.

Draft 2

Elephants behave differently in social groups depending on their gender. In elephant groups, females develop lifelong relationships with one another, and help to raise each other's babies. When a baby's mother dies, aunts, grandmothers, and friends act as the orphan's mother. Male elephants also have strong relationships with one another. In male groups, there is a firm hierarchy. Older male elephants teach the younger ones, and have control of them. This organization helps keep the peace when food and water are limited because the young males know that the older ones eat and drink first.

D Now use the questions below to revise each of your summary paragraphs.   REVISED DRAFT

☐ Does your topic sentence state the main idea of the section you are summarizing?
☐ Did you include all the important information from the section?
☐ Did you present the information in the same general order as the original section?
☐ Did you paraphrase by combining ideas, using synonyms, or changing the parts of speech where appropriate?

EDITING PRACTICE

Read the information below.

When you use synonyms, make sure your synonym:
- has the same meaning as the original word.
- fits in the context of the sentence.

Correct one mistake with an underlined synonym in each of the paraphrases (1–3). Use a thesaurus to help you.

1. DNA is a <u>tiny</u> molecule containing a code that gives the body <u>instructions</u> for the growth of cells.

   Paraphrase: DNA is a <u>small</u> molecule that contains <u>lessons</u> for a person's cell development.

2. Because each person's DNA is <u>distinctive</u>, it is a <u>valuable</u> tool for identification.

   Paraphrase: Every individual's DNA is <u>diverse</u>, so it is <u>useful</u> in identifying people.

3. Using DNA phenotyping, scientists can <u>determine</u> traits such as a person's eye color, natural hair color, the possible shapes of their facial features, and their geographic <u>ancestry</u>.

   Paraphrase: DNA phenotyping allows scientists to <u>control</u> characteristics such as eye and hair color, facial structure, as well as geographic <u>origin</u>.

FINAL DRAFT **E** **Follow these steps to write a final draft.**

1. Check your revised draft for mistakes with using synonyms.
2. Now use the checklist on page 253 to write a final draft. Make any other necessary changes.

UNIT REVIEW
Answer the following questions.

1. How is DNA technology useful in helping detectives solve crimes? Name two ways.

   _____

   _____

   _____

2. What are some ways of paraphrasing information?

   _____

   _____

   _____

3. Do you remember the meanings of these words? Check (✔) the ones you know. Look back at the unit and review the ones you don't know.

   Reading 1:

   ☐ analysis AWL   ☐ commit AWL   ☐ detective AWL

   ☐ determine   ☐ examine   ☐ heal

   ☐ mystery   ☐ prove   ☐ reveal AWL

   ☐ suspect

   Reading 2:

   ☐ archaeologist   ☐ carry out   ☐ combination

   ☐ identity AWL   ☐ mention   ☐ moreover

   ☐ obtain AWL   ☐ sample   ☐ suffer from

   ☐ unclear

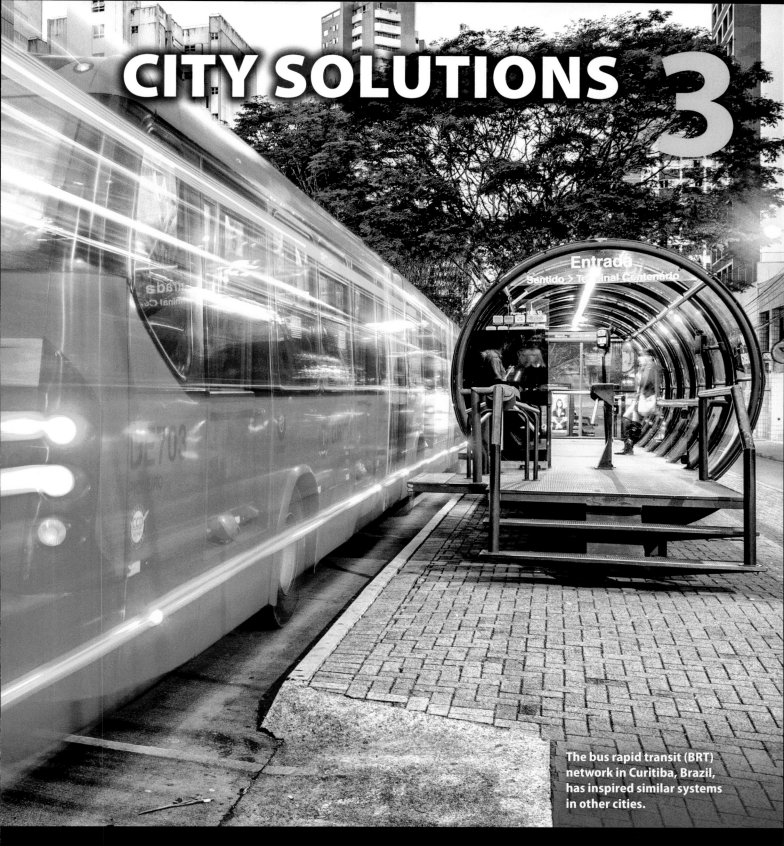

CITY SOLUTIONS 3

The bus rapid transit (BRT) network in Curitiba, Brazil, has inspired similar systems in other cities.

THINK AND DISCUSS

1 What are the biggest cities in your country? How would you describe them?

2 What is your favorite city? What do you like about it?

EXPLORE THE THEME

A Look at the information on these pages and answer the questions.

1. What overall trends have occurred in the world's urban population since 1950?

2. Which region had the fastest percentage urban growth from 1950 to 1990? How about from 1990 to 2015?

3. Which regions are projected to urbanize fastest between now and 2050?

B Match the words in yellow to their definitions.

_____ (adj) related to a city

_____ (n) the process of increasing

_____ (adj) having a large number of people and buildings close together

AN URBAN SPECIES

Urban areas of more than a million people were rare until the early 20th century. Today, there are over 30 cities of more than 10 million people. These **dense** areas can have more than 500 inhabitants per square mile (over 195 people per square kilometer).

Growth in these high-density cities is likely to increase even more in the future as populations rise and migration from rural areas continues. In fact, two-thirds of the world's population may live in cities by 2050.

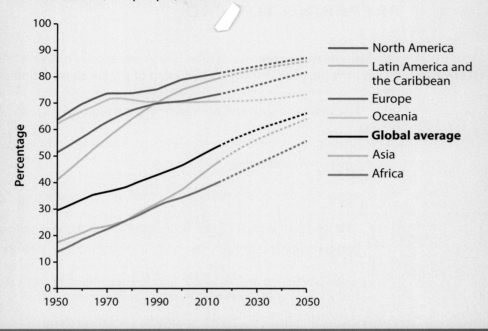

Growing Urbanization

Percentage of population living in urban areas of more than 300,000 people, 1950–2050

- North America
- Latin America and the Caribbean
- Europe
- Oceania
- **Global average**
- Asia
- Africa

With a population of about 3 million people, Dubai is the most populous city in the United Arab Emirates.

Reading 1

PREPARING TO READ

BUILDING
VOCABULARY

A The words and phrases in blue below are used in Reading 1. Read the sentences. Then match the correct form of each word or phrase to its definition.

> Houses in the **suburbs** are relatively cheap compared to those in the city center.
>
> Some studies show that employees with flexible working arrangements are happier and more **productive**.
>
> Many governments have policies that support low-**income** families.
>
> One negative **aspect** of city living is traffic congestion—cities **tend to** have a higher **concentration** of cars on the roads, especially during peak hours.
>
> Major cities such as Tokyo continue to **spread out** as their populations grow.

1. _____ (n) a part or side of something

2. _____ (v) to cover a huge area

3. _____ (n) money that a person earns

4. _____ (adj) able to achieve a significant amount or result

5. _____ (v) to usually do something or be a certain way

6. _____ (n) a huge amount or number of something in one place

7. _____ (n) an area outside of a large city that has homes and businesses

USING
VOCABULARY

B Discuss these questions with a partner.
1. Would you rather live in a city center, a **suburb**, or a rural area? Why?
2. What **aspects** of city life appeal to you? Which aspects don't you like?

PREDICTING

C Read the title and the headings in the reading passage. What do you think the passage is mainly about? Check your idea as you read.

a. a comparison of large cities in the past and those in the present

b. the environmental challenges that growing cities are facing

c. the positive impacts of urbanization on people and the environment

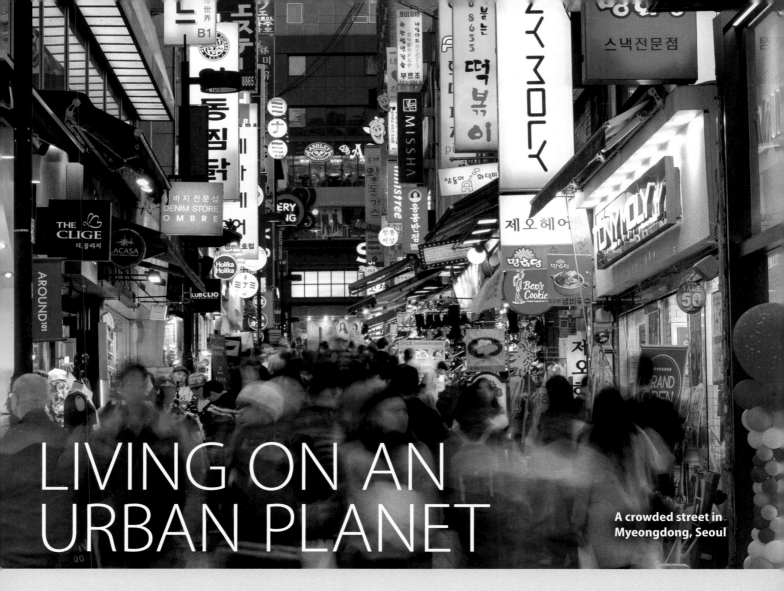

LIVING ON AN URBAN PLANET

A crowded street in Myeongdong, Seoul

🎧 1.05

A   Consider this: in 1800, less than 3 percent of the world's population lived in cities, but by 2050, this could increase to over 66 percent. The trend is clear and the conclusion inescapable—humans have become an **urban** species.

CITIES AS SOLUTIONS?

B   In the 19th and early 20th centuries, large urban areas began to grow and spread. Many people viewed cities largely in negative terms—crowded, dirty, unhealthy places full of disease and crime. People feared that as cities got bigger, living conditions would get worse. Recent decades, however, have seen a widespread change in attitudes toward urbanization.[1] Many experts believe that urbanization is good news. Although negative **aspects** such as pollution and urban slums remain serious problems, many urban planners now believe big cities might help solve the problem of Earth's growing population.

[1] **Urbanization** is the process by which cities grow.

The trading floor of the
New York Stock Exchange

Harvard economist Edward Glaeser is one person who believes that cities bring largely positive benefits. According to Glaeser, cities are "the absence of space between people." This closeness reduces the cost of transporting goods, people, and ideas, and allows people to be more productive. Successful cities also attract and reward smart people with higher wages, and they enable people to learn from one another. According to Glaeser, a perfect example of how information can be shared in a big city is the trading floor of the New York Stock Exchange. There, employees share information in one open, crowded space. "They value knowledge over space," he says. "That's what the modern city is all about."

Another champion[2] of urbanization is environmentalist Stewart Brand. According to Brand, living in cities has a smaller impact on the environment than living in suburbs and rural areas. Cities allow half of the world's population to live on about 4 percent of the land. City roads, sewers,[3] and power lines are shorter and require fewer resources to build and operate. City apartments require less energy to heat, cool, and light than houses in other areas. Most

[2] If you are a **champion** of something, you support or defend it.
[3] **Sewers** are large underground channels that carry waste matter and rainwater away.

importantly, Brand points out that people living in dense cities drive less. They can walk to many destinations and use public transportation. As a result, cities tend to produce fewer greenhouse gas emissions per person than suburbs.

Because of these reasons, it may be a mistake to see urbanization as evil. Instead, we should view it as an inevitable part of development, says David Satterthwaite of London's International Institute of Environment and Development. For Satterthwaite and other urban planners, rapid growth itself is not the real problem. The larger issue is how to manage the growth. There is no one model for how to manage rapid urbanization, but there are hopeful examples. One is Seoul, South Korea.

SEOUL'S SUCCESS STORY

Since the 1960s, Seoul's population has increased from fewer than 3 million to more than 10 million people. In the same period, South Korea has also gone from being one of the world's poorest countries to being richer than many countries in Europe. How did this happen? Large numbers of people first began arriving in Seoul in the 1950s. The government soon recognized that economic development was essential for supporting its growing urban population. It therefore began to invest in South Korean companies. This investment eventually helped corporations such as Samsung and Hyundai grow and develop. A major contributing factor for South Korea's economic success was the large number of people who came to Seoul to work.

"You can't understand urbanization in isolation from economic development," says economist Kyung-Hwan Kim of Sogang University. The growing city paid for the buildings, roads, and other infrastructure that helped absorb even more people. South Korea's growth cannot be easily copied. However, it proves that a poor country can urbanize successfully and incredibly fast.

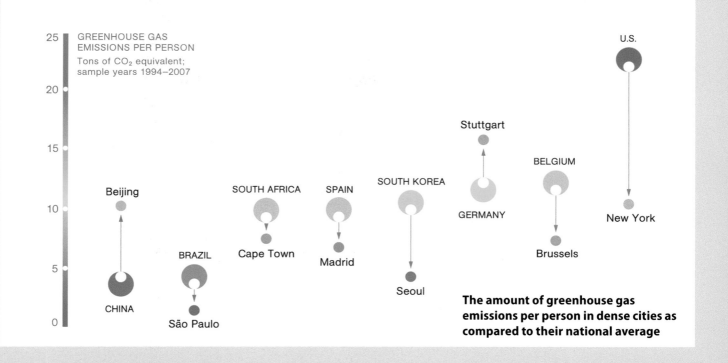

GREENHOUSE GAS
EMISSIONS PER PERSON

Tons of CO_2 equivalent;
sample years 1994–2007

The amount of greenhouse gas emissions per person in dense cities as compared to their national average

MANAGING URBANIZATION

Despite success stories such as Seoul, urban planners around the world continue to struggle with the problem of how to manage urbanization. While they used to worry mainly about city density, urban planners today are focusing on urban sprawl—the way big cities are spreading out and taking over more and more land.

Shlomo Angel is an urban planning professor at New York University and Princeton University. He thinks rising incomes and cheaper transportation are two main reasons for urban sprawl. "When income rises, people have money to buy more space," he says. With cheaper transportation, people can afford to travel longer distances to work. In the second half of the 20th century, for example, many people in the United States moved from cities to suburban areas. This trend led to expanding suburbs, which led to more energy use and increased air pollution and greenhouse gas emissions.

Today, many planners want to bring people back to downtown areas and make suburbs denser. Some ways to densify suburbs include creating walkable town centers, high-rise apartment buildings, and more public transportation. This would make people less dependent on cars. "It would be a lot better for the planet," says Edward Glaeser, if people are "in dense cities built around the elevator rather than in sprawling areas built around the car."

Shlomo Angel believes that planning can make a big difference in the way cities are allowed to grow. However, good planning requires looking decades ahead—reserving land for parks and public transportation, for example, before the city grows over it. It also requires looking at growing cities in a positive way, as concentrations of human energy. With the Earth's population headed toward 9 or 10 billion, dense and carefully planned cities are looking more like a solution—perhaps the best hope for lifting people out of poverty without wrecking[4] the planet.

[4] To **wreck** something means to completely destroy or ruin it.

UNDERSTANDING THE READING

SUMMARIZING

A Read the first sentence of a summary of "Living on an Urban Planet." Check (✓) four other sentences to complete the summary.

Because most of the world's population will live in cities, it's important to plan and manage cities well so they can benefit society.

☐ 1. Urbanization has a lot of benefits, such as the easy exchange of ideas and the reduction of human impact on the environment.

☐ 2. Seoul experienced many problems as a result of its rapid population growth between 1960 and 2000.

☐ 3. Seoul's successful urbanization is an example of how urbanization can bring positive impacts to cities and countries.

☐ 4. Although some cities have managed to urbanize well, urban planners today are concerned with managing the expansion of large cities.

☐ 5. The second half of the 20th century saw many people in the United States moving out of cities.

☐ 6. Careful long-term planning is key to growing cities that can accommodate the world's future population.

UNDERSTANDING
MAIN IDEAS

B Match each section of the reading passage to its main idea.

_____ 1. Paragraph B

_____ 2. Paragraph C

_____ 3. Paragraph D

_____ 4. Paragraphs F–G

_____ 5. Paragraph J

_____ 6. Paragraph K

a. Urbanization is better for the environment.

b. By reducing distance, cities bring largely positive benefits.

c. Proper urban planning can bring positive results to cities.

d. Recently, attitudes toward living in cities have become more positive.

e. Planners want to reduce the need for cars in suburban areas.

f. Well-managed urbanization in the 20th century helped a poor country achieve rapid economic development.

IDENTIFYING
PROS AND CONS

C Answer the questions below with information from the reading passage.

1. According to Edward Glaeser, what are two benefits of living in cities? (paragraph C)

_____

2. According to Stewart Brand, what is one benefit of dense cities? What is one example he gives? (paragraph D)

_____

3. According to David Satterthwaite, what is the main challenge related to urbanization? (paragraph E)

_____

D Read the following quotes from the passage. Which main or supporting idea from the paragraph does each quote support? Discuss with a partner.

1. "They value knowledge over space. That's what the modern city is all about." (paragraph C)

   _____

   _____

2. "You can't understand urbanization in isolation from economic development." (paragraph G)

   _____

   _____

3. "When income rises, people have money to buy more space." (paragraph I)

   _____

   _____

4. "It would be a lot better for the planet [if people are] in dense cities built around the elevator rather than in sprawling areas built around the car." (paragraph J)

   _____

   _____

E Do you think that city life is mainly beneficial? Why or why not? Complete the sentence below. Include at least two reasons. Then share your ideas with a partner.

Overall, I think urbanization has a **positive / negative** impact on human societies because

_____

_____

Shanghai has experienced rapid urbanization since the 1980s.

DEVELOPING READING SKILLS

READING SKILL Analyzing Visual Information

When you first look at a graph, read the title, subtitle, caption, and/or legend (key). Ask yourself what information is being presented. What do the lines, colors, or symbols mean? What is the purpose of the graph? Then underline important words in the title or caption that tell you about the content. Ask yourself how the graph supports the ideas in the reading passage. How does it help you understand the author's ideas better?

ANALYZING VISUAL INFORMATION

A Work with a partner. Look at the graph below and answer the questions.

1. Look at the title, subtitle, and legend. What is the main purpose of the graph?
2. Underline the sentence in the reading passage that the graph relates to.
3. How does the graph support the sentence in the reading passage?

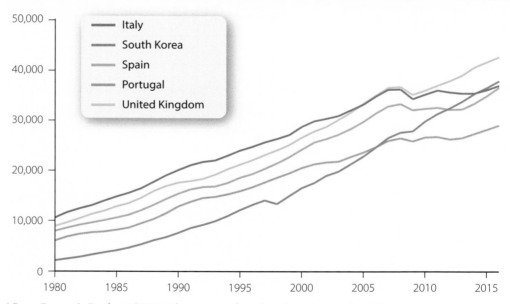

South Korea Overtakes Europe
Growth in GDP[1] per capita (against selected European countries) 1980–2016

[1]Gross Domestic Product (GDP) is the amount of goods and services produced in one year.

ANALYZING VISUAL INFORMATION

B Look at the infographic in the reading passage and answer the questions. Discuss your answers with a partner.

1. What do the red and green colors indicate? _____
2. What is the main purpose of the chart?
   a. to show the emissions goals of certain cities and countries
   b. to show how some countries have reduced their emissions in the last 25 years
   c. to show how most cities have lower per capita emissions than their countries
3. Which paragraph in the passage does the graph support? _____

Video

FARMING UNDERGROUND

A World War II air raid shelter in London is converted into a farm.

BEFORE VIEWING

A Read the title and the photo caption. Why do you think people would create farms underground? Discuss with a partner.

B Read the information about food miles—the distance food travels from where it's produced to people's plates—and answer the questions.

How big an impact do "food miles" have on the environment? In some parts of the world, food—such as grains, fruit, and vegetables—travels over 2,400 kilometers to get to consumers. In 2016, the United Kingdom imported about half of its food from other countries. This food is flown or shipped into the country and then transported to towns and cities in trucks. Food transportation trucks produce a quarter of transport-related greenhouse gas emissions—a major cause of global warming. And with an expanding population, these issues are only likely to increase. If producers and consumers are serious about slowing global warming, growing—and buying—more food locally could reduce "food miles."

1. How do "food miles" affect the environment?

   _____

2. Are the problems related to "food miles" likely to increase or decrease in the future? Why?

   _____

3. What do you think is one way to help reduce "food miles" where you live? Note your idea and discuss with a partner.

   _____

C The words and phrases in **bold** below are used in the video. Read the sentences. Then match the correct form of each word or phrase to its definition.

> One way to be more **carbon-neutral** is to drive less and walk more.
>
> **LEDs** save money and energy because they use 90 percent less power than traditional light bulbs.
>
> The **distribution** of food by air and land can cause greenhouse gas emissions.
>
> By **utilizing** new farming technologies—such as **hydroponic farming**—we can use fewer resources to produce the food we need.

1. _____ (n) the act of supplying goods

2. _____ (v) to use something

3. _____ (n) a device that produces light, usually used in electronics

4. _____ (adj) adding no more carbon to the atmosphere than the amount you take in

5. _____ (n) a method of growing plants in mineral-rich water

WHILE VIEWING

A ▶ Watch the video. Check (✓) the reasons Steven Dring and Richard Ballard built an underground farm.

☐ 1. to make young people aware of how food is grown
☐ 2. to grow new types of plants
☐ 3. to cut down on food miles
☐ 4. to help solve environmental problems
☐ 5. to provide food for the growing population of London
☐ 6. to use less water than traditional farming

B ▶ Watch the video again. For each statement below, circle T for true, F for false, or NG if the information is not given.

1. Steven Dring and Richard Ballard built the tunnels. **T F NG**

2. According to Dring, the population in London will increase by two million in 10 years. **T F NG**

3. The underground farm receives funding from the government. **T F NG**

4. Dring and Ballard want to grow more plants in the future. **T F NG**

AFTER VIEWING

A Steven Dring says, "We've still got kids in the U.K. who think that spaghetti is grown on trees." Why is this a problem? How can the underground farm help solve it? Discuss with a partner.

B What challenges do you think underground farms in cities might face? Think of two ideas. Then share them with a partner.

Reading 2

PREPARING TO READ

BUILDING
VOCABULARY

A The words in blue below are used in Reading 2. Complete the sentences with the correct words. Use a dictionary to help you.

attempt	basically	consumption	enhance
increasingly	industrial	majority	safety
phenomenon	varied		

1. One way to improve the _____ of city neighborhoods is to have regular police patrols.

2. According to Stewart Brand, city living actually reduces energy _____ because the _____ of people have access to public transportation and don't have to drive so much.

3. The _____ of urbanization is becoming _____ common as more and more cities continue to grow and develop.

4. Manchester used to be a(n) _____ city; from cotton to chemicals, there was a(n) _____ group of factories and businesses there.

5. Economist Edward Glaeser _____ sees cities as places where there is an absence of space between people.

6. The _____ to clean up a small river in downtown Seoul was a success—it helped _____ the attractiveness of the area.

USING
VOCABULARY

B Discuss these questions with a partner.
1. What are two ways to **enhance** the quality of life in cities?
2. What can you do to reduce your energy **consumption**?

PREDICTING

C Reading 2 is an interview with Richard Wurman, an urban planner. Wurman studied various cities to learn more about the effects of global urbanization.

What kinds of information about the cities do you think he collected? Discuss with a partner. Then check your ideas as you read.

_____

_____

THE URBAN VISIONARY

🎧 1.06

A When architect and urban planner Richard Wurman learned that the majority of Earth's population lived in cities, he became curious. He wondered what the effects of global urbanization will be. With a group of business and media partners, Wurman set out on a five-year study—a project called 19.20.21—to collect information about urbanization, focusing on the world's largest urban concentrations, or megacities.

B The project's aim is to standardize the way information about cities—such as health, education, transportation, energy consumption, and arts and culture—is collected and shared. The hope is that urban planners will be able to use these objective data to enhance the quality of life for people in cities while reducing the environmental impact of urbanization.

Q: What draws people to cities?

C **Wurman:** People flock to cities because of the possibilities for doing things that interest them. Those interests—and the economics that make them possible—are based on people living together. We really have turned into a world of cities. Cities cooperate with each other. Cities trade with each other. Cities are where you put museums, where you put universities, where you put the centers of government, the centers of corporations. The inventions, the discoveries, the music and art in our world all take place in these intense gatherings of individuals.

Q: Tell us about 19.20.21.

D **Wurman:** For the first time in history, more people live in cities than outside them. I thought I'd try to discover what this new phenomenon really means. I went to the Web, and I tried to find the appropriate books and lists that would give me information, data, maps, so I could

> **"**One has to understand [a city's problems] in context and in comparison to other places.**"**

understand. And I couldn't find what I was looking for. I couldn't find maps of cities to the same scale. Much of the statistical information is gathered independently by each city, and the questions they ask are often not the same. There's no readily available information on the speed of growth of cities. Diagrams on power, water distribution and quality, health care, and education aren't available, so a metropolis[1] can't find out any information about itself relative to other cities and, therefore, can't judge the success or failure of programs.

[1] A **metropolis** is a large, important, busy city.

So I decided to gather consistent information on 19 cities that will have more than 20 million people in the 21st century. That's what 19.20.21 is about. We'll have a varied group of young cities, old cities, third-world cities, second-world cities, first-world cities, fast-growing cities, slow-growing cities, coastal cities, inland cities, industrial cities, [and] cultural cities. Much of this can be presented online, but we're also planning to have exhibits and urban observatories so that cities around the world can see themselves relative to others.

Q: What are some of the cities you're looking at?

Wurman: What inspires me is being able to understand something, and understanding often comes from looking at extremes. So the cities that pop out are the ones that are clearly the largest, the oldest, the fastest-growing, the lowest, the highest, the densest, the least dense, [or] the largest in area. The densest city is Mumbai. The fastest-growing is Lagos.[2] For years, the largest city was Mexico City, but Tokyo is now the biggest … There are cities that are basically spread out, like Los Angeles. Then there are classic cities, which you certainly wouldn't want to leave out, like Paris. I find the data on cities to be endlessly fascinating. Just look at the world's 10 largest cities through time. The biggest city in the year 1000 was Córdoba, Spain. Beijing was the biggest city in 1500 and 1800, London in 1900, New York City in 1950, and today [it's] Tokyo.

[2]In 2017, Dhaka was the densest city, and Zinder was the fastest-growing.

Today, Plaza de la Corredera in Córdoba is a popular place for visitors to the city.

Q: Cities are increasingly challenged to sustain their infrastructure and service. Can they survive as they are now?

Wurman: Nothing survives as it is now. All cities are cities for the moment, and our thoughts about how to make them better are thoughts at the moment. There was great passion 30 years ago for the urban bulldozer,[3] that we had to tear down the slums, tear down the old parts of cities, and have urban renewal. That lasted for about 10, 15 years, until it didn't seem to work very well. And yet the reasons for doing it seemed justified at that moment … It shows that the attempt to make things better often makes things worse. We have to understand before we act. And although there are a lot of little ideas for making things better—better learning, increased safety, cleaner air—you can't solve the problem with a collection of little ideas. One has to understand them in context and in comparison to other places.

[3]A **bulldozer** is a large vehicle used for knocking down buildings.

THE URBAN OBSERVATORY

Wurman's team has created an interactive online exhibit called the Urban Observatory. Hoping to make the world's data "understandable and useful," the website has maps that compare different cities according to a variety of themes. These themes include the types of occupations people have, the types of transportation available, and the quality of public spaces, such as parks.

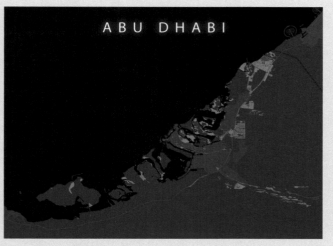

▲ The maps above show the distribution of green spaces in three major cities.

UNDERSTANDING THE READING

A Choose the best alternative title for the reading passage.

UNDERSTANDING MAIN IDEAS

   a. An Idea for Sharing Urban Data

   b. An Idea for Improving Urban Areas

   c. An Idea for Controlling Urban Expansion

B Match each section in the passage to its purpose.

UNDERSTANDING PURPOSE

_____ 1. Paragraph B   a. to state what the project wants to achieve

_____ 2. Paragraph C   b. to give reasons why more people are moving to cities

_____ 3. Paragraph D   c. to give advice on how cities should manage their development

_____ 4. Paragraphs E–F

_____ 5. Paragraph G   d. to describe the types of data included in the project and what they show

                      e. to explain the challenges Wurman faced when studying urbanization

C Complete the concept map using information from paragraphs A, B, D, and E. Write no more than two words or a number in each space.

UNDERSTANDING DETAILS

Origins

- created by Richard Wurman, an [1]_____ and urban planner
- Wurman was curious how [2]_____ will change the world
- he set up 19.20.21 with a team of people working in [3]_____ and [4]_____
- the project was expected to last for [5]_____

Aims

- to [6]_____ the collection of city data so that it's easier to compare, e.g., all city maps use the same scale
- the data can then be used by [7]_____ to improve city living
- Wurman hopes urbanization can then have a more positive [8]_____

19.20.21

Methods

- data is collected from the world's largest cities
- study focuses on cities with populations of over [9]_____ people
- looks at how people use transportation, how much [10]_____ they consume, etc.
- information will be shared [11]_____ and via exhibits and other events

D Find the following words and phrases in the reading passage. Use context to identify their meanings. Then circle the best option to complete the definitions.

> draw (paragraph C)   pop out (paragraph F)
>
> flock (paragraph C)   slum (paragraph G)
>
> relative to (paragraph D)

1. Things that *draw* people to a city make them want to **go there** / **stay away**.

2. When people *flock* to a place, they go in **small** / **large** numbers.

3. *Relative to* something means **in comparison with** / **connected to** it.

4. If information *pops out*, you notice it more because it is **detailed** / **obvious**.

5. *Slums* are parts of cities where living conditions are very **poor** / **good**.

E Look at the maps in the reading passage and answer the questions below.

1. What do the maps show?

   _____

2. Which city has the greatest amount? Which has the least?

   _____

3. How might this information be useful for cities?

   _____

   _____

F Read the statements below. Which of the people in this unit—Glaeser, Brand, Angel, or Wurman—would agree most strongly with each one? Write a name for each statement. More than one answer is possible. Then share your answers with a partner.

1. Overall, people living in cities have a smaller carbon footprint.   _____

2. It's better to make decisions about a city after looking at it alongside others.   _____

3. Cities are efficient and important places for people to share ideas and information.   _____

4. Proper planning is the way to manage urban growth and overcome problems.   _____

Writing

EXPLORING WRITTEN ENGLISH

A Read the sentences (a–c) and notice the underlined verbs. Match each sentence to the most suitable description. NOTICING

a. In 2017, Steven Dring and Richard Ballard <u>set up</u> an underground farm in London.

b. Richard Wurman's team <u>has created</u> an online exhibit for the Urban Observatory.

c. Edward Glaeser <u>has written</u> a number of books about cities.

_____ 1. The action happened at an unspecified time in the past.

_____ 2. The action happened several times in the past.

_____ 3. The action happened at a specific time in the past.

LANGUAGE FOR WRITING Using the Simple Past and the Present Perfect

We use the simple past to describe actions that began and ended in the past.

The Highline—a green space in New York City—**opened** to the public in 2009.

We use the present perfect tense to talk about:

1. something that happened several times in the past.

Planners **have redeveloped** this area three times.

2. something that happened at an unspecified time in the past.

The Urban Observatory **has gathered** data from many different cities.

Note: To form the present perfect, use _have_ or _has_ and the past participle of a main verb.

B Circle the correct options to complete the sentences.

1. Large numbers of people **moved** / **have moved** to Seoul during the 1950s.

2. In the 1950s, the South Korean government **invested** / **has invested** in local companies such as Samsung and Hyundai in order to support the country's economic growth.

3. Before the 20th century, South Korea **was** / **has been** one of the world's poorest countries.

4. Overall, life **improved** / **has improved** for South Koreans during the past few decades.

5. In 1961, the life expectancy in South Korea was 51 years. Since then, it **increased** / **has increased** to 79 years.

The first paragraph of an essay is the **introductory paragraph**. This paragraph contains the thesis statement and general information about the essay. It can also include a **hook**—an opening sentence to make the reader interested. The hook can be a surprising fact, an interesting question, or an imaginary situation related to the topic. See the first sentence of paragraph A, Reading 1, for an example.

A **thesis statement** is usually the last sentence in the introductory paragraph. It expresses the main idea of an entire essay. Here's an example of a thesis statement for a problem-solution essay:

> *With more convenient public transportation and pedestrian-only streets, Morristown is now an environmentally friendly and healthy place for its residents.*

A good thesis statement gives the writer's position about the topic and states the main points of the essay.

Note: In an introduction, you should avoid using *I* unless you are writing a personal essay. For example, you should avoid saying *I am going to write about . . . .*

C Read the following pairs of thesis statements. Choose the one in each pair that you think is better. Share the reasons for your answers with a partner.

1. a. Life is a lot better in Philadelphia than it was a few years ago for several good reasons.
   b. Life is a lot better in Philadelphia today because there is less crime and more job opportunities.

2. a. Two recent changes have improved the city of San Pedro: new streetlights and better roads.
   b. Most residents of San Pedro are very pleased with the recent infrastructure improvements.

D Choose the best opening hook for each essay topic. Then discuss with a partner.

1. **Topic:** making parking in the city center more convenient
   a. I used to avoid going downtown because it always took me a really long time to find parking.
   b. How long is too long to look for parking downtown? Ten minutes? Fifteen minutes? An hour?

2. **Topic:** improving road safety in cities
   a. Each year, more than 800 people are hit by cars in San Francisco.
   b. A lot of people get hit by cars in San Francisco while they're trying to cross the street.

3. **Topic:** managing traffic congestion in cities
   a. Traffic is terrible in my city because there are too many cars on the road and as a result, it takes a really long time to get anywhere.
   b. Imagine this: It's 8 a.m. You have 30 minutes to get to your job on the other side of town. The traffic is terrible—you'll never make it.

E Match the topics in exercise D to their thesis statements below. One statement is extra.

_____ a. With the introduction of a new subway line and increased housing in the city, there should now be fewer cars on the roads during peak hours.

_____ b. In response to the problem, the government has set stricter rules on where you can leave your car in the city center.

_____ c. To ensure the well-being of all road users, city planners have now put more stoplights and created more areas where cars can't go.

_____ d. The increased number of garages in the central district has made it easier for drivers to find a space to leave their cars when they visit.

> **WRITING SKILL** Writing a Concluding Paragraph
>
> The last paragraph of an essay is the **concluding paragraph**. This paragraph usually includes a **summary statement** and sometimes leaves the reader with a **final thought** about the topic. The summary statement paraphrases the thesis statement. Notice in the summary statement below how the author restates the thesis statement in the Writing Skill box in different words.
>
> _Improved public transportation and pedestrian-only streets have given Morristown cleaner air and a more sustainable future._
>
> Here are two ways to leave the reader with a final thought.
>
> - Make a prediction: _The effects of these improvements to life in Morristown may encourage more people to move here._
> - Ask a question: _Will these improvements inspire city officials to make even more environmentally friendly changes in Morristown?_

F Write a summary statement for each thesis statement in exercise E.

_____

_____

_____

_____

_____

_____

G Choose one of the summary statements in exercise F and write a final thought.

_____

_____

WRITING TASK

GOAL You are going to write a problem-solution essay on the following topic:

Describe a problem that a city or town had, and explain one thing that was done to solve it.

BRAINSTORMING **A** Think of a city or town that is better to live in now than it used to be. Make a list of improvements that were made. Think about areas such as housing, environmental issues, traffic, public transportation, and job opportunities. Do research if necessary.

PLANNING **B** Follow these steps to make notes for your essay.

Step 1 Choose the problem that you want to write about. Note it in the outline, and note two effects of the problem as your supporting ideas.

Step 2 Describe the best solution to the problem. Note two ways it helped solve the problem.

Step 3 Write a thesis statement that states the problem and the solution. Add a hook to your introduction.

Step 4 Write a summary statement and add a final thought for the concluding paragraph.

OUTLINE
Introductory Paragraph
Hook: _____

Thesis Statement: _____

_____

The Problem: _____

Supporting Idea 1 / Details: _____

_____

Supporting Idea 2 / Details: _____

_____

The Solution: _____

Supporting Idea 1 / Details: _____

_____

Supporting Idea 2 / Details: _____

_____

Concluding Paragraph
Summary Statement: _____

Final Thought: _____

REVISING PRACTICE

The draft below is similar to the one you are going to write. Follow the steps to create a better second draft.

1. Add the sentences (a–c) in the most suitable spaces.
   a. It was dirty and dark, with a lot of noise from the cars rushing overhead.
   b. What other improvements might make the city an even more beautiful place to live and visit?
   c. Imagine your shock when you visit San Francisco for the first time, and you have to walk under an ugly freeway to get to the bay.

2. Now fix the following problems (d–f) in the essay.
   d. Cross out one sentence that does not relate to the topic sentence in paragraph B.
   e. Correct a mistake with the simple past or present perfect in paragraph B.
   f. Correct a mistake with the simple past or present perfect in paragraph C.

A

_____ It isn't what you expected. Parts of the city are actually unattractive. However, one improvement that has made the city a more beautiful place for residents and tourists is tearing down the Embarcadero freeway.

B

For three decades until the early 1990s, the Embarcadero freeway was one of the least attractive parts of San Francisco. The two-level freeway completely blocked the view of the bay and sites in the bay, such as Angel Island and Alcatraz. Visitors can take ferries to Alcatraz and take a tour of the old prison. In addition, pedestrians had to walk underneath this 150,000-ton cement structure in order to get from downtown to the bay. Walking under the freeway has not been a pleasant experience. _____

C

In 1989, part of the freeway has been destroyed by an earthquake; two years later, the city authorities decided to take the whole thing down and renovate the area. One way that this has helped make San Francisco more beautiful is by giving people access to the bay. People are able to walk or jog along the Embarcadero or just enjoy views of the Bay Bridge, the water, and the hills and neighboring cities on the other side of the bay. Tearing down the freeway has also allowed residents and tourists to see the beautiful Ferry Building, one of San Francisco's most important buildings. The Ferry Building was closed for decades, but since the renovation, it has been open, and now houses great shops and restaurants. The once ugly Embarcadero has become a place that residents and tourists want to visit.

D

The removal of the Embarcadero freeway has made the waterfront area attractive and accessible for both visitors and San Franciscans. Today, most people don't even remember the old freeway. _____

D **Now use the questions below to revise your essay.**

☐ Does your introductory paragraph have an interesting hook and a clear thesis statement?

☐ Did you include enough details to explain the problem and the solution in your body paragraphs?

☐ Does your concluding paragraph have a summary statement and a final thought?

EDITING PRACTICE

Read the information below.

In sentences using the present perfect, remember to:
• use the correct form of *have.*
• use the correct form of the past participle of the main verb.

Correct one mistake with the present perfect in each of the sentences (1–5).

1. The city have made a lot of changes over the past 10 years.

2. Residents have enjoy the renovations to the city center and the public parks.

3. The new subway system has make it easier to get across town.

4. It is now safer for people to ride their bikes to work because the government has add bicycle lanes to busy streets.

5. San Francisco city planners has created a beautiful walkable area alongside the bay.

E **Follow these steps to write a final draft.**

1. Check your revised draft for mistakes with the simple past and the present perfect.

2. Now use the checklist on page 253 to write a final draft. Make any other necessary changes.

UNIT REVIEW
Answer the following questions.

1. Why might living in cities be better than living in the suburbs? List two reasons.

_____

_____

_____

2. What should you include in a thesis statement?

_____

_____

_____

3. Do you remember the meanings of these words? Check (✔) the ones you know. Look back at the unit and review the ones you don't know.

Reading 1:

☐ aspect AWL   ☐ concentration AWL   ☐ dense
☐ growth   ☐ income AWL   ☐ productive
☐ spread out   ☐ suburb   ☐ tend to
☐ urban

Reading 2:

☐ attempt   ☐ basically   ☐ consumption AWL
☐ enhance AWL   ☐ increasingly   ☐ industrial
☐ majority AWL ☐ phenomenon AWL   ☐ safety
☐ varied AWL

DANGER ZONES

Mount Sinabung—an active
volcano in Sumatra, Indonesia

ACADEMIC SKILLS

READING Understanding referencing and cohesion
WRITING Writing a process essay
GRAMMAR Using parallel structures
CRITICAL THINKING Inferring

THINK AND DISCUSS

1 What extreme natural events can be dangerous to humans?
2 Why do you think some people live in areas that are affected by extreme natural events?

A Look at the information on these pages and answer the questions.

1. Where in the world do most of the following occur?
   - earthquakes
   - volcanoes
   - cyclones

2. What do many of the places affected by natural hazards have in common?

B Match the correct form of the words in blue to their definitions.

_____ (n) danger

_____ (adv) in every part

_____ (n) a sudden event that causes suffering and loss

WORLD OF HAZARDS

Natural hazards occur throughout the world, but mostly happen in certain vulnerable areas. For example, most earthquakes and volcanoes occur at or near plate boundaries. Large storm systems (known as cyclones in the Indian Ocean, hurricanes in the Atlantic, and typhoons in the Pacific) form in the tropics and cause serious coastal flooding.

Unfortunately, as the map shows, many of the world's most highly populated areas are also the most hazardous. With more people, the cost of natural hazards is significant. In 2016, natural disasters in Asia resulted in over 80 billion dollars in damage cost.

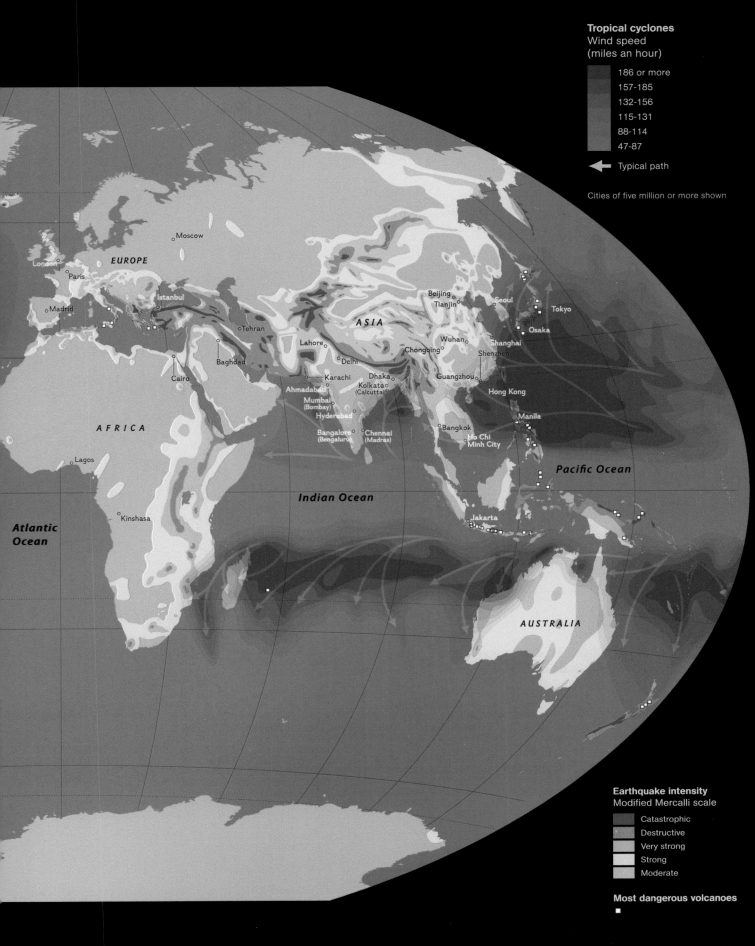

Tropical cyclones
Wind speed
(miles an hour)

186 or more
157-185
132-156
115-131
88-114
47-87

← Typical path

Cities of five million or more shown

Moscow

EUROPE

London

Paris

Madrid

Istanbul

Tehran

AFRICA

Lagos

Kinshasa

Baghdad

Cairo

Lahore

Delhi

Karachi

Ahmadabad

Mumbai
(Bombay)

Hyderabad

Bangalore
(Bengaluru)

ASIA

Dhaka

Kolkata
(Calcutta)

Chennai
(Madras)

Beijing

Tianjin

Wuhan

Chongqing

Seoul

Tokyo

Osaka

Shanghai

Shenzhen

Guangzhou

Hong Kong

Bangkok

Ho Chi
Minh City

Manila

Jakarta

Pacific Ocean

Indian Ocean

Atlantic
Ocean

AUSTRALIA

Earthquake intensity
Modified Mercalli scale

Catastrophic
Destructive
Very strong
Strong
Moderate

Most dangerous volcanoes
■

Reading 1

PREPARING TO READ

BUILDING
VOCABULARY

A The words and phrases in blue below are used in Reading 1. Read the paragraph. Then match the correct form of each word or phrase to its definition.

Every year, **deadly** earthquakes kill thousands of people and cause massive **destruction** to buildings. A system that **forecasts** when a natural disaster is about to occur and **alerts** people would potentially save many lives. With enough warning, people could **get out** of the area and avoid the disaster. Scientists and researchers are trying to develop systems like this, but the process can be expensive and the systems don't work **effectively** all of the time. Hopefully, one day, **affordable** and accurate early-warning systems will save lives in vulnerable places around the world.

1. _____ (v) to warn

2. _____ (v) to predict

3. _____ (n) severe damage

4. _____ (v) to leave; to escape

5. _____ (adj) not too expensive

6. _____ (adv) in a way that works well

7. _____ (adj) so dangerous that it can cause death

USING
VOCABULARY

B Discuss these questions with a partner.

1. What kinds of natural **disasters** occur in your country?

2. How do officials in your country **alert** people when a natural **hazard** might occur?

BRAINSTORMING

C What are two ways in which scientists predict natural hazards such as earthquakes and tornadoes? Discuss with a partner.

PREDICTING

D Skim the first two paragraphs of the reading passage. How do you think animals might sense danger? Note two ways. Then check your ideas as you read.

_____

_____

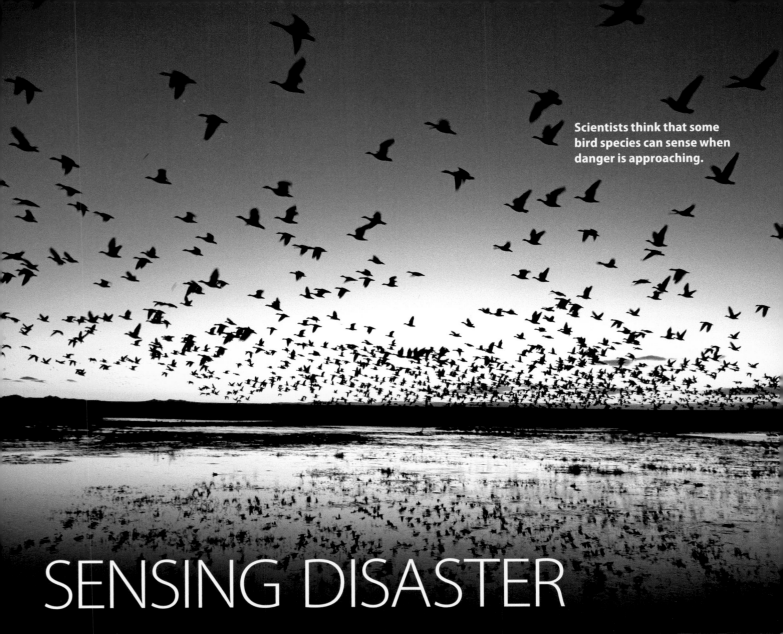

Scientists think that some bird species can sense when danger is approaching.

SENSING DISASTER

🎧 1.07

A   Twenty-three hundred years ago, hordes[1] of mice, snakes, and insects fled the Greek city of Helike on the Gulf of Corinth. "After these creatures departed, an earthquake occurred in the night," wrote the ancient Roman writer Claudius Aelianus. "The city subsided;[2] an immense wave flooded and Helike disappeared."

B   Scientists have long suspected that animals might have a "sixth sense." This sense **alerts** them when natural **hazards**—like earthquakes and tornadoes—are about to strike. Until recently, though, we have had to rely on informal reports of changes in animal behavior. However, scientists have now begun to detect evidence that suggests animals can indeed make predictions.

---

[1] **Hordes** are large moving groups.
[2] To **subside** is to go down to a lower or the normal level.

A tapir captured by a motion-triggered camera in Panama

A NATURAL WARNING

In 2011, a research team began a study of animal behavior in Yanachaga National Park in the Peruvian Amazon. In order to track animal movements, the team placed motion-triggered cameras throughout the park. On a single day, the cameras typically recorded up to 15 animal sightings.[3] Then the researchers noticed a change: Over a three-week period, the sightings dropped to fewer than five a day. In the last few days, there were no animal sightings at all.

The researchers were puzzled: this was highly unusual behavior, especially in a rain forest area normally filled with wildlife. But then, at the end of the three-week period, disaster struck. On August 24, the area was hit by a 7.0 magnitude earthquake. Could the animals have left the area—or found places to hide—because they sensed the earthquake was coming?

"As far as we know, this is the first time that motion-triggered cameras have documented this phenomenon prior to an earthquake," says lead researcher Dr. Rachel Grant. She believes the findings could have important consequences for earthquake prediction. "Animals have the potential to be reliable forecasters of earthquakes and could be used alongside other monitoring systems," she says. Cameras that track animal movements could therefore be used as an affordable early warning system.

Scientists are not certain why animal movements might change before earthquakes. However, Grant has a theory. Prior to an earthquake, large forces stress the Earth's surface and change the atmosphere. The atmospheric changes can, in turn, cause increased serotonin[4] levels in animals and humans, leading to unpleasant feelings of restlessness.[5] Two weeks before the earthquake

[3] Sightings are occasions in which something is observed.

[4] Serotonin is a chemical in the body that affects the sleep-wake cycle.
[5] Restlessness is a state of not being able to relax.

in Peru, a significant atmospheric change was recorded. Eight days before the quake, it became even more intense, possibly causing the animals to leave the area.

When it comes to predicting earthquakes, rodents such as rats appear to be the most sensitive animals in the rain forest. "What was interesting was that rodents were the first to disappear," Grant says. "They were nowhere to be seen eight days before the earthquake … That they should completely disappear was amazing." Grant believes that recent research in China and Japan may help explain why this happened. According to these studies, rats' sleeping and waking patterns are disturbed in the days leading up to an earthquake. These changes may alert them to a coming disaster.

FOLLOW THE BIRDS

Like rats, birds may also be sensitive to subtle changes in the environment. In fact, scientists have recently learned that some birds may be able to sense severe storms before they arrive.

In 2014, a team of U.S. scientists studied the migration patterns of golden-winged warblers. To track the birds' movements, the researchers attached small, lightweight geolocators that recorded the birds' locations. In April, the team expected to find the warblers in the Cumberland Mountains of eastern Tennessee, where they breed and raise their young. But the birds were not there. Instead, they discovered that most of the birds had flown to Florida; one had even traveled to Cuba.

Several days later, the birds arrived back in Tennessee—after a mysterious round-trip journey of more than 900 miles (1,500 kilometers). The researchers finally worked out what may have prompted the trip. At around the time the birds left Tennessee, a severe weather system was approaching the Midwest region. The deadly storms created more than 80 tornadoes and left at least 35 people dead.

Scientists theorize the warblers were alerted by infrasound—a type of low-frequency noise—produced by the storms. Humans can't hear infrasound, but birds can. It appears the warblers detected the weather system and decided to get out of the way. "We were completely blown away by this behavior," says researcher Gunnar Kramer, a population ecologist at the University of Minnesota. "It shows that the birds can do more than we give them credit for."

Eventually, scientists hope that signs from the natural world might help us forecast earthquakes and serious weather events more effectively. Even a few minutes' warning could be enough for people to avoid the destruction that severe storms and earthquakes can cause. Over two thousand years ago, it seems the animals in Helike had an important message to share. It's only now that we're really paying attention.

A golden-winged warbler

UNDERSTANDING THE READING

SUMMARIZING **A** Complete the summary of the passage using suitable words. Write one word in each space.

Scientists think that animals might be able to [1]_____ some natural hazards. By studying their [2]_____, scientists have observed that animals seem to be sensitive to small [3]_____ in the atmosphere in the days before the hazard strikes. For example, in one study, animals were observed leaving just before a(n) [4]_____. In another study, birds left an area just before a destructive [5]_____ arrived.

UNDERSTANDING A PROCESS **B** How do researchers think animals sense earthquakes? Put the events (a–e) in order.

a. animals leave the area
b. serotonin levels in animals rise
c. forces stress the surface of Earth
d. animals become restless
e. Earth's atmosphere changes

Several days before the earthquake:

UNDERSTANDING MAIN IDEAS **C** Use the information from the section "Follow the Birds" to answer the questions.

1. What was the purpose of the geolocators?

_____

2. Why were the researchers surprised to find the warblers in Florida and Cuba?

_____

3. What probably caused the birds to leave Tennessee?

_____

4. Why does Kramer say "birds can do more than we give them credit for"?

_____

UNDERSTANDING DETAILS **D** Read the statements about the section "A Natural Warning." For each statement, circle T for true, F for false, or NG if the information is not given.

1. In the three-week period before a 7.0 earthquake in Peru, there were more animal sightings than usual. **T F NG**

2. According to Grant, this is the first time that motion-triggered cameras have recorded animals leaving an area before an earthquake. **T F NG**

3. There was a change in the atmosphere two weeks before the earthquake in Peru. **T F NG**

4. Serotonin levels in people are not affected by changes in the atmosphere. **T F NG**

5. The research in China and Japan was part of a wider study that observed the behavior of several animal species. **T F NG**

E Find and underline the following **bold** words and phrases in the passage. Use context to identify their meanings. Then match the sentence parts to form definitions.

_____ 1. Paragraph E: If someone has **documented** something,

_____ 2. Paragraph H : If you are **sensitive** to the surrounding environment,

_____ 3. Paragraph H: If something is **subtle**,

_____ 4. Paragraph J: When someone **prompts** you to do something,

_____ 5. Paragraph K: When something **blows** you **away**,

a. they make you act in that way.

b. it impresses you greatly.

c. it is not easy to notice.

d. they have made a record of it.

e. you are aware of what is happening around you.

CRITICAL THINKING   **Inferences** are logical guesses about information a writer doesn't directly say. You make inferences based on information suggested—but not necessarily stated—in a text. When you make an inference, be sure there is evidence in the text to support it. For example, in paragraph E, we can infer that using animals as disaster warning systems is probably cheaper compared to other types of warning systems, even though it is not explicitly stated.

F Check (✓) the two statements that can be inferred from the excerpt below. Discuss the reasons for your answers with a partner.

"In 2014, a team of U.S. scientists studied the migration patterns of golden-winged warblers. To track the birds' movements, the researchers attached small, lightweight geolocators that recorded the birds' locations. In April, the team expected to find the warblers in the Cumberland Mountains of eastern Tennessee, where they breed and raise their young. But the birds were not there. Instead, they discovered that most of the birds had flown to Florida; one had even traveled to Cuba."

☐ 1. The scientists wanted to study the behavior of birds in Florida.

☐ 2. The researchers used geolocators to find the birds in Florida and Cuba.

☐ 3. The birds live in Tennessee the whole year round.

☐ 4. It is unusual for the birds to travel south in April.

In 2011, lemurs in the National Zoo ▶ in Washington, D.C., started making alarm calls 15 minutes before an earthquake struck the area.

DEVELOPING READING SKILLS

> **READING SKILL** Understanding Referencing and Cohesion
>
> Writers often use **referents** to refer to a noun or an idea that appeared previously in the passage. This helps connect ideas and avoid repetition. The noun or idea that is being referred to is called an **antecedent**.
>
> ANTECEDENT
> *Scientists have long suspected that animals might indeed have a "sixth sense." … Until*
>
> *recently, they have had to rely on informal reports of changes in animal behavior.*
> REFERENT
>
> Referents are usually:
> - pronouns (*he, she, they, it,* etc.).
> - possessive adjectives (*his, her, our, its,* etc.).
> - demonstrative pronouns (*this, that, these, those*).
>
> If you are not sure what a referent is referring to, look at the earlier part of the sentence or sentences that appeared before it. When you find a noun or an idea that might be the antecedent, read the words around it. Check that the context matches the context of the sentence with the referent. The referent and the antecedent have to agree in gender and number, e.g., if the referent is *they*, look for plural nouns.

UNDERSTANDING REFERENCING

A Read the sentences from the reading passage. Underline the antecedent that the referent in **bold** refers to.

1. In the last few days, there were no animal sightings at all. The researchers were puzzled: **this** was highly unusual behavior, especially in a rain forest area normally filled with wildlife.

2. "As far as we know, this is the first time that [we] have documented this phenomenon prior to an earthquake," says lead researcher Dr. Rachel Grant. **She** believes the findings could have important consequences for earthquake prediction.

3. Two weeks before the earthquake in Peru, a significant atmospheric change was recorded. Eight days before the quake, **it** became even more intense, …

4. In April, the team expected to find the warblers in the Cumberland Mountains of eastern Tennessee, where **they** breed and raise their young.

UNDERSTANDING REFERENCING

B Read the paragraph from the passage. Underline the antecedent that each referent in **bold** refers to, and draw an arrow to it.

When it comes to predicting earthquakes, rodents such as rats appear to be the most sensitive animals in the rain forest. "What was interesting was that <u>rodents</u> were the first to disappear," Grant says. "**They** were nowhere to be seen eight days before the earthquake … That **they** should completely disappear was amazing." Grant believes that recent research in China and Japan may help explain why **this** happened. According to **these** studies, rats' sleeping and waking patterns are disturbed in the days leading up to an earthquake. **These** changes may alert **them** to a coming disaster.

Video

HURRICANES

BEFORE VIEWING

A Read the caption and look at the picture. What do you think are some effects of hurricanes? Make some notes and discuss with a partner.

PREDICTING

B Read the information below and complete the meanings of the words and phrases in **bold**.

LEARNING ABOUT THE TOPIC

Hurricanes form over warm ocean waters. When a hurricane nears the coast, it creates a **storm surge**. Wind and rain from hurricanes can cause a lot of damage, but storm surges are the most destructive aspect of this type of storm. When a hurricane **makes landfall**, a large amount of water rushes over the land and destroys structures on the shore. **Debris** then joins the fast-moving water, crashing into and damaging even more structures.

1. A storm surge is _____ .

2. To make landfall is to _____ .

3. Debris is _____ .

C The words in **bold** below are used in the video. Read the sentences. Then match each word to its definition.

Some hurricanes can be over 1,000 miles in **diameter**.

Hurricanes can cause **catastrophic** damage, destroying buildings and killing people.

Thunderstorms start to form when warm, **moist** air rises to form clouds. They are less likely to occur when the air is dry.

1. _____ (adj) a little wet

2. _____ (adj) extremely bad or destructive

3. _____ (n) the length of a straight line drawn through the center of a circle

WHILE VIEWING

A ▶ Watch the video. Check (✓) the topics that are mentioned. Three are extra.

☐ 1. what hurricanes are   ☐ 5. the effects of hurricanes

☐ 2. how hurricanes form   ☐ 6. protecting your home from a hurricane

☐ 3. where hurricanes form   ☐ 7. the biggest hurricane ever recorded

☐ 4. differences between hurricanes and cyclones   ☐ 8. how scientists try to predict hurricanes

B ▶ Watch the video again. Write short answers to the questions.

1. How is the eye of the hurricane different from the wall?

_____

2. What is a "hurricane hunter"? What does it do?

_____

3. What other kinds of technology are helping scientists to predict hurricanes?

_____

AFTER VIEWING

A Have you heard about any hurricanes in the news recently? What impacts did the hurricane(s) have? Discuss with a partner.

B Would studying animal behavior help predict a hurricane? Which animal would you study? Discuss with a partner.

_____

_____

Reading 2

PREPARING TO READ

A The words in **blue** below are used in Reading 2. Complete the sentences with the correct form of the words. Use a dictionary to help you.

BUILDING
VOCABULARY

accumulate	collapse	entire	crack	eruption
explode	threaten	pressure	continuous	vast

1. A strong hurricane can result in the destruction of a(n) _____ city.

2. The smoke and ash from a volcanic _____ can spread over _____ areas of land.

3. Since 1659, the Central England Temperature series has kept a(n) _____ record of temperatures in parts of England.

4. Natural disasters often _____ the lives of many people when they occur in highly populated places.

5. Earthquakes occur when _____ inside Earth's crust _____ over time and is then released. Large earthquakes can create huge _____ in roads and cause buildings to shake violently and _____.

6. In 2011, an earthquake and a tsunami caused several nuclear reactors in Japan to _____, leading to a nuclear disaster.

B Discuss these questions with a partner: Have you ever seen a volcanic **eruption**? What are some volcanic eruptions you know of?

USING
VOCABULARY

C The prefix *super-* means "above" or "beyond." In what two ways do you think a "supervolcano" might be different from other volcanoes? Discuss with a partner.

BRAINSTORMING

_____

_____

D Look at the photos and headings in the reading passage. What topics do you think the passage covers? Check your ideas as you read.

PREDICTING

☐ 1. what a supervolcano is

☐ 2. the effects of a supervolcano eruption

☐ 3. where the world's supervolcanoes are located

☐ 4. when Yellowstone's supervolcano might erupt

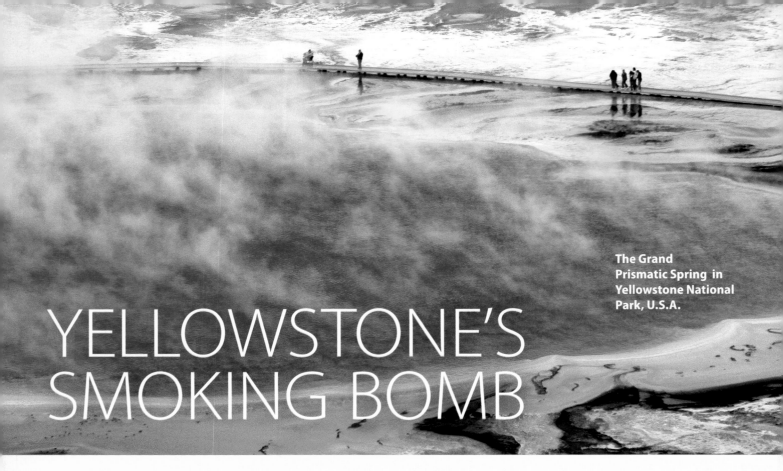

The Grand Prismatic Spring in Yellowstone National Park, U.S.A.

YELLOWSTONE'S SMOKING BOMB

🎧 1.08

A   Yellowstone National Park, the oldest and most famous national park in the United States, sits on top of one of the biggest volcanoes on Earth. Yellowstone's volcano is so big that many scientists call it a *supervolcano*. As the name suggests, supervolcanoes are much bigger and more powerful than ordinary volcanoes, and their eruptions can be exceptionally violent and destructive. When volcanoes erupt, they can kill plants and animals for miles around. When a supervolcano explodes, it can threaten whole species with extinction by changing the climate across the entire planet.

WHAT CAUSES A SUPERVOLCANO TO ERUPT?

B   No supervolcano has erupted in recorded human history. However, in the 2.1 million years that Yellowstone has sat over the supervolcano, scientists believe that the park has experienced three super-eruptions. Geologists who study Yellowstone's supervolcano have pieced together the sequence of events that probably cause a super-eruption. First, an intense plume of heat pushes up from deep within Earth. The extreme heat melts rock and creates a huge chamber a few miles below the surface. The chamber slowly fills with a pressurized mix of magma (melted rock), water vapor, carbon dioxide, and other gases. As additional magma accumulates in the chamber over thousands of years, the land on the surface above it begins to move up to form a dome, inches at a time. As the dome moves higher, cracks form along its edges. When the pressure in the magma chamber is released through the cracks in the dome, the gases suddenly explode, creating a violent super-eruption and emptying the magma chamber. Once the magma chamber is empty, the dome collapses, leaving a giant caldera, or crater, in the ground. Yellowstone's caldera, which covers a 25-by-37-mile (or 40-by-60-kilometer) area in the state of Wyoming, was formed after the last super-eruption, some 640,000 years ago.

(continued on page 90)

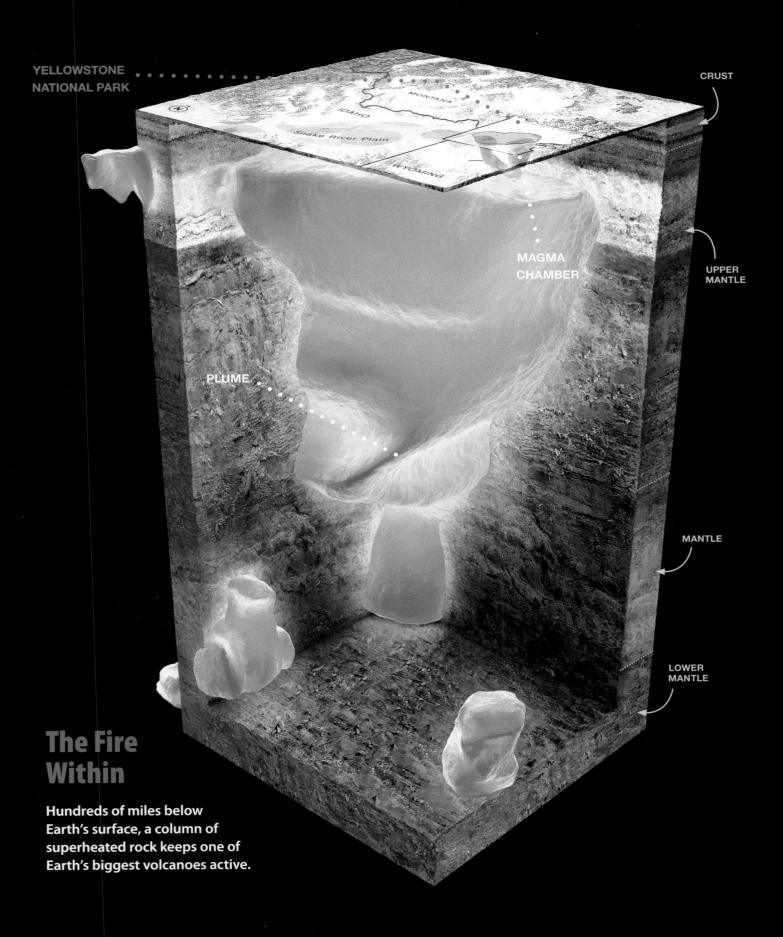

CRUST

MONTANA

IDAHO

Snake River Plain

WYOMING

MAGMA
CHAMBER

UPPER
MANTLE

PLUME

MANTLE

LOWER
MANTLE

The Fire Within

Hundreds of miles below
Earth's surface, a column of
superheated rock keeps one of
Earth's biggest volcanoes active.

A WAKING GIANT?

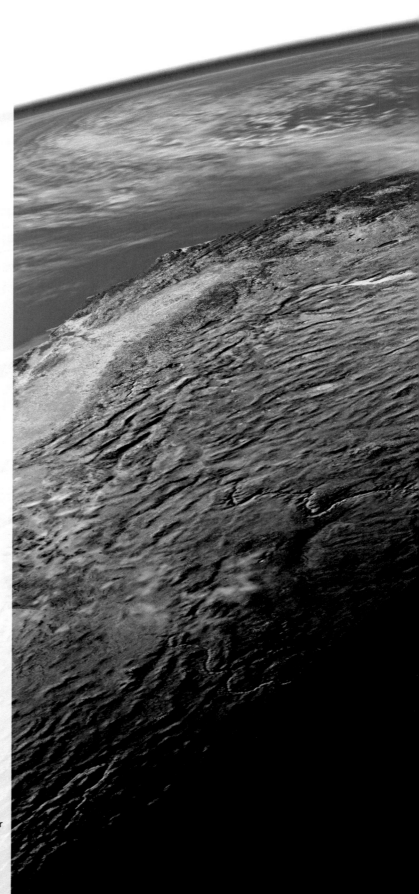

1870: Army officer Gustavus Doane explores the region that will later become Yellowstone National Park. He notices there is a huge open space—or a basin—surrounded by mountains and concludes that it is the crater of a huge extinct volcano.

1950s: Harvard graduate student Francis Boyd discovers a thick layer of heated and compacted[1] ash at Yellowstone and determines that it is the result of a geologically recent eruption.

1970s: Supervolcano expert Bob Smith of the University of Utah finds that land near the caldera has risen by some 30 inches (76 centimeters) in three decades, proving the supervolcano is alive.

1985: A number of small earthquakes strike the area, causing the land to sink. Over the next decade, it sinks eight inches (20 centimeters).

2004–2007: The ground above the caldera rises upward at rates as high as 2.8 inches (7 centimeters) a year.

2007–2010: The ground rise slows to one centimeter or less a year, but the ground has risen about 10 inches (25 centimeters) in just a few years. "It's an extraordinary uplift," says Smith, "because it covers such a large area and the rates are so high."

---

[1] If something is **compacted**, it is densely packed or pressed together as a result of external pressure.

Fire and debris rise from deep within Earth under Yellowstone in this artist's view of a supervolcanic eruption.

HOW VIOLENT IS A SUPER-ERUPTION?

After each super-eruption at Yellowstone, the whole planet felt the effects. Scientists theorize that gases rising high into the atmosphere mixed with water vapor to create a haze that reduced sunlight, causing a period of cooling across the globe. It is estimated that the combined debris from the three eruptions was so vast, it could have filled the Grand Canyon.

The most recent catastrophic eruption, about 640,000 years ago, poured out 240 cubic miles (1,000 cubic kilometers) of rock, lava, and ash. A column of ash rose some 100,000 feet (30 kilometers) into the atmosphere, and winds carried ash and dust across the western half of the United States and south to the Gulf of Mexico. Closer to the supervolcano, thick clouds of ash, rocks, and gas—superheated to 1,470 degrees Fahrenheit (800 degrees Celsius)—rolled over the land. This volcano's lava and debris destroyed everything within its devastating range, filling entire valleys and forming layers hundreds of feet thick.

WILL THE SUPERVOLCANO ERUPT AGAIN?

Predicting when an eruption might occur is extremely difficult, in part because scientists still do not understand all the details of what is happening under the caldera's surface. Moreover, they have kept continuous records of Yellowstone's activity only since the 1970s—a tiny slice of geologic time—making it hard to draw conclusions. However, scientists theorize that Yellowstone's magma chamber expands periodically from a plume of hot rock moving up from deep inside Earth. As the chamber expands, it pushes the land above it upward. According to this theory, when the plume of rock decreases, the magma cools and becomes solid, allowing the land above to fall back.

Scientists believe that Yellowstone has probably seen a continuous cycle of rising and falling land over the past 15,000 years. Geophysicist and supervolcano expert Bob Smith of the University of Utah believes the rise-and-fall cycle of Yellowstone's caldera will likely continue. "These calderas tend to go up and down, up and down," he says. "We call this a caldera at unrest. The net effect over many cycles is to finally get enough magma to erupt. And we don't know what those cycles are."

So is the supervolcano going to explode again? Some kind of eruption is highly likely at some point. The chances of another catastrophic super-eruption are anyone's guess. It could happen in this century, or 100,000 years from now. No one knows for sure.

THE YELLOWSTONE ERUPTIONS

Three major blasts have shaken Yellowstone National Park during the past 2 million years. The smallest of these, 1.3 million years ago, produced 280 times more material than the 1980 eruption of Mount St. Helens. After the two biggest eruptions, winds carried material from Yellowstone across much of the United States.

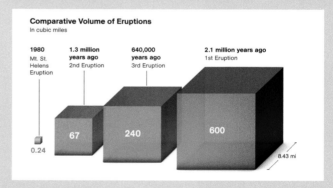

Comparative Volume of Eruptions
In cubic miles

1980 Mt. St. Helens Eruption	1.3 million years ago 2nd Eruption	640,000 years ago 3rd Eruption	2.1 million years ago 1st Eruption
0.24	67	240	600

8.43 mi

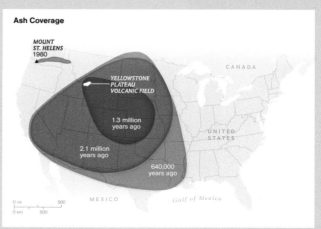

Ash Coverage

MOUNT ST. HELENS 1980

YELLOWSTONE PLATEAU VOLCANIC FIELD

CANADA

1.3 million years ago

2.1 million years ago

640,000 years ago

UNITED STATES

MEXICO   Gulf of Mexico

0 mi   500
0 km   500

UNDERSTANDING THE READING

A Complete the summary of the reading passage using suitable words. Write no more than three words in each space.

Supervolcanoes are different from normal volcanoes because they are
[1] _____ in size and [2] _____ . One supervolcano is located
under [3] _____ and has been there for at least [4] _____ .
Scientists believe that there have been three [5] _____ during that period.
A supervolcano's eruption is so violent that the whole planet can feel its effects. The ash
and rock that it releases into the air can block [6] _____ and cause global
temperatures [7] _____ . It is difficult to predict when a supervolcano will
erupt. Scientists think that Yellowstone's caldera has been at unrest for the past
[8] _____ years, and that there is a high chance that the supervolcano will
erupt again.

B Use information from the sidebar "The Yellowstone Eruptions" to answer the questions.

1. What is the main purpose of the information in this section?
   a. to describe the ages and sizes of several different volcanoes in North America
   b. to compare the size and extent of Yellowstone's eruptions with a more recent volcanic eruption
   c. to show how the volume of Yellowstone's eruptions has steadily increased over time

2. About how much material was produced by the most recent super-eruption?

   _____

3. Which eruption covered the largest amount of the United States with ash?

   _____

4. Which paragraphs from the reading passage does the sidebar mostly relate to?

   _____

C Check (✓) the two best inferences based on the information in paragraphs C and D. Then discuss the reasons for your answers with a partner.

☐ 1. The most recent super-eruption caused the extinction of many plant and animal species.

☐ 2. Yellowstone's supervolcano does not erupt very frequently.

☐ 3. Scientists probably found evidence of volcanic ash from the supervolcano in the western United States and the Gulf of Mexico.

D Label the illustration below to show the stages in a supervolcano eruption (a–f).

a. The chamber becomes empty, leaving a huge crater in the ground.
b. A plume of extreme heat rises from deep within Earth.
c. Columns of ash may rise many kilometers into the air.
d. Pressure forces gases to explode upward through cracks in the dome.
e. The chamber pushes the surface of the land to form a dome.
f. The intense heat melts rock, creating a chamber just below the surface.

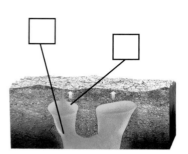  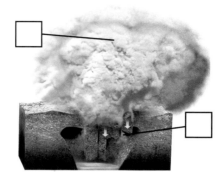

Before the Eruption   **The Volcano Erupts**   **After the Eruption**

E Find the following underlined words and phrases in the reading passage. Use context to identify their meanings. Then circle the best option to complete the definitions.

1. Paragraph A: You use <u>exceptionally</u> to describe something that is true to a very **large / slight** degree.

2. Paragraph B: To <u>piece together</u> means to **research / understand** how something works.

3. Paragraph E: A <u>slice</u> of something is a **section / demonstration** of it.

4. Paragraph E: If something happens <u>periodically</u>, it happens **once / several times**.

F Answer these questions. Then discuss with a partner.

1. What three pieces of evidence from the timeline "A Waking Giant?" show that a supervolcano exists under Yellowstone and is still alive?

_____

_____

2. Refer to paragraphs E–G. What are two reasons why it is difficult for scientists to predict when the supervolcano will erupt again?

_____

_____

Writing

EXPLORING WRITTEN ENGLISH

A Read the sentences below. For each sentence, what do the underlined words have in common in terms of their grammatical form and tense? Discuss with a partner.

NOTICING

1. Some scientists have begun <u>studying</u> and <u>recording</u> animal movements to try to prove that animals can make predictions.

2. Dr. Rachel Grant believes that prior to an earthquake, large forces <u>stress</u> Earth's surface and <u>change</u> Earth's atmosphere.

3. Yellowstone National Park is the <u>oldest</u> and <u>most famous</u> national park in the United States.

4. Supervolcanoes are <u>much bigger</u> and <u>more powerful</u> than ordinary volcanoes.

5. Before an eruption, a supervolcano's chamber slowly fills with a pressurized mix of <u>magma</u> (melted rock), <u>water vapor</u>, <u>carbon dioxide</u>, and <u>other gases</u>.

6. A volcano's <u>lava</u> and <u>debris</u> destroy everything within its devastating range.

LANGUAGE FOR WRITING Using Parallel Structures

When you join two ideas in one sentence, both ideas have to be in the same grammatical form and tense. In addition, the two parallel ideas should come immediately before and after *and*. Look at these examples.

Parallel nouns:

Idea 1: *Property gets damaged in earthquakes.*

Idea 2: *Earthquakes damage buildings.*

Property *and* ***buildings*** *get damaged in earthquakes.*

Parallel verbs:

Idea 1: *Learn about earthquake safety online.*

Idea 2: *Phone numbers for local shelters can be found online.*

You can ***learn*** *about earthquake safety and* ***find*** *phone numbers for local shelters online.*

Parallel adjectives:

Idea 1: *The people were hungry.*

Idea 2: *They also needed to sleep.*

The people were ***hungry*** *and* ***tired***.

B Complete the sentences (1–5) by combining the two ideas with parallel structures.

1. Idea 1: When it starts to rain, streets will be slippery.
   Idea 2: Slippery streets can be a danger.

   When it starts to rain, streets will be _____ and
   _____.

2. Idea 1: People can prepare for a hurricane by buying extra food.
   Idea 2: They also need extra water.

   To prepare for a hurricane, people can _____ and
   _____.

3. Idea 1: People need to be cautious.
   Idea 2: People aren't aware of dangers.

   People should _____ and _____
   of dangers.

4. Idea 1: People are frightened of hurricanes.
   Idea 2: Hurricanes cause damage to property.

   Hurricanes _____ people and
   _____ property.

5. Idea 1: Houses were crushed by the tornado.
   Idea 2: The tornado carried cars away.

   The tornado was so strong that it _____ and
   _____.

WRITING SKILL Writing a Process Essay

A process essay explains how to do something, such as how to apply for financial aid or use a computer program. Each body paragraph describes one or more tasks or steps required for accomplishing the goal. The body paragraphs can be organized:

- in order of importance (in your opinion).
- chronologically (if the steps should happen in a particular time order).

Each body paragraph begins with a topic sentence that describes the task(s) or the step(s). The details in the paragraph include important information that helps the reader understand the process.

Use the following transition words and phrases to connect the body paragraphs and help the reader follow the order of the tasks or the steps.

The first step is …	*First, …*
Most importantly, …	*The most important thing …*

Second, …	*Then, …*	*Next, …*
After that, …	*Another important thing is …*	

Before doing the next step, …	*The last step is …*

C Put the steps below in the best order (1–6). Then write the steps out in order using appropriate transition words.

Planning for a vacation:

_____ Download movies or shows to watch on your flight.

_____ Pack your bags.

_____ Search flights and hotels.

_____ Reserve a flight and a hotel room.

_____ Choose a place to go.

_____ Check the weather.

I'm planning for a vacation. First, I need to _____

_____

_____

_____

_____

_____

D Choose one of the steps in exercise C. Brainstorm for details and examples to elaborate on it. Take some notes below.

Step: _____

Details: _____

_____

E Using your ideas in exercise D, write two to three sentences to describe the step you chose. Then share your sentences with a partner.

_____

_____

_____

_____

_____

WRITING TASK

GOAL You are going to write a process essay on the following topic:

Choose one type of natural hazard. Describe how residents of an affected city can prepare for it.

BRAINSTORMING **A** Decide on a natural hazard you will write about. List the types of risk there are for residents and the kinds of damage the natural hazard can cause. Then list ways that residents can prepare for it. Do research if necessary.

PLANNING **B** Follow these steps to make notes for your essay.

Step 1 Decide on the two most important tasks that residents should do in order to prepare for the natural disaster. State the natural hazard you are going to discuss and complete the thesis statement.

Step 2 For each body paragraph, write a topic sentence that describes one method of preparation.

Step 3 Note two or three details for each body paragraph, e.g., why this type of preparation is helpful, how it can be done, what kind of harm it might prevent.

Step 4 Make notes for a hook in the introductory paragraph. Then write a summary statement and add a final thought in the concluding paragraph.

OUTLINE

Introductory Paragraph

Hook: _____

Thesis Statement: To prepare for _____ ,

residents should _____ and _____ .

Body Paragraphs

Topic Sentence 1: _____

_____

Details: _____

Topic Sentence 2: _____

_____

Details: _____

Concluding Paragraph

Summary Statement: _____

_____

Final Thought: _____

FIRST DRAFT **C** Use the information in your outline to write a first draft of your essay.

REVISING PRACTICE

The draft below is a process essay about ways to prepare for travel emergencies. Follow the steps to create a better second draft.

1. Add the sentences (a–c) in the most suitable spaces.
   a. In addition, travelers should pack a first-aid kit containing bandages, pain relievers, antibiotic creams, and any other necessary items.
   b. Another important thing for people to consider is what they might need in the event that they lose items such as passports and credit cards.
   c. To prepare for a travel emergency, travelers should think about their medical needs and consider what they might need in case of the theft or loss of important items.

2. Now fix the following problems (d–f) in the essay.
   d. Cross out one sentence in paragraph A that does not relate to the essay topic.
   e. Correct a mistake with a transition word or phrase in paragraph B.
   f. Correct a mistake with parallel structure in paragraph C.

A

When most people plan a vacation, they spend a lot of time choosing a hotel or deciding what sites they want to see. The best places to look for cheap flights and hotel rooms are discount travel websites. However, they may not plan for possible travel emergencies. _____

B

First importantly, thinking about medical needs beforehand can save travelers a lot of time and trouble. They should pack enough medication to last for the whole trip, so they don't have to refill prescriptions while they're traveling. They should also keep their prescription medications in the original bottles, so they will know the details of the medication if they do need to get a refill. _____

C

_____ It's a good idea to know the phone numbers of their embassies or consulates in case their passports are stolen. Travelers should also have pictures of their passports on their phones and keeping copies in different parts of their luggage. This way, it will be easier to get replacement passports if necessary. Finally, travelers should know the phone numbers of their credit card companies so they can cancel their cards immediately after they are lost or stolen.

D

If people are prepared for emergencies before they leave for a vacation, they will avoid ruining a trip with serious problems. A little bit of planning ahead of time can save travelers a lot of problems later.

D Now use the questions below to revise your essay.

REVISED DRAFT

- ☐ Does your introductory paragraph have a hook and a clear thesis statement?
- ☐ Did you include enough details in your body paragraphs to explain the tasks or steps?
- ☐ Did you use transition words and phrases correctly?
- ☐ Does your concluding paragraph have a summary statement and a final thought?

EDITING PRACTICE

Read the information below.

In sentences with parallel structure, remember that:

- the ideas have to be in the same form, so when combining sentences you may have to shift words around, change a verb tense, or change the form (e.g., change a verb to an adjective).
- the two parallel ideas should come immediately before and after *and*.

Correct one mistake with parallel structures in each of the sentences (1–5).

1. People can prepare for fires by creating an escape plan and discuss it with family members.

2. Keep important papers and putting medicine in one place.

3. If you need to take pets with you, pet carriers are important to have and extra pet food.

4. To walk around your house and identify things you will need to take.

5. Pack a bag with clothes for each family member and necessities.

FINAL DRAFT **E** Follow these steps to write a final draft.

1. Check your revised draft for mistakes with parallel structures.

2. Now use the checklist on page 253 to write a final draft. Make any other necessary changes.

UNIT REVIEW
Answer the following questions.

1. According to scientists, what is one reason that animals might be able to predict natural hazards?

_____

_____

_____

2. What are two ways that you can organize ideas in a process essay?

_____

_____

_____

3. Do you remember the meanings of these words? Check (✔) the ones you know. Look back at the unit and review the ones you don't know.

Reading 1:

☐ affordable   ☐ alert   ☐ deadly

☐ destruction   ☐ disaster   ☐ effectively

☐ forecast   ☐ get out   ☐ hazard

☐ throughout

Reading 2:

☐ accumulate AWL   ☐ collapse AWL   ☐ continuous

☐ crack   ☐ entire   ☐ eruption

☐ explode   ☐ pressure   ☐ threaten

☐ vast

THE TRAVEL BUSINESS

5

In 2016, more than 5 million people visited Abu Dhabi's Sheikh Zayed Grand Mosque.

ACADEMIC SKILLS

READING	Analyzing causes and effects
WRITING	Writing a cause-effect essay
GRAMMAR	Using if (then)

THINK AND DISCUSS

1 What benefits can tourism bring to a city?
2 What problems can tourism cause?

EXPLORE THE THEME

A Look at the information on these pages and answer the questions.

1. Look at the list of the top most visited cities. Why do you think so many people go to those places?
2. What are some positive effects of mass tourism?

B Match the words in yellow **to their definitions.**

_____ (v) to keep in good condition

_____ (n) the system by which a government's industry and money are organized

_____ (adj) special; very different

Osaka was the world's 17th most popular destination in 2016. Among the city's most distinctive landmarks is Shitennō-ji—one of the oldest temples in Japan.

Top 10 destination cities by international overnight visitors (2016)

1 Bangkok 21.5 million	4 Dubai 15.3 million	5 New York 12.8 million	6 Singapore 12.1 million
2 London 19.9 million	7 Kuala Lumpur 12.0 million	9 Tokyo 11.7 million	10 Seoul 10.2 million
3 Paris 18.0 million	8 Istanbul 12.0 million		

TRENDS IN TRAVEL

A recent study of global travel shows some surprising trends. While Paris and London have always been popular with businesspeople and tourists, the world's most visited city is Bangkok, which had over 21 million overnight travelers in 2016. The fastest-growing destination in terms of visitors who stay overnight is Osaka. In terms of how much money visitors spend in the city, Dubai ranks number one—visitors spent over $31 billion there in 2016.

For many of these destinations, mass tourism—large groups of people visiting popular destinations on organized trips—is critical to the success of their **economy**. Tourists spend money at hotels, shops, restaurants, and attractions—providing jobs for thousands of people. Tourism dollars also help cities build and **maintain** roads, parks, and other amenities, which benefit both visitors and locals.

Fastest-growing destination cities
(Rank in growth rate, 2016)

1	2	3
Osaka	Chengdu	Abu Dhabi

Reading 1

PREPARING TO READ

BUILDING VOCABULARY **A** The words and phrases in blue below are used in Reading 1. Read the paragraph. Then match the correct form of each word or phrase to its definition.

Mass tourism isn't the only way to travel. One **alternative** is to experience another country by studying there. Many universities form **partnerships** with schools in other parts of the world to allow their students to learn about other cultures. Overseas students may also choose to stay in their host country during vacations, particularly if they are able to **earn a living** through part-time jobs, such as working in a café or restaurant.

1. _____ (v) to get money to pay for things that you need

2. _____ (n) a way of working with another person, group, or organization

3. _____ (n) something you can choose instead of another thing

BUILDING VOCABULARY **B** Read the sentences. Choose the best definitions for the words in blue.

1. Many cities **preserve** their historic buildings, so tourists can see how the city used to look.
   a. to make additional copies of   b. to protect from harm

2. It may be **necessary** to get a visa before you are allowed to enter a country.
   a. essential; required   b. useful; recommended

3. Economic development must be **sustainable** in order to benefit future generations.
   a. able to continue in the long term   b. able to affect many places

4. Mass tourism can have **harmful** effects on cities, such as increasing pollution levels.
   a. unusual; surprising   b. damaging; dangerous

USING VOCABULARY **C** Discuss these questions with a partner.

1. What are some **distinctive** travel destinations in your country or region?

2. Which historic places or buildings in your area have been **preserved**?

BRAINSTORMING **D** What are the positive and negative effects of large numbers of tourists visiting a natural area, such as a beach or a forest? Discuss with a partner.

PREDICTING **E** Read the first paragraph of the reading passage. The prefix *geo-* refers to the Earth. How do you think "geotourism" is different from mass tourism? Check your ideas as you read.

THE NEW FACE OF TOURISM

🎧 1.09

A The twenty-first century has seen significant growth in mass tourism. This growth brings an increased risk of endangering the sites that make a place unique and worth visiting. However, a new kind of tourism approach—geotourism—may offer a solution.

B Jonathan Tourtellot is founding director of the Destination Stewardship Center. Its mission is to protect and maintain the world's distinctive places through wisely managed tourism. Tourtellot is an advocate of the *geotourism* approach, a term he came up with to describe the core strategy for achieving this goal. He believes that as mass tourism continues to grow and move into places that saw few visitors in the past, geotourism will be a good long-term plan. "The challenge of managing tourism in a way that protects places instead of overrunning[1] them," says Tourtellot, "is simply going to become larger."

C Geotourism is an alternative to mass tourism, which can have harmful effects on local people and on the environment. Many of the systems that support mass tourism—large hotels, chain restaurants,[2] tour companies— are often owned and run by companies based outside the tourist areas. Chain restaurants may not always serve local food. Large tour companies do not always hire local experts and guides, even though these people might have the most insight into the area's history and culture. Much of the money made from this type of tourism does not, therefore, benefit the local economy. In addition, with mass tourism, visitors do not usually have much contact with the local people. This limits their understanding of the nature and culture of the places they visit.

D In contrast, geotourism is like a partnership between travelers and locals. For example, geotravelers stay in hotels owned by local residents who care about protecting the area and the environment. Geotravelers eat in restaurants that serve regional dishes. They buy from local merchants and craftspeople and hire local travel guides. They also try to see traditional music, dance, and theater. As a result, these travelers gain a broader understanding of the area's history and culture. Moreover, the money they spend stays in the local community. This helps local people earn a living; it is also necessary in order to protect the area for future travelers. In this way, geotourism benefits both sides of the partnership—the travelers and the locals.

[1] If a place is **overrun**, it is fully occupied.
[2] **Chain restaurants** are owned by the same company and have standardized products and services.

Geotourism Pioneer:
An Interview with
Jonathan Tourtellot

Q: How would you differentiate among ecotourism, sustainable tourism, and geotourism?

Tourtellot: Ecotourism focuses specifically on natural areas. I'm convinced that there are elephants roaming Africa and trees growing in Costa Rica that would not be there without ecotourism. Sustainable tourism … seems to say, "Keep everything the way it is." We needed a term that would bring the ecotourism principle out of its niche[3] and cover everything that makes travel interesting. Geotourism is defined as tourism that sustains or enhances the geographical character of a place—the environment, heritage, aesthetics,[4] culture, and well-being of local people.

Q: What happens when tourism is badly managed?

Tourtellot: It can destroy a place. Coasts, for example, are extremely vulnerable. Coasts are important for biodiversity because much of marine life has its nurseries[5] in coastline areas. So development there is a highly sensitive issue. Same thing goes for attractive mountainsides like the Rockies of the West. That's why when development occurs on a large scale, it's important that it be … well planned.

Q: What happens to a destination after years of heavy traffic?

Tourtellot: Here's an example—at the Petrified Forest [in northeast Arizona], it's very easy to bend down, pick up a little bit of petrified wood, and pocket it. People think it's only one pebble[6] in such a vast area, so it makes no difference if they take it. But since millions of visitors over the years have thought the same thing, all of the pebbles have disappeared—meaning there's been an enormous loss of what makes the Petrified Forest so special. So, when you're talking about an entire location like a town, a stretch of coastline, a wild area, or a national park, it's important to listen to park rangers when they tell you where to go and not go, what to do and not do.

---

[3] A **niche** is a special area of demand for a product or a service.
[4] **Aesthetics** relates to the appreciation and study of beauty.
[5] Marine-life **nurseries** are places where young sea creatures can begin growing into adults.

[6] A **pebble** is a small, round stone.

According to a survey by the Destination Stewardship Center, the Norwegian Fjords are one of the world's best examples of geotourism.

Q: What happens when tourism is managed well?

Tourtellot: It can save a place. When people come [to] see something special and unique to an area—its nature, historic structures, great cultural events, beautiful landscapes, even special cuisine—they are enjoying and learning more about a destination's geographical character … [T]ravelers spend their money in a way that helps maintain the geographical diversity and distinctiveness of the place they're visiting. It can be as simple as spending your money at a little restaurant that serves a regional dish with ingredients from local farmers, rather than at an international franchise[7] that serves the same food you can get back home.

Q: How else can tourism help benefit a destination?

Tourtellot: Great tourism can build something that wasn't there before. My favorite example is the Monterey Bay Aquarium in California. It was built in a restored cannery[8] building on historic Cannery Row—which is a good example of **preserving** a historical building rather than destroying it. The aquarium, which has about 1.8 million visitors each year, brought people's attention to the incredible variety of sea life right off the coast of California. And it played a major role in the development of the Monterey Bay National Marine Sanctuary. Once people saw what was there, they wanted to protect it.

[7] A **franchise** is allowed to sell another company's products.

[8] A **cannery** is a factory where food is canned.

UNDERSTANDING THE READING

UNDERSTANDING
KEY TERMS

A Check (✓) the three best statements to complete the definition of *geotourism*.

According to Jonathan Tourtellot, geotourism _____ .

☐ 1. focuses on bringing people to natural areas

☐ 2. has positive effects on local economies

☐ 3. helps preserve the environment

☐ 4. benefits international tour companies

☐ 5. is good for both travelers and locals

UNDERSTANDING
MAIN IDEAS

B Check (✓) four statements that summarize Tourtellot's main ideas.

☐ 1. Geotourism is similar to ecotourism, but is mainly concerned with controlling pollution caused by tourists.

☐ 2. Tourism that is not well planned can cause significant environmental damage, particularly along coastlines.

☐ 3. When a place has a lot of visitors over a long period of time, the visitors can destroy some of the characteristics that made the site special.

☐ 4. When tourism is well planned, people learn about the geography of an area and help support it at the same time.

☐ 5. Tourism can help preserve places that might otherwise be lost.

☐ 6. The basic idea of geotourism is "keep everything the way it is."

UNDERSTANDING
PURPOSE

C Match each place mentioned in the reading passage to the main reason (a–d) Tourtellot mentions it.

_____ 1. Costa Rica

_____ 2. The Rockies

_____ 3. The Petrified Forest

_____ 4. Monterey Bay Aquarium

a. an unusual landscape that has been significantly damaged by tourism

b. a region where careful development planning is important

c. an example of how geotourism can help preserve a historical site

d. a place where ecotourism has had a positive environmental impact

> **CRITICAL THINKING** Writers often make arguments by contrasting the advantages of an idea with the disadvantages. You can **evaluate** their argument by asking:
>
> • Is there enough evidence to support each argument?
>
> • Does the writer present both sides of the argument?
>
> • Is the presented evidence fair and up to date?
>
> • Does the evidence relate logically to the argument?

D Complete the notes comparing geotourism and mass tourism with suitable words.

IDENTIFYING ARGUMENTS

Advantages of Geotourism	Disadvantages of Mass Tourism
• allows tourism growth to be managed in the long term	• does not promote local food or culture
• people support the _____ by using local hotels or restaurants	• people spend money that doesn't go to _____
• visitors gain a deeper understanding of the area's _____	• people gain a limited _____ of the places they visit
• careful development can help preserve _____ and educate people about the area	• unmanaged tourist numbers can cause natural areas to _____ their original beauty

E Work with a partner. Answer the questions below.

CRITICAL THINKING: EVALUATING ARGUMENTS

1. What might be some disadvantages of geotourism?

   _____

   _____

2. Consider the pros and cons of geotourism and mass tourism (refer to your answers in 1, exercise D, and exercise A-2 in Explore the Theme). Are you convinced by the writer's argument that geotourism is better than mass tourism? Why or why not?

   _____

   _____

The Petrified Forest receives around 800,000 visitors every year.

DEVELOPING READING SKILLS

READING SKILL Analyzing Causes and Effects

Recognizing causes and effects can help you understand a writer's main arguments. The following words and phrases are used to signal cause-effect relationships.

For introducing causes:

if, because of, when, as, one effect of

For introducing effects:

as a result, one result (of…) is, so, therefore, consequently, (this) leads/led to

             CAUSE   EFFECT

Tourism brings money into a community. **As a result***, governments can make improvements that benefit local residents.*

                  CAUSE   EFFECT

Because of *the money brought into a community by tourism, governments can make improvements that benefit local residents.*

Sometimes, writers do not use signal words to show cause-effect relationships; in these cases, you need to infer the meaning from the context.

IDENTIFYING CAUSES
AND EFFECTS

A Read the sentences. Underline words that signal causes and circle those that signal effects.

1. As ecotourism can bring many benefits, many local and national governments are looking at ways to preserve their distinctive natural areas.

2. In Costa Rica, for example, an interest in developing ecotourism led to the creation of several national parks and reserves where wildlife is protected.

3. The creation of national parks and reserves requires large numbers of skilled workers. Consequently, many people who are out of work may become employed.

4. The government of Costa Rica created a successful international ecotourism marketing campaign. As a result, tourism to the country increased dramatically.

ANALYZING CAUSES
AND EFFECTS

B Complete the chart with the causes and effects of geotourism / mass tourism. Use information from paragraphs C and D in the passage.

Cause	Effect
1.	1. The money made does not help the local economy.
2.	2. People don't know much about the nature and culture of the places they visit.
3. Travelers eat and shop at local businesses.	3.
4. The money spent by travelers goes to the local community.	4.

ANALYZING CAUSES
AND EFFECTS

C Which of the cause-effect sentence(s) in paragraphs C and D contained a signal word or phrase? Which required inferring from the context? Discuss with a partner.

Video

GALÁPAGOS TOURISM

Giant land tortoises on
Santa Cruz island, Galápagos

BEFORE VIEWING

A What effect might tourists and tourism activities have on animal species that live on remote islands? Discuss with a partner.

PREDICTING

B Read the information about the Galápagos Islands. Then answer the questions.

LEARNING ABOUT
THE TOPIC

The Galápagos Islands are located 620 miles (1,000 km) off the coast of Ecuador. Thousands of different species live on the islands, many of which cannot be found anywhere else on Earth. The naturalist Charles Darwin studied the animals of the Galápagos—particularly the finches (a bird species) and tortoises. From his study of finches, Darwin saw how animals change to adapt to their environments. This research inspired his development of the theory of evolution, which he described in detail in his 1859 book *On the Origin of Species*. Today, tourists from around the world are able to interact closely with the islands' animals.

1. What is special about the animals on the Galápagos Islands?

   _____

2. How did the Galápagos Islands contribute to our scientific knowledge?

   _____

C The words and phrases in **bold** below are used in the video. Read the sentences. Then match the correct form of each word or phrase to its definition.

> **Contaminants**, such as gasoline and other fuels, can contribute to water pollution.
>
> Tourism can bring **revenue** to a place, but it can also bring problems.
>
> Jonathan Tourtellot believes that by managing tourism, we can avoid **ruining** destinations for future travelers.
>
> A global cyberattack by a computer virus, WannaCry, was a **wake-up call** for many countries to strengthen their cyber security measures.

1. _____ (n) money that a company or an organization receives
2. _____ (n) a substance that makes something unsuitable for use
3. _____ (v) to destroy or severely damage something
4. _____ (n) an event that is serious enough to make people aware of a big problem

WHILE VIEWING

A ▶ Watch the video. Check (✓) the main ideas of the video.

☐ 1. Human presence on the islands has increased significantly in the last few decades.
☐ 2. Tourist revenue has been used for some major construction projects on the islands.
☐ 3. Tourism is negatively affecting the natural environment of the islands.
☐ 4. The local people have started adopting more environmentally friendly practices.

B ▶ Watch the video again. Check (✓) the actions that are being taken to make the islands greener.

☐ 1. Older oil tanks have been replaced with more modern ones.
☐ 2. The number of tourists on the islands has been restricted.
☐ 3. Gas stations have barriers to prevent oil leaks.
☐ 4. Cars will be replaced with vehicles that are more environmentally friendly.
☐ 5. The locals are reducing their waste and recycling more.

AFTER VIEWING

A Read the statements below. Which do you agree with more? Why? Discuss with a partner.

1. Banning tourists from the islands is the most effective way to protect the natural environment.

2. Tourism on the islands should be allowed, as long as more efforts are made to manage its growth.

B Work with a partner. Can you think of other ways that the environment on the Galápagos Islands could be protected? Use ideas from Reading 1 or your own ideas.

Reading 2

PREPARING TO READ

A The words in blue below are used in Reading 2. Read the paragraphs. Then match the correct form of each word to its definition.

BUILDING VOCABULARY

A key **objective** of geotourism is to make sure places are environmentally friendly. Some hotels, for example, not only provide **comfort** to their visitors; they also have sustainable practices such as using **renewable** energy sources like solar power for electricity. Hotel companies are also encouraged to assess the **ecological** impact of any new projects before they start building.

Another **vital** part of geotourism is to raise people's **awareness** of the history and culture of the places they visit. For example, tours may include visits to **landmarks** that have **spiritual** meaning to the local people, such as Chichén Itzá in Mexico, where ceremonies for the gods were often performed. These visits are often more **enriching** when tourists have the chance to interact with local people employed as **official** guides.

1. _____ (n) a goal

2. _____ (n) a state of ease or well-being

3. _____ (n) knowledge that something exists

4. _____ (adj) able to be replaced naturally

5. _____ (adj) necessary or extremely important

6. _____ (adj) providing more appreciation or enjoyment

7. _____ (adj) relating to a government or an organization

8. _____ (n) a building or structure with historical or cultural significance

9. _____ (adj) relating to a higher purpose rather than just material needs

10. _____ (adj) relating to the relationship between living things and their surroundings

B Think back to the last time you traveled to a new place. What was your main **objective**: to relax, to learn something, to meet people, or something else? Discuss with a partner.

USING VOCABULARY

C Skim the reading passage and answer the questions. Then check your ideas as you read.

SKIMMING

1. What types of natural places does the reading passage describe?

_____

2. What do these places have in common? List one or two things.

_____

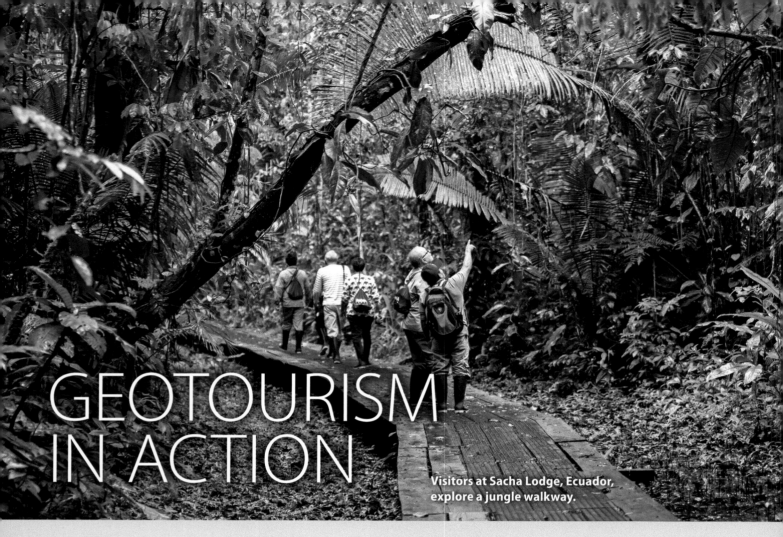

GEOTOURISM IN ACTION

Visitors at Sacha Lodge, Ecuador, explore a jungle walkway.

🎧 1.10

A As public awareness grows of the negative effects of mass tourism, more travel companies are providing options that enhance—rather than harm—local cultures and environments. The following examples from around the world show how innovative local programs can promote sustainable tourism that benefits tourists, locals, and the environment.

ECOLODGES IN ECUADOR

B Located in the Amazon basin, Ecuador is one of South America's most popular places for tourists. Ecolodges now provide a sustainable travel option for these tourists. First developed in the 1990s, an ecolodge is a type of hotel that helps local economies and protects the environment. Many of the lodges are built with renewable materials that are found locally. The lodges allow people in the community to sell locally made products to guests; some are also owned and operated by local people.

C Ecolodges not only help local economies and the environment, they also enable visitors to gain a deeper understanding of the region. There are ecolodges throughout the country, so visitors can choose to stay in the rain forest, in the mountains, or at an island beach. Visitors at Sani Lodge in the rain forest, for example, are surrounded by over 500 species of tropical birds and a thousand species of butterflies. In the Andes, guests can go hiking and explore volcanic glaciers. On the Galápagos, visitors can watch giant tortoises lay their eggs.

D These lodges let visitors interact with local people and learn about local culture, too. For example, at some ecolodges, guests learn how to make dishes using local ingredients. At Sani Lodge, local families invite guests into their homes. In 2015, the owners of Sani Lodge won the World Legacy Travel Award for their efforts to promote sustainable tourism. This kind of tourism, says company director Jascivan Carvalho, leads to "a deeper, more enriching experience for travelers, and for locals, whose livelihoods improve."

ADVENTURE TREKKING IN NEPAL

E Nepal has been an important trekking destination for over a hundred years. Until recently, however, most tour guides and porters were male. In 1993, three sisters—Lucky, Dicky, and Nicky Chhetri—had an idea. They were running a restaurant and lodge in Pokhara, a popular base for trekkers. When some female guests complained of poor treatment by male porters, the sisters decided to act. They would start their own trekking business—one run by women, for women. They launched their partnership—3 Sisters Adventure Trekking— with two main goals: to give local women

opportunities to work in the tourism industry, and to give female trekkers the choice of female guides for greater comfort and security.

F The sisters also created a nonprofit organization—Empowering Women of Nepal (EWN). The organization trains and hires local women as guides. The training program includes classes in English, health, and awareness of ecological issues. At the end of the program, the trainees get on-the-job experience as guides, earning the same wages as male guides. Some graduates of the program use their earnings to continue their education, while others start their own businesses.

G These improvements to the women's social and financial situations are good for both their families and the rest of the community. The interaction between local guides and tourists from all over the world creates a vital cultural exchange, too. "I learned to become an ambassador for my country," says one of the graduates of the program.

A local guide from 3 Sisters Adventure Trekking with a trekker on Suriya Peak in Nepal

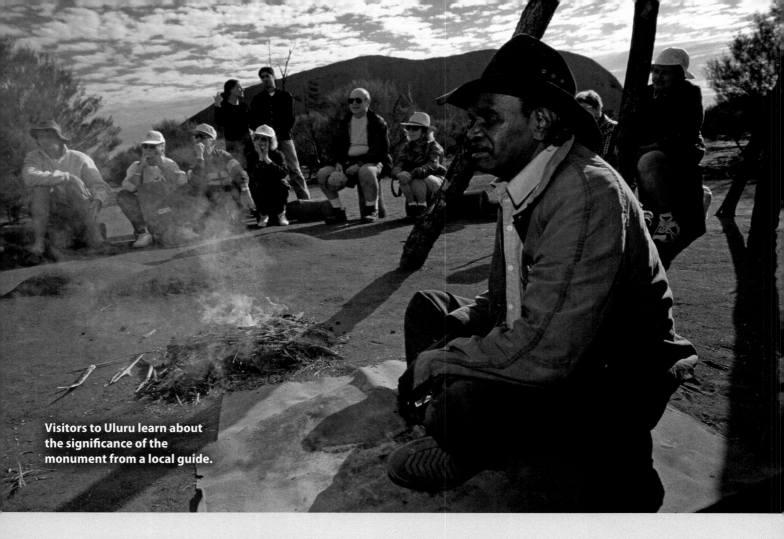

Visitors to Uluru learn about the significance of the monument from a local guide.

CULTURAL TOURS IN AUSTRALIA

Uluru is a giant rock formation that stands in the desert of central Australia. Also known as Ayer's Rock, the famous landmark is an Australian icon and a hot spot for tourists. But for the local Anangu—meaning "we people"— Uluru is the heart of a region where they have lived for more than 20,000 years. Until recently, many visitors came to Uluru with the objective of climbing it. However, the Australian government and several tour companies are asking visitors not to do this. In fact, the government of Australia has now introduced an official policy to stop visitors from climbing the monument.

The concerns over climbing Uluru are partly because it is dangerous—the rock stands nearly 350 meters high (over 1,140 feet) and has steep sides. However, it is also a sacred site for the Anangu people, the traditional owners of the rock. For the Anangu, climbing Uluru is a spiritual experience. The government's and tour companies' efforts have had a positive effect. While 74 percent of visitors climbed Uluru in 1990, that number dropped to less than 30 percent by 2015.

Adventure Tours and SEIT Outback Australia are just two of the companies that work to educate visitors about the culture of Uluru. Some of these tour companies hire indigenous guides who can share the perspectives of the local people. Instead of taking tourists to the top of the rock, tour guides lead tourists around Uluru on the paths that Anangu ancestors walked. The guides tell traditional stories about how the world was born and how people are connected to the land. Through these travel experiences, visitors can leave Uluru culturally richer than when they arrived.

UNDERSTANDING THE READING

A Look at the main ideas (1–6) from the reading passage. Match each section of the passage (a–c) with two main ideas.

UNDERSTANDING MAIN IDEAS

a. Ecolodges in Ecuador

b. Adventure Trekking in Nepal

c. Cultural Tours in Australia

_____ 1. The main focus is on providing employment for local women and services for female travelers.

_____ 2. Visitors stay in a type of hotel accommodation that benefits the environment and the financial well-being of local communities.

_____ 3. An education program helps local people learn skills that they can use in their communities.

_____ 4. Visitors have the opportunity to experience a wide variety of natural environments.

_____ 5. Greater awareness of local concerns has reduced the negative impact of tourism on the site.

_____ 6. Tour guides emphasize how the site is culturally and historically significant for the local people.

B Match each paragraph or section from the passage to the best description (1–7).

UNDERSTANDING DETAILS

| B | C | D | E | F–G | H–I | J |

_____ 1. welcoming visitors into local homes

_____ 2. the evolution of a new type of green travel lodge

_____ 3. a wide variety of environmental experiences on offer

_____ 4. a training program that offers local women a better future

_____ 5. understanding a place from a traditional cultural perspective

_____ 6. the origins of a more gender-balanced approach to trekking

_____ 7. reasons why climbing a sacred landmark is now discouraged

Uluru is one of Australia's most well-known landmarks.

C Find and underline the following words and phrases in **bold** in the reading passage. Use context to identify their meanings. Then write the part of speech and your own definition of each word or phrase.

1. **livelihood** (paragraph D)   Part of speech: _____

   Meaning: _____

   _____

2. **ambassador** (paragraph G)   Part of speech: _____

   Meaning: _____

   _____

3. **hot spot** (paragraph H)   Part of speech: _____

   Meaning: _____

   _____

4. **indigenous** (paragraph J)   Part of speech: _____

   Meaning: _____

   _____

D Underline the word(s) that signal a cause-effect relationship in the excerpt below. What effect does ecotourism have on travelers and locals? Discuss with a partner.

Director of the company, Jascivan Carvalho, says that this kind of travel experience can lead to

"a deeper, more enriching experience for travelers, and for locals, whose livelihoods improve."

E Read Jonathan Tourtellot's definition of geotourism from Reading 1. What are some examples from the reading that relate to his definition? Note them in the chart.

"Geotourism is defined as tourism that sustains or enhances the geographical character of a place—the environment, heritage, aesthetics, culture, and well-being of local people."

Ecolodges in Ecuador	Adventure Trekking in Nepal	Cultural Tours in Australia

F Which of the three destinations do you think is the best example of geotourism? Why? Note your ideas and discuss your reasons in a small group.

Place: _____

Reason(s): _____

_____

Writing

EXPLORING WRITTEN ENGLISH

A Read the sentences and underline the part that describes a cause. Circle the part that describes an effect.

NOTICING

1. If tourists stay at large international hotels, they often interact less with locals.

2. Tourists don't necessarily help the local economy if they only eat at chain restaurants.

LANGUAGE FOR WRITING Using *if ... , (then) ...*

One way to express a cause-effect relationship that is generally true is to use sentences with *if*. In these sentences, the *if*-clause introduces a condition or cause that leads to the effect or result expressed in the other clause.

        CAUSE   EFFECT
__If__ tourism is managed well, both tourists and local people benefit.

You can reverse the order of the clauses.

            EFFECT   CAUSE
Both tourists and local people benefit __if__ tourism is managed well.

You can also use a modal (*can, should, might, must*) in the effect clause.

        CAUSE   EFFECT
__If__ tourism is badly managed, it __can__ destroy a place.

Note: Use a comma when the *if*-clause comes first. Use the present tense in the *if*-clause and the present tense or a modal in the effect clause.

B Underline the sentence in each pair (1–4) that is a cause. Then combine the sentences using *if*-clauses.

1. You buy locally made products. You support the local economy.

   _____

2. Forests and beaches might be ruined. Too many people visit them.

   _____

3. Female trekkers feel more comfortable and safe. The porters are female.

   _____

4. Tourists can learn about local customs. They stay at an ecolodge.

   _____

C Use your own ideas to complete each sentence with a cause or an effect.

1. If _____ , it may harm the environment.

2. If tourists use local guides, _____ .

3. Visitors can have an enriching travel experience if _____ .

4. _____ if you meet locals when you travel.

WRITING SKILL Writing a Cause-Effect Essay

One type of cause-effect essay explains how a situation (a cause) produces another situation (an effect). For example, an essay could explain the effects of population growth on an area. The thesis statement in this type of essay states that the focus is on the effects of a particular cause.

In a cause-effect essay that focuses on effects, each body paragraph includes a topic sentence that states the effect. One body paragraph could focus on the most important effect; the next paragraph could focus on a less important effect. Another way to organize body paragraphs is to focus first on the effects on one group (e.g., humans), and then focus on a different group (e.g., animals) in another paragraph.

A well-developed body paragraph includes at least two supporting ideas that include reasons, facts, and examples to help a reader understand your topic sentence. One strategy for adding effective details is to think about questions (*who, why, when, where, what*) that a reader might have about your topic sentence. If your supporting ideas do not adequately answer these questions, then you should add more details.

ANALYZING A
CAUSE-EFFECT
OUTLINE

D The paragraph outline below is for an essay about how vacation rentals (houses that are rented to tourists) affect cities. Use the notes (1–4) to complete the outline.

1. neighborhood businesses lose money
2. may have to lay off employees or shorten their hours
3. they can harm neighborhoods
4. more vulnerable to burglars

Topic Sentence: *One negative effect of vacation rentals is that _____.*

Supporting Idea 1: *changes the character of a neighborhood*

Details:

• *neighborhoods become empty on weekdays / during off-peak*

• _____

Supporting Idea 2: _____

Details:

• *local businesses don't have enough customers in off-season*

• _____

E The draft paragraph below is about the effects of the redevelopment of a national park. A reader has noted some questions asking for more information. Add the details (a–d) that the writer could use to improve the paragraph.

IMPROVING A CAUSE-EFFECT PARAGRAPH

One positive effect of the redevelopment of Ghana's Kakum National Park was that it greatly improved the local economy. ____ In the 1990s, Conservation International formed partnerships to make the park more attractive to tourists. ____ These improvements had positive financial effects on the community. ____ When the project was finished, there were many more visitors to the park. ____ This increase in tourism continues to bring money into the local economy.

Why did the park need to be redeveloped?

How was the park made attractive to tourists?

How did the community benefit?

How many more visitors were there?

a. fewer than 1,000 visitors in 1991; over 180,000 a year today
b. local people did the work; the project used local materials
c. had suffered for many years from deforestation and lack of investment
d. built visitors' center, wildlife exhibitions, restaurants, shops, camping facilities, a canopy walk—a special walkway (takes visitors through treetops of rain forest)

F Rewrite the paragraph, inserting the information from the notes in the highlighted spaces.

WRITING A CAUSE-EFFECT PARAGRAPH

WRITING TASK

GOAL You are going to write a cause-effect essay on the following topic: What are the positive—or negative—effects of tourism on a place that you know well?

BRAINSTORMING **A** Think of a place you know well that is popular with tourists. List some positive and negative effects that tourists have on this place.

PLANNING **B** Follow these steps to make notes for your essay.

Step 1 Decide whether to write about the positive or the negative effects in your essay. Write your thesis statement in the outline.

Step 2 Choose two effects and note them in the outline.

Step 3 Add two supporting ideas and details about each effect.

Step 4 Write a summary statement and add a final thought.

OUTLINE

Introductory Paragraph

Thesis Statement: _____

_____

Body Paragraphs

Effect 1: _____

Supporting Idea 1 / Details: _____

_____

Supporting Idea 2 / Details: _____

_____

Effect 2: _____

Supporting Idea 1 / Details: _____

_____

Supporting Idea 2 / Details: _____

_____

Concluding Paragraph

Summary Statement: _____

_____

Final Thought: _____

FIRST DRAFT **C** Use the information in the outline to write a first draft of your essay.

REVISING PRACTICE

The draft below is a cause-effect essay about the effects of vacation rentals on cities. Follow the steps to create a better second draft.

1. Add the sentences (a–c) in the most suitable spaces.
   a. In some cities, the vacation rental business has reduced the number of available apartments by 20 to 30 percent.
   b. Vacation rentals also have negative effects on housing in a community.
   c. As a result, they may have to lay off some of their employees or limit their hours.

2. Now fix the following problems (d–f) in the essay.
   d. Correct a mistake with an *if . . . , (then) . . .* sentence in paragraph B.
   e. Cross out one sentence in paragraph C that does not relate to the essay topic.
   f. Correct a mistake with an *if . . . , (then) . . .* sentence in paragraph C.

A

In the sharing economy, anyone can be an entrepreneur. People can make money with ridesharing, by renting out their cars, or even by renting out their homes. While allowing people to stay in your home for a few days a month might be a nice way to make some extra money, vacation rentals have negative effects on communities.

B

One negative effect of vacation rentals is that they can harm neighborhoods. For example, they can change the character of neighborhoods, particularly those in popular destinations. Low numbers of tourists on weekdays or in the off-peak season can mean nearly empty neighborhoods, making the areas easy targets for burglars. Vacation rentals can also cause neighborhood businesses to lose money. If vacation rentals are empty for days at a time, so small grocers and other neighborhood businesses don't have a lot of customers. _____

C

_____ First of all, short-term vacation rentals can cause housing shortages, as landlords rent apartments out to tourists instead of making them available to permanent residents. _____ In addition, vacation rentals drive up housing prices in a community. If there are fewer apartments available rents tend to go up, forcing people with average incomes to move outside of the city. Rental companies don't always know everything about the home or apartment owners' backgrounds.

D

Short-term vacation rentals have harmful effects on communities. They can negatively impact the character and economy of a neighborhood, and lead to housing shortages and higher rents. When tourism takes over a neighborhood and drives local residents away, is it even the same place anymore?

D **Now use the questions below to revise your essay.**

- ☐ Does your introduction have a clear thesis statement?
- ☐ Did you include enough details to explain the effects in your body paragraphs?
- ☐ Do all your sentences relate to the thesis statement?
- ☐ Does your concluding paragraph have a summary statement and a final thought?

EDITING PRACTICE

Read the information below.

In sentences with *if*-clauses that describe general truths, remember:
- that the *if*-clause introduces the condition or cause.
- to use a comma after the *if*-clause when it comes first in a sentence.
- to use the present tense in the *if*-clause, and the present tense or a modal in the effect clause.

Correct one mistake with *if*-clauses in each of the sentences (1–5).

1. If prices are too high people might stop traveling.

2. If travel journalists will write about the importance of protecting destinations, they might educate tourists.

3. If tourists only eat at chain restaurants, they didn't learn anything about local food.

4. Tourists show disrespect to the local culture, if they climb Uluru.

5. Local communities can benefit if tourism will promote local businesses.

FINAL DRAFT **E** **Follow these steps to write a final draft.**

1. Check your revised draft for mistakes with *if*-clauses.
2. Now use the checklist on page 253 to write a final draft. Make any other necessary changes.

UNIT REVIEW
Answer the following questions.

1. What are two things you learned about geotourism?

_____

_____

_____

2. What are some signal words or phrases that introduce causes or effects?

_____

_____

_____

3. Do you remember the meanings of these words? Check (✔) the ones you know. Look back at the unit and review the ones you don't know.

Reading 1:

- ☐ alternative AWL
- ☐ distinctive AWL
- ☐ earn a living
- ☐ economy AWL
- ☐ harmful
- ☐ maintain AWL
- ☐ necessary
- ☐ partnership AWL
- ☐ preserve
- ☐ sustainable AWL

Reading 2:

- ☐ awareness AWL
- ☐ comfort
- ☐ ecological
- ☐ enriching
- ☐ landmark
- ☐ objective AWL
- ☐ official
- ☐ renewable
- ☐ spiritual
- ☐ vital

INFORMATION DESIGN 6

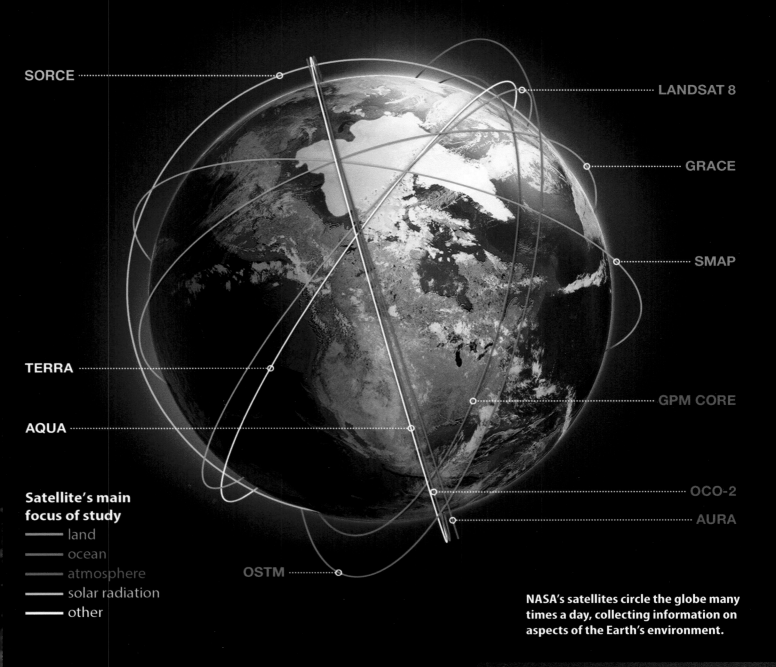

SORCE

LANDSAT 8

GRACE

SMAP

TERRA

GPM CORE

AQUA

OCO-2

AURA

Satellite's main focus of study
- land
- ocean
- atmosphere
- solar radiation
- other

OSTM

NASA's satellites circle the globe many times a day, collecting information on aspects of the Earth's environment.

ACADEMIC SKILLS

READING	Identifying arguments and counterarguments
WRITING	Writing a persuasive essay
GRAMMAR	Describing visual information
CRITICAL THINKING	Evaluating visual data

THINK AND DISCUSS

1. What does the infographic above show?
2. What are some other ways in which information and data can be presented visually?

A Look at the information on these pages and answer the questions.

1. What does the infographic show?

2. Do you think it's an effective infographic? Why or why not?

B Match the words and phrases in blue to their definitions.

_____ (v) to communicate

_____ (v) to be noticeable or easy to see

_____ (v) to understand the meaning of something

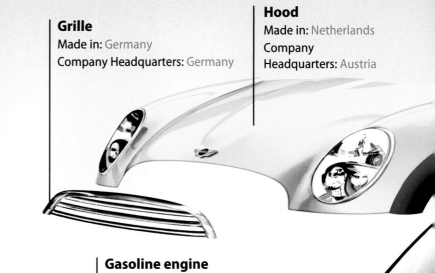

Grille
Made in: Germany
Company Headquarters: Germany

Hood
Made in: Netherlands
Company Headquarters: Austria

Gasoline engine
Made in: Brazil
Company Headquarters: Brazil

Diesel engine
(not shown)
Made in: Japan
Company Headquarters: Japan

Front and rear bumpers
Made in: U.K.
Company Headquarters: Canada

UNDER THE HOOD

When you think of infographics, you might think of pie charts and line graphs—or you might picture more complex images such as the globe on the previous page. But infographics can take almost any form. With a single infographic, designers are now able to convey complicated information and help us interpret the meaning of vast data sets.

The infographic on these pages, for example, has a 3-D design that allows a viewer to understand a large amount of information about a car in a small amount of space. In the image, the outer shell of a BMW Mini has been lifted away from the car's body so that the viewer can see its inner workings. This treatment lets each piece of the car stand out as an individual part. In addition, the infographic allows a viewer to see a bigger story—although the car is made by a German company, it is actually a global product.

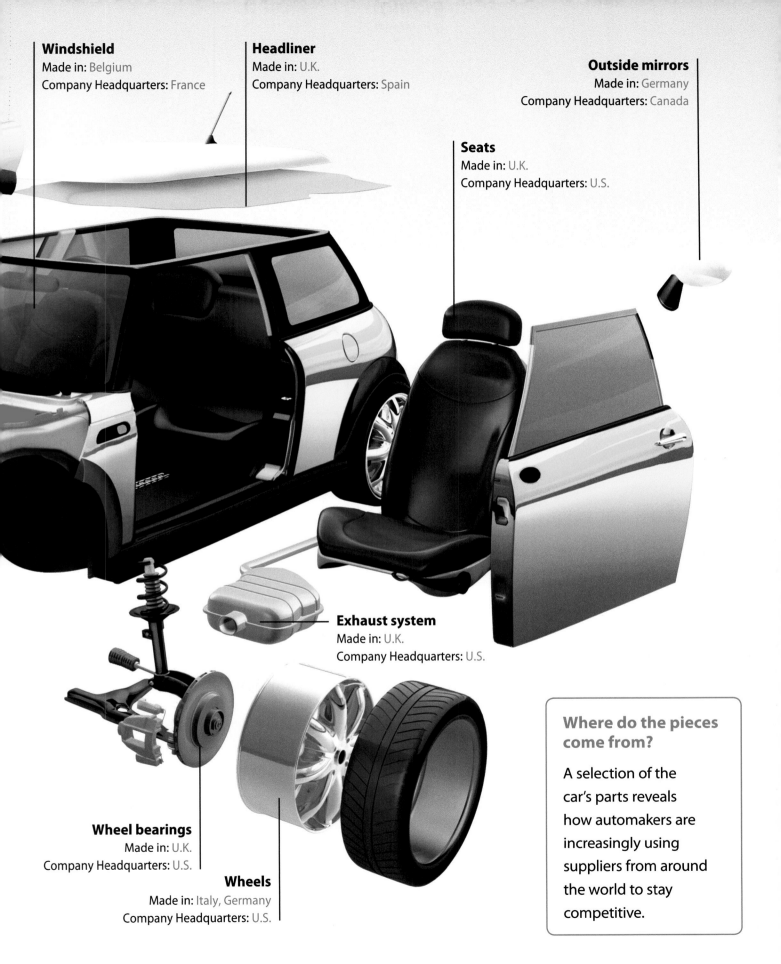

Windshield
Made in: Belgium
Company Headquarters: France

Headliner
Made in: U.K.
Company Headquarters: Spain

Outside mirrors
Made in: Germany
Company Headquarters: Canada

Seats
Made in: U.K.
Company Headquarters: U.S.

Exhaust system
Made in: U.K.
Company Headquarters: U.S.

Wheel bearings
Made in: U.K.
Company Headquarters: U.S.

Wheels
Made in: Italy, Germany
Company Headquarters: U.S.

Where do the pieces come from?

A selection of the car's parts reveals how automakers are increasingly using suppliers from around the world to stay competitive.

Reading 1

PREPARING TO READ

BUILDING
VOCABULARY

A The words in blue below are used in Reading 1. Read the sentences. Then match the correct form of each word to its definition.

Good journalists aim to present the news in an **objective** manner without inserting their own opinions into their reports.

People with poor **vision** correct their eyesight by wearing glasses or contact lenses.

In order to make their products seem more effective, companies might **deliberately** include **misleading** information in their advertisements.

One **downside** to using information from the Internet is that the source may not be reliable.

Most people have strong opinions about whale hunting. Not many people are **neutral** about the issue.

When writing a report, it's important to check that the points make sense and don't contain **faulty** logic.

1. _____ (n) a disadvantage

2. _____ (adv) on purpose or intentionally

3. _____ (n) the ability to see

4. _____ (adj) containing mistakes; inaccurate

5. _____ (adj) based on facts, not personal bias

6. _____ (adj) not having an opinion about something

7. _____ (adj) making someone believe something that is not true

USING
VOCABULARY

B Discuss these questions with a partner.

1. What do you think are the **downsides** to using information from the Internet?

2. What kinds of **misleading** information have you seen online?

BRAINSTORMING

C What are some benefits of infographics for people working in business, education, or journalism? Discuss with a partner.

PREDICTING

D Skim the first sentence of each paragraph in the reading passage. What do you think the passage is about? Check your idea as you read.

a. the purposes of different types of infographics

b. the history of data visualization

c. the pros and cons of using infographics

THE RISE OF VISUAL DATA

Facebook CEO Mark Zuckerberg presents a graphic showing the global connections of Facebook users.

🎧 2.01

A Visual data—charts, maps, and infographics—are more prevalent[1] than ever. Every day, we are exposed to visual data in print, in online media, and in the apps we use. Why is visual data so common today? And are there any downsides to living in a world of visual data?

THE POWER OF VISUALS

B The human brain can interpret a complex concept more quickly when it is presented visually than when it is explained on printed text. A 2014 study at the Massachusetts Institute of Technology (MIT), for example, showed that humans can interpret an image of a "smiling couple" after seeing it for only 13 milliseconds—nearly 10 times faster than the blink of an eye. To explain all the details of the "smiling couple" in writing would take significantly longer. As Mary Potter, professor of brain and cognitive sciences at MIT, explains, "What vision does is find concepts. That's what the brain is doing all day long—trying to understand what we're looking at."

[1]Something that is **prevalent** is widespread or common.

Data visualization journalist and educator Alberto Cairo thinks that "words alone are not powerful enough to communicate effectively … you also need visuals." Visual data is most effective when there is an "aha" moment—when the information provides "spontaneous insight." These visuals immediately create understanding of complex concepts. Cairo cites a chart (Figure 1) that shows the sudden rise in global temperatures as an example of this. With its sharp curve upward, the chart quickly conveys how rapidly our planet is warming.

Visual data also appears to make information seem more credible. A study carried out at Cornell University in New York showed that 67 percent of participants believed information when they read it in a document without a graph. However, when a graph was included, 96 percent believed the same information. Alberto Cairo agrees that "a message looks more scientific when you put charts in it." He points out that visual data can also mislead, because it makes textual information look more serious and academic than it perhaps is.

THE PITFALLS OF VISUAL DATA

Even though graphs may look credible, they can be misleading, especially if faulty logic is used to present information. Figure 2, for example, shows the rise and fall of the performance of athletes who appeared on the cover of *Sports Illustrated* magazine. The graph appears to imply there is a cause-effect relationship between two events: being on the cover of the magazine leads to poor performance afterward.

In fact, athletes usually appear on magazine covers when they are at the peak of their performance. After this stage, it is most probable that athletes' performance will eventually decline. So, although there may be a correlation between two events, that does not mean that one event has a direct effect on the other.

Another way charts can mislead is when a scale is inappropriate. Figure 3 illustrates the effectiveness of two drugs, and there seems to be a big difference between them. However, the difference looks greater than it really is.

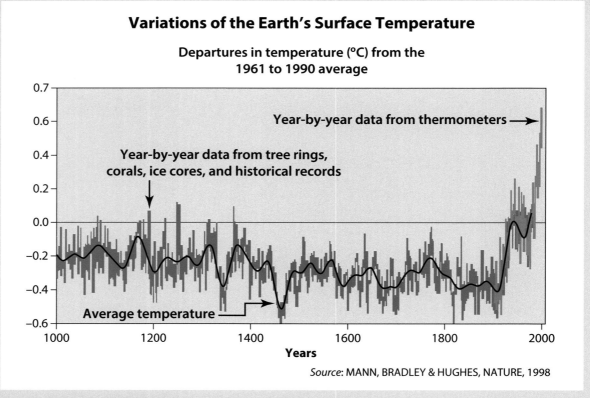

Figure 1: Average global temperature over 1,000 years

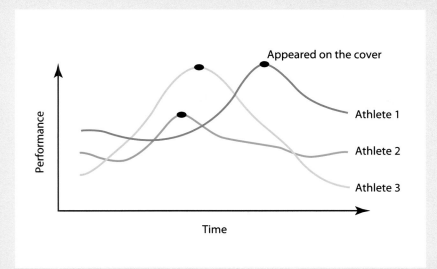

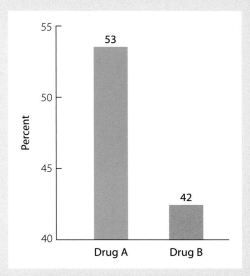

Figure 2: Performance of athletes before and after appearing on the cover of *Sports Illustrated* magazine

Figure 3: Effectiveness of Drug A

This is because the numbers on the vertical axis go only from 40 percent to 55 percent—making it look like Drug A is five times more effective than Drug B. In fact, the difference between the two drugs is only about 10 percent. In addition, the color of the bar for Drug A makes that data stand out more and seem more important—and positive—than Drug B.

Some visuals may be unintentionally misleading. Others, however, may be deliberately designed to influence the viewer. According to Cairo, deliberately misleading visuals are designed to make a point, not to objectively present facts. While he thinks this may be valid in advertising or PR, it's not a good example of objective journalistic communication. Cairo believes that while designers may never be able to approach information in a completely neutral way, they should at least try: "That is what journalism is."

VISUALIZING THE FUTURE

According to Geoff McGhee—a data visualizer at Stanford University—new forms of visual data are pushing the boundaries of what we can process. Unlike traditional visual data, these new types of visuals use thousands of data points, such as the map showing global connections on Facebook (the first image in this reading passage). Many of these modern visualizations feature a huge number of thin, overlapping,[2] and semi-transparent[3] lines. The 3-D effect allows viewers to "see through" points to look at others behind.

Some journalists worry that complex visualizations such as these may make beautiful data art, but risk confusing readers instead of enlightening them. For Alberto Cairo, the key issue with visualization is not complexity or beauty, but whether the public is reliably informed. When creators of visual data are balanced and honest, he says, "great visualizations change people's mind for the better."

[2]When two lines are **overlapping**, part of one line covers part of the other line.
[3]If something is **semi-transparent**, you can see through it, but not completely.

UNDERSTANDING THE READING

SUMMARIZING **A** Read the first sentence of a summary of the passage. Check (✓) three other sentences to complete the summary.

Infographics are more common today, but data visualizers should take into consideration certain issues.

☐ 1. Visual data is not as effective as text, but it is more interesting to look at and makes information seem more trustworthy.

☐ 2. It is easier and faster to interpret large amounts of information through visual data than through text.

☐ 3. There are many benefits to using visual data, but charts and graphs can be misleading.

☐ 4. Most infographics on the Internet unintentionally use incorrect data.

☐ 5. In the future, infographics will be easier to create and less confusing than they are now.

☐ 6. Data visualization may become more complex in the future, but it is important that it remains clear and accurate.

UNDERSTANDING DETAILS **B** Write answers to these questions. Then share your answers with a partner.

1. According to Alberto Cairo, when is visual data most effective?

_____

2. What does Cairo think is one benefit of including charts in a document?

_____

3. What ways of presenting visual data can result in inaccurate information? List three ways.

_____

_____

_____

4. What is a main difference between modern infographics and traditional charts such as line graphs?

_____

INTERPRETING VISUAL INFORMATION **C** Read the descriptions below. Match each one to a figure from the passage (1–3).

_____ a. the y-axis has a misleading scale

_____ b. shows a trend that is increasing

_____ c. presents a misleading comparison

_____ d. illustrates performance levels over time

_____ e. shows the relative success of two products

_____ f. provides quick insight into complex information

_____ g. implies an incorrect cause-effect relationship

_____ h. allows various data to be compared against an average

D Find and underline the following words in **bold** in the reading passage. Use context to identify their meanings. Match the sentence parts to complete the definitions.

1. Paragraph D: If something is **credible**, _____
2. Paragraph E: If you **imply** something, _____
3. Paragraph F: If there is a **correlation** between two things, _____
4. Paragraph H: If something is done **unintentionally**, _____

a. it is not done on purpose.
b. it is believable or trustworthy.
c. you suggest it without stating it directly.
d. there is a meaningful connection between them.

> **CRITICAL THINKING**   In order to **evaluate visual data**, ask yourself: Does the infographic show an accurate representation of relationships between two or more things, or is it biased to show one perspective? Is the scale misleading or exaggerated in some way? Is the creator of the infographic neutral?

E Study the two graphs below. How are they different?

_____

Which scale would be more suitable for each situation below?

_____ a. for looking in detail at the monthly changes in the U.S.'s GDP

_____ b. for comparing with another country's GDP in the same time period

Falling Gross Domestic Product (GDP) in the United States

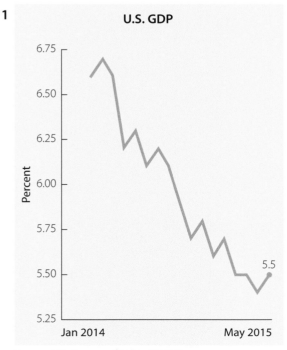

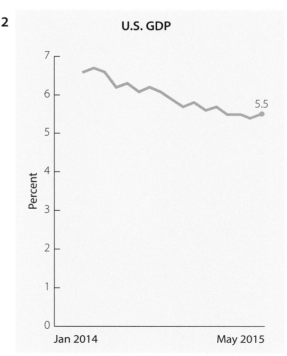

Source: U.S. Bureau of Labor Statistics

F Look back at Units 1–5 and find an infographic that you think best follows the principles of objective design. Find another infographic that you think could be improved. Discuss your reasons with a partner.

DEVELOPING READING SKILLS

> **READING SKILL** Identifying Arguments and Counterarguments
>
> Writers often acknowledge counterarguments—the arguments on the other side of the issue—in addition to presenting their own arguments. Concession words and phrases are often used to signal counterarguments. Some examples are *while, even though, though,* and *although.*
>
> COUNTERARGUMENT   WRITER'S ARGUMENT
> **While** *it may seem difficult to make good infographics,* <u>anyone can create them with the right software</u>.

IDENTIFYING ARGUMENTS

A Find the following concession words and phrases in the reading passage. Then underline the writer's argument and draw two lines under the counterargument.

1. even though (paragraph E)

2. although (paragraph F)

3. while (paragraph H)

4. while (paragraph H)

IDENTIFYING ARGUMENTS

B Choose the correct paraphrase of each main argument in exercise A. Then share your answers with a partner.

1. a. Graphs that look impressive sometimes contain inaccurate information.

   b. Misleading information is sometimes included to make charts attractive.

2. a. More evidence is needed to show that the two events affect each other.

   b. Two events that are connected are not necessarily in a cause-effect relationship.

3. a. Deliberately misleading visuals are used in advertising or PR to help make a point.

   b. It is unacceptable for journalists to include misleading information in visual data.

4. a. It is important for graphic designers to present information in the most neutral way possible.

   b. It is impossible for graphic designers to be completely neutral about the issues they write about.

IDENTIFYING COUNTERARGUMENTS

C Match each argument (a–c) to a counterargument (1–3).

1. While including charts and graphs is useful in reports, _____

2. Although charts and graphs may not always be necessary, _____

3. Though they sometimes seem simple, _____

a. a screen with nothing but text on it is uninteresting and unattractive.

b. charts and graphs can communicate a lot of information in small spaces.

c. they should be used only if they relate to the points made.

Video

Jer Thorp created this graphic to show exoplanets—planets outside of our solar system—discovered by the Kepler space telescope.

326.01

PAINTING WITH NUMBERS

BEFORE VIEWING

A Read the caption above and discuss the answers to these questions with a partner.

PREDICTING

1. What might the different sizes and colors of the circles represent?
2. What do you think the locations of the circles represent?

B Read the information about data artists. In what ways are Thorp's and Nightingale's infographics similar? Discuss your answer with a partner.

LEARNING ABOUT THE TOPIC

Jer Thorp is a data artist—someone who combines art and science to better communicate complex information. According to Thorp, an early example of an infographic was by Florence Nightingale—a nurse during the Crimean War (1853–1856). One of her graphics (right) showed that, contrary to popular belief, most soldiers were dying of treatable diseases rather than from injuries during the war. Her work reduced soldiers' deaths by over 60 percent, and is an example of how infographics can change public opinion.

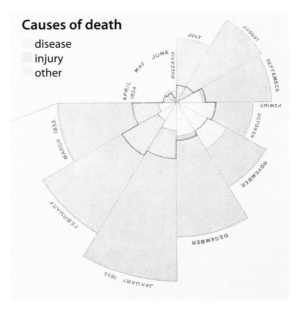

Causes of death
- disease
- injury
- other

C The words in **bold** below are used in the video. Read the sentences. Then match the correct form of each word to its definition.

> Police use maps to **plot** the **incidence** of crimes in an area. This can help them identify areas that need extra security.
>
> A complicated issue can be explored from different **angles**.
>
> One **strategy** to creating an effective infographic is to use objective data.

1. _____ (n) the number of times an event happens

2. _____ (v) to mark data on a map or chart

3. _____ (n) a particular perspective of something

4. _____ (n) a way of doing something to achieve a goal

WHILE VIEWING

UNDERSTANDING
MAIN IDEAS

A ▶ Watch the video. What benefits of using visual data are mentioned?

☐ 1. It makes data easier to remember.

☐ 2. It simplifies complex data.

☐ 3. It helps us see things we've never seen before.

☐ 4. It makes data more interesting.

UNDERSTANDING
DETAILS

B ▶ Watch the video again. Complete the sentences about what each graphic shows.

1. John Snow's map shows where people _____

_____

2. The "Just Landed" visualization shows _____

_____

AFTER VIEWING

REACTING TO
THE VIDEO

A Read the quote from the video about Thorp's "ooh-aah" approach to creating graphics. Then discuss the questions with a partner.

"The first thing I want people to do is I want them to say 'ooh' when they see the visualization, but that 'ooh' is useless unless there's an 'aah.' I want that learned moment that comes from really being able to discover something that you didn't understand before."

1. What makes people say "ooh" about an infographic?

2. What makes people say "aah"?

CRITICAL THINKING:
APPLYING

B Work in a small group. Choose three infographics in this book. For each, decide if there is a balance of "ooh" and "aah."

Reading 2

PREPARING TO READ

A The words and phrases in **blue** below are used in Reading 2. Complete the sentences with the correct form of the words or phrases. Use a dictionary to help you.

BUILDING VOCABULARY

| context | propose | publication | have to do with | reliance |
| universal | nevertheless | statistic | emphasize | gesture |

1. _____ such as comics and magazines tend to have more images, compared to journal articles that usually contain more data and _____ .

2. Sometimes, speakers use simple _____ while giving a speech, especially when they want to _____ certain points and draw people's attention to them.

3. People who create infographics may not be totally neutral about the data they are using. _____ , Alberto Cairo thinks that they should try to present the data in the most objective way possible.

4. Although it is helpful to include visuals in an essay, you should make sure that they are suitable for the _____ in which they are used.

5. When you see a chart or graph, ask yourself: what does it _____ the topic?

6. Visuals such as photos and infographics are like a(n) _____ language—there is little _____ on text to convey meaning.

7. Data artist Jer Thorp _____ that we can use the "ooh-aah" approach when evaluating the effectiveness of visual information.

B Discuss these questions with a partner.

USING VOCABULARY

1. What are some common **gestures** in your culture or country? What do they mean?

2. What are some topics that have **universal** appeal around the world?

C Work with a partner. What does the color red make you think of? What about the color green?

BRAINSTORMING

D Look at the images and read the first paragraph of the reading passage. What kinds of cultural differences in visual design do you think you will read about? Discuss with a partner. Then check your ideas as you read.

PREDICTING

VISUAL CULTURE

🎧 2.02

A When we think of language, we usually think of words, but visuals are also a part of communication. And like written language, visual symbols are not universal. An English speaker, for example, may place their hand near their chest as a gesture to mean "me," while a Japanese speaker is likely to point at their nose to indicate the same. Similarly, the way visual information is used can vary depending on the cultural context.

B Take the color of money. Charles Apple, an American visual journalist, was working for a newspaper in South Africa when green was proposed as a color for the business section. The newspaper preferred blue, however, and for a simple reason: not every country has green money.

C And that's not all. "In the United States, red usually has a connotation[1] of losses or deficits," Apple says, "but that's not true in all countries." Xan Sabaris, a Spanish infographic artist who has worked for the Beijing-based *China Daily*, agrees: "For the Western culture, red has negative connotations. In China, it's the opposite. You could see Chinese newspapers where stock market charts use green for negative values and red for positive ones."

D Shapes are influenced by culture, too. Antonio Farach, from Honduras, and Adonis Durado, from the Philippines, both work at the *Times of Oman*. Farach noticed how subtle details play a role. In

[1]A **connotation** is an idea that a word makes you think of, apart from its meaning.

Western cultures, he says, "rounded corners are more accepted than in Arabic countries. In typography, Arabs prefer blade-like typefaces ..."

Sometimes the differences are not so subtle. "The big difference is orientation," says Durado. "Arabs write and read from right to left." This sometimes means inverting, or flipping, images, but this can present challenges. "[N]ot all images can just be flipped," says Durado, citing examples such as maps.

Konstantinos Antonopoulos, a Greek designer working for *Al Jazeera English* in Qatar, remarks how different publications within the same company often need different visuals for the same stories. *Al Jazeera Arabic*, for example, "has a strong visual language, spearheaded by the brilliant typography of the Arabic alphabet." But the company may change the visuals for its publications in Turkey or the Balkans, for example. "[They] have their own visual languages," Antonopoulos explains.

The color of money varies around the world.

Graphics director Alberto Lucas López moved from Spain to work for the *South China Morning Post* in Hong Kong. He thinks that some differences in style have to do with Chinese writing. "I could clearly see the parallelism[2] between the Chinese characters and the visual preferences," he says. His

[2]**Parallelism** is a likeness or connection between two or more things.

E
F
G

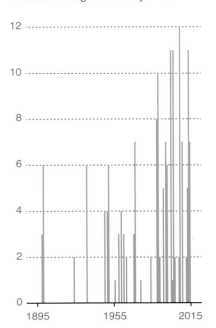

Months of severe drought
Palmer Drought Severity Index

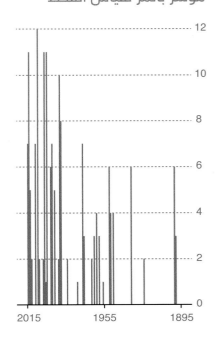

شهور القحط الشديد
مؤشر بالمر لقياس القحط

▲ **The same graph presented in English (left) and Arabic (right) editions of the same publication**

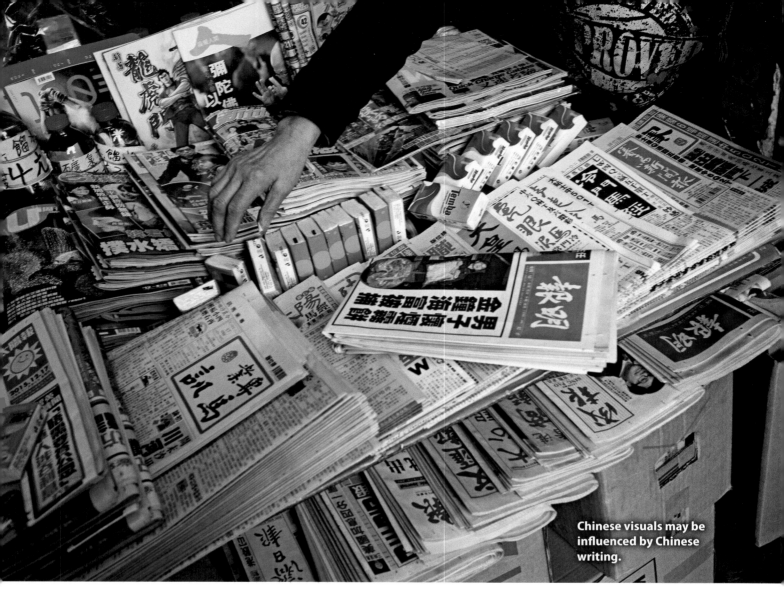

Chinese visuals may be influenced by Chinese writing.

theory is that Chinese visuals are heavily influenced by Chinese writing: complex symbols with many elements compressed in a reduced space. Nevertheless, López feels it's important to respect these differences: "Sometimes we see as incorrect what is different from our view of clear structures, strict order, and synthesis. But it's just a different visual culture."

Cultural differences can also influence what gets designed in the first place. Felipe Memoria, a Brazilian designer working in New York, has noticed how sports reporting differs in Brazil and the United States. He speculates that in

contrast to Brazilians, Americans are "really into data." The result: greater reliance on infographics—charts, statistics, and graphs—in American sports publications.

These journalists and designers have had to adapt, but they're also making their contributions to the cultures they've adopted. Nick Mrozowski, an American designer who worked for many years in Portugal, emphasizes the positives of this exchange of ideas. He brought some of his American design preferences to the job, but, he says, "I'm also certain that I absorbed a great deal more from Portugal's talented creatives than I left behind."

UNDERSTANDING THE READING

A Check (✓) the three main ideas of the reading passage.

UNDERSTANDING MAIN IDEAS

☐ 1. Different cultures use colors to mean different things.

☐ 2. Information should be presented in a visual style that is culturally appropriate.

☐ 3. Today's designers of visual data are struggling to keep up with cultural changes.

☐ 4. People today generally prefer modern infographics to more traditional visual styles.

☐ 5. Cultural differences influence the amount and type of infographics that publications choose to include.

B What points do the experts in the passage make? Answer the questions in your own words.

UNDERSTANDING SUPPORTING IDEAS

1. What does Charles Apple say about the use of the color green?

   _____

2. What does Xan Sabaris point out about the color red?

   _____

3. What challenges about creating visual data do Antonio Farach and Adonis Durado describe?

   _____

4. What does Alberto Lucas López say about the connection between Chinese writing and visual data?

   _____

5. What point does Nick Mrozowski make about his experience in Portugal?

   _____

C Work with a partner. Based on the information from the passage, in which publication would you most likely find the following features (1–6)? Why? Discuss with a partner, using evidence from the passage to give reasons.

CRITICAL THINKING: APPLYING

a. an American publication   b. a Chinese publication   c. an Arabic publication

_____ 1. a diagram where information goes from right to left

_____ 2. a line graph where red shows rising prices

_____ 3. a financial report with green design elements showing profit

_____ 4. graphics with a lot of data packed in a small space

_____ 5. a sports article with a variety of data and infographics

_____ 6. a font style that uses mostly sharp, blade-like edges

D Find and underline the following words in **bold** in the reading passage. Use context to identify their meanings. Then match the sentence parts to complete the definitions.

1. Paragraph C: **Deficits** are _____
2. Paragraph E: **Orientation** refers to _____
3. Paragraph E: **Inverting** something means _____
4. Paragraph G: If something is **compressed**, it is _____
5. Paragraph H: If you are **into** something, you are _____

a. losses.
b. very interested in it.
c. pressed tightly together.
d. turning it inside out or upside down.
e. the direction in which something is pointed.

E Read the guidelines for selecting charts and graphs for an academic essay. Which do you think are most important? Rank them (1 = most important, 5 = least important). Then work in a group and add two more guidelines that you think are important.

The chart/graph should …

_____ be visually interesting.

_____ use simple typefaces.

_____ be appropriate for your audience.

_____ be based on logical data.

_____ have an objective scale.

Additional guidelines:

_____

_____

F Find a magazine or newspaper that is published in your country. Note answers to the questions below. Then discuss them with a partner.

1. What colors are mainly used in this publication? Why do you think this is?

_____

_____

2. List three things you notice about the design in this publication, e.g., the use of text and images, how the elements are arranged, etc. What impact do you think the designer wanted to create through these?

_____

_____

_____

_____

Writing

EXPLORING WRITTEN ENGLISH

A Match each underlined phrase with the most suitable percentage amount (a–e).

NOTICING

1. The numbers on the vertical axis make it look like Drug A is <u>five times more</u> effective than Drug B.

2. As shown in Figure 1, <u>about a third</u> of the population did not vote.

3. <u>Approximately half</u> the class prefers to take tests on Mondays, as shown in Figure 1.

4. Figure 3 shows that <u>more than a third</u> of the students speak three languages.

5. <u>The majority</u> of the school's students have part-time jobs, as shown in Figure 2.

_____ a. 500 percent

_____ b. 71 percent

_____ c. 38 percent

_____ d. 49.4 percent

_____ e. 33 percent

LANGUAGE FOR WRITING Describing Visual Information

When you include graphs and charts in an essay, label them sequentially (e.g., Figure 1, Figure 2, etc.) so they are easier to refer to. You can use the following phrases to refer to figures within an essay:

Figure 1 shows (that) …

As Figure 1 illustrates, …

As seen/shown in Figure 1, …

Note: Use a comma before or after phrases that include *as*.

It can sometimes be easier for your reader to visualize the data if you use words and phrases instead of numbers (e.g., *a quarter* instead of *25 percent*). You can also use modifiers that round up or down important quantities from a chart (e.g., *less than twenty kilos* instead of *19.8 kilos*). Using words and phrases like these can make your message more meaningful and impactful.

Below are some words and phrases that express quantities.

a quarter of	*a third of*	*two-thirds of*
two-fifths of	*a half of*	*two times / five times more*
approximately	*the majority of*	*twice / five times as much*
about	*almost all*	*less than*
more than	*nearly*	

B Look at the bar graph below. Then complete the sentences using the words and phrases in the box. One is extra.

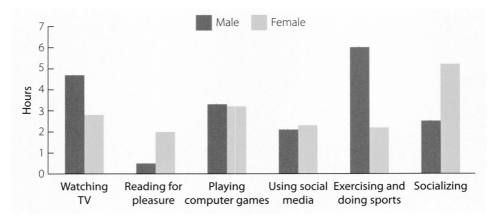

Figure 1: Time spent on the weekend by 18–24-year-olds

half	twice	a third
more than	four times	less than

1. As Figure 1 shows, women read for pleasure _____ as much as men.

2. Men and women spend _____ three hours playing computer games.

3. Women spend almost _____ as much time socializing as men, as seen in Figure 1.

4. Women spend about _____ as much time as men exercising and doing sports, as illustrated in Figure 1.

5. As shown in Figure 1, women watch _____ three hours of TV during the weekend.

C Write two more sentences about the graph in exercise B using words and phrases that express quantity.

1. _____

2. _____

WRITING SKILL Writing a Persuasive Essay

In a persuasive essay, you choose one side of an issue and persuade your reader to agree with your position. You present your position in your thesis statement and support it with reasons that show why you think it's correct.

The body paragraphs in a persuasive essay should include good reasons and convincing details that show why your position is correct. Convincing details include facts, direct quotes, and data based on evidence.

Charts and graphs that show the data you're referring to can make your arguments even stronger. They make your argument more credible and provide evidence that what you are saying is true. For example, if you are arguing that self-driving cars are more dangerous than traditional cars, a chart or graph that compares accident rates for each type of vehicle will make your argument more convincing.

The topics for your persuasive essay should not be:

- just factual (e.g., *Tigers are an endangered species.*).
- very subjective (e.g., *Tigers are more beautiful than leopards.*).
- too broad (e.g., *Animals should be protected.*).

The thesis statement in a persuasive essay should state your position about the topic. A good thesis statement should focus on a specific part of the topic. Compare these examples of thesis statements.

- *Keeping exotic animals as pets is a bad idea.* [too general]
- *Having exotic animals such as tigers and chimpanzees as pets is harmful for both the animals and the people who keep them.* [more specific]

D For each item (1–3), choose the better topic to use in a persuasive essay. Then discuss with a partner why the other topics are not good ones for a persuasive essay.

1. a. High schools should require students to wear uniforms.
   b. Some high schools require students to wear uniforms.
2. a. Socializing in person is more fun than using social media.
   b. Socializing in person is a better way to get to know people than using social media.
3. a. Airports should be made safer than they are now.
   b. Airports should screen passengers before they board planes.

E Imagine you are writing a persuasive essay on the topic of "We should eat insects instead of meat and fish." Work with a partner to answer the questions below.

1. Choose the more suitable thesis statement for the topic. Why do you think it's better?
   a. Eating insects is generally better than eating meat and fish.
   b. Eating insects rather than meat and fish is healthier and more environmentally friendly.

2. Check (✔) two reasons that best support the thesis statement.
   - ☐ a. Insects are packed with nutrition.
   - ☐ b. We need protein in our diets.
   - ☐ c. Farmers care more for animals and fish.
   - ☐ d. Eating insects produces less waste than eating meat or fish.

3. Check (✔) the four best details to include in the essay's body paragraphs. Why are the other details not as good?
   - ☐ a. Only 20 percent of an insect is thrown away.
   - ☐ b. More than half of a cow is wasted.
   - ☐ c. Eating meat is very wasteful.
   - ☐ d. Insects have as much protein as meat and fish.
   - ☐ e. Insects have 10 times as much vitamin B_{12} as salmon.
   - ☐ f. People from some cultures enjoy eating insects.

WRITING TASK

GOAL You are going to write a persuasive essay on a topic of your choice. Use at least one chart, graph, or other visual data to support your argument.

BRAINSTORMING **A** Choose one of the topics below for your essay or write your own topic idea.

☐ Self-driving cars are the best solution to transportation problems.
☐ University education should be free.
☐ Hunting of whales should be banned.
☐ _____

Decide your position on the topic. List reasons for your position and some counterarguments. Look for visual data to support at least one of your reasons. Use the online search terms below or add your own.

> distracted drivers' accidents graph   global tuition fees chart   whale-hunting graph

PLANNING **B** Follow these steps to make notes for your essay.

Step 1 Choose the two best reasons for your position. Decide which infographic(s) you will use to support your argument.

Step 2 Write your thesis statement in the outline and note your two best reasons.

Step 3 Add details that explain your reasons. Include details about the visual data.

Step 4 Write a summary statement for your conclusion.

OUTLINE

Introductory Paragraph

Thesis Statement: _____

_____

Body Paragraphs

Reason 1: _____

Details: _____

_____

Reason 2: _____

Details: _____

_____

Concluding Paragraph

Summary Statement: _____

_____

FIRST DRAFT **C** Use the information in the outline to write a first draft of your essay.

REVISING PRACTICE

The draft below is a persuasive essay about whether people should eat insects rather than meat and fish. Add the sentences (a–c) in the most suitable spaces.

a. As resources become scarce and the global population increases, perhaps someday more people will consider sitting down for a meal of crickets and worms.

b. One reason insects make a good food source is that consuming them produces much less waste than eating meat or fish.

c. As illustrated in Figure 2, crickets have as much protein as salmon, chickens, and cows.

A

Does a meal of fried crickets and marinated worms sound tasty to you? While insects are already a desirable source of protein in some parts of the world, they are not very popular worldwide. However, there are good reasons for eating insects instead of meat and fish.

B

_____ When we eat chicken or beef, we generally only eat the muscles and throw away the rest. As Figure 1 shows, the majority of a cricket's body can be used as food—only one-fifth is wasted. Conversely, with most other protein sources, such as fish, chicken, and cattle, much more of the animal is wasted. Only about half of a salmon or a chicken is used as food, and less than half of a cow is consumed. This means the majority of the animal's body is thrown away.

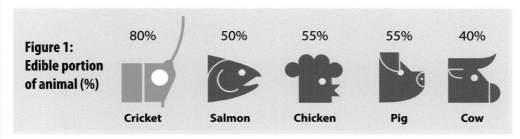

Figure 1: Edible portion of animal (%)

Cricket	Salmon	Chicken	Pig	Cow
80%	50%	55%	55%	40%

C

Another reason we should eat insects is that they are packed with nutrition. Many insects are rich in protein. _____ They also contain much less fat, making them a healthy choice. In addition, insects such as crickets are a good source of vitamins and minerals. They have 10 times as much vitamin B_{12} as salmon, almost five times as much magnesium as beef, and more calcium than milk.

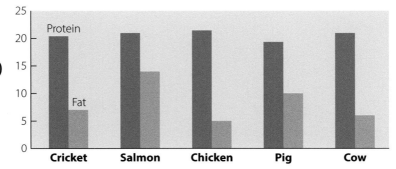

Figure 2: Nutritional value of animal (%)

The percent of protein and fat in crickets is similar to that of most meats.

D

It's clear that there are benefits to replacing meat and fish with insects. In addition to being less wasteful and equally nutritious, insects are available all over the world and they reproduce rapidly. _____

D   Now use the questions below to revise your essay.

- ☐ Does your thesis statement clearly state your position on the issue?
- ☐ Did you include enough facts and data to support your reasons?
- ☐ Do you have at least one infographic to support your reasons?
- ☐ Does your concluding paragraph have a summary statement?

EDITING PRACTICE

Read the information below.

When describing visual data, remember to:
- use a comma before or after phrases that include *as* (e.g., *As Figure 2 shows*, …).
- capitalize the "F" in "Figure" when referring to specific graphs or diagrams.
- make sure there is a noun-verb agreement after expressions describing quantity (e.g., *a third of, a quarter of, a majority of*, etc.).

Correct one mistake with language for describing visual data in each of the sentences (1–5).

1. Much of the animal is wasted: less than half are used for food.

2. A quarter of people spends more than four hours a day online.

3. As figure 1 illustrates, approximately a third of the animal is wasted.

4. Two-fifths of the students studies in the school library.

5. As Figure 3 shows more than half of the class prefers to use their phones to take notes.

FINAL DRAFT   **E**   Follow these steps to write a final draft.

1. Check your revised draft for mistakes with describing visual data.
2. Now use the checklist on page 253 to write a final draft. Make any other necessary changes.

UNIT REVIEW
Answer the following questions.

1. What are two things that designers should keep in mind when they create infographics?

   _____

   _____

   _____

2. What are some concession words and phrases that signal counterarguments?

   _____

   _____

   _____

3. Do you remember the meanings of these words? Check (✔) the ones you know. Look back at the unit and review the ones you don't know.

   Reading 1:
   - ☐ convey
   - ☐ deliberately
   - ☐ downside
   - ☐ faulty
   - ☐ interpret AWL
   - ☐ misleading
   - ☐ neutral AWL
   - ☐ objective AWL
   - ☐ stand out
   - ☐ vision

   Reading 2:
   - ☐ context AWL
   - ☐ emphasize AWL
   - ☐ gesture
   - ☐ have to do with
   - ☐ nevertheless AWL
   - ☐ propose
   - ☐ publication AWL
   - ☐ reliance AWL
   - ☐ statistic AWL
   - ☐ universal

GLOBAL CHALLENGES 7

If all the ice in the world melted, coastal cities such as New York would be mostly underwater.

THINK AND DISCUSS

1 What are some potential effects of rising sea levels?
2 Why do you think sea levels are rising?

A Look at the information on these pages and answer the questions.

1. What does the size of each area on the map represent? What do the different colors represent?

2. What do you think this map will look like 30 years from now?

B Match the words and phrases in blue to their definitions.

_____ (adv) at this moment

_____ (adj) connected to

_____ (adv) concerning the whole planet

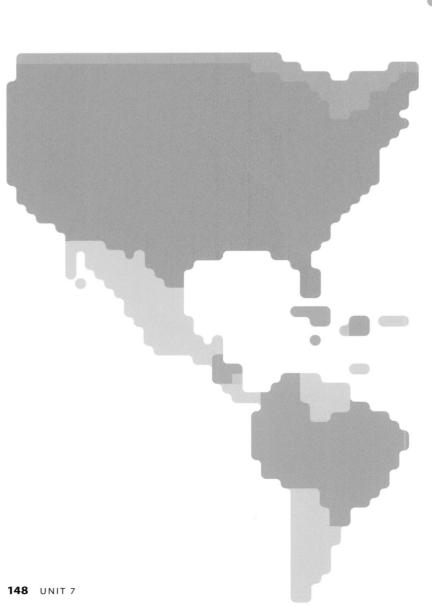

Key

Size indicates the GDP of an area.

Color indicates gross domestic product per person (2009).

- More than $40,000
- $25,000 to $40,000
- $9,514 to $24,999 — World average $9,514
- $3,000 to $9,513
- Less than $3,000

OUR HUMAN IMPACT

What impact do we have on Earth's resources? One way to measure this is to look at Gross Domestic Product (GDP)—the amount of goods and services produced in one year. GDP numbers are **related to** consumption—the using up of resources. A high GDP per capita equates with a higher standard of living, which in turn is likely to mean a higher rate of natural resource consumption.

This map shows GDP levels **worldwide**. Each area is sized according to its GDP, rather than to its physical area. The colors indicate the GDP per person in each area. As the map shows, wealthier regions such as North America **currently** have the highest GDP levels—and therefore the greatest environmental impact—but emerging economies such as China and India are catching up fast.

Reading 1

PREPARING TO READ

A The words and phrases in blue below are used in Reading 1. Read the sentences. Then match the correct form of each word or phrase to its definition.

> Many scientists believe that climate change is a **crucial** global issue today.
>
> Cars and factories **generate** greenhouse gases, which contribute to global warming.
>
> Warming temperatures are causing Arctic sea ice to **shrink** rapidly. Eventually, all the sea ice may **vanish** completely.
>
> Because of the **exceptional** increase in global temperatures, sixteen of the warmest years ever recorded have occurred since 2000.
>
> Scientists are identifying **practical** ways that individuals and countries can help solve this problem, such as by **focusing on** alternative energy sources.

1. _____ (v) to disappear

2. _____ (adj) extremely important

3. _____ (adj) likely to be effective or useful

4. _____ (v) to produce or create

5. _____ (adj) much greater than usual

6. _____ (v) to pay attention to

7. _____ (v) to get smaller

B Discuss these questions with a partner.

1. What is a **crucial** problem in your town or city right now?

2. What are some **practical** ways that you can deal with it?

C Note your answers to these questions. Then discuss with a partner.

1. What do you think is the most important environmental issue that we face today?

_____

2. What are two ways to educate people about this environmental issue?

_____

D Read the first paragraph and the three interview questions in the reading passage. What topics do you think DiCaprio will talk about? Discuss with a partner. Then check your ideas as you read.

A NEED FOR CHANGE

🎧 2.03

A   Oscar-winning actor Leonardo DiCaprio likes to say that he makes his living in made-up worlds. Now DiCaprio, a UN Messenger of Peace, has produced a documentary about a very real concern: climate change. He shot *Before the Flood* all over the world—this time playing himself.

B   DiCaprio became a climate activist after a 1998 meeting with former U.S. Vice President Al Gore, an early advocate for climate change education. The meeting inspired him to launch the Leonardo DiCaprio Foundation. The foundation has awarded over 60 million dollars to individuals and organizations that are working to protect wildlife, indigenous communities, and the planet.

C   In the documentary *Before the Flood*, DiCaprio investigates the impact of climate change around the globe. In his introductory speech at the film's London premiere, DiCaprio said, "We wanted to make a film that gave people a sense of urgency, [and] that made them understand what particular things are going to solve the problem." In late 2016, *National Geographic* interviewed DiCaprio about *Before the Flood*. This interview was edited for length and clarity.

Q: Who do you hope to reach with the film?

D   **DiCaprio:** We all have a role to play in saving our planet. This film is meant to educate everyone, from global leaders to everyday citizens, on the threat of climate change. There are practical steps we all must take—today—to hasten[1] the adoption of renewable and clean-energy technologies across the planet. For the film we interviewed inspiring figures, from Pope Francis and President Obama, who both have the ability to galvanize[2] millions of people, to activists like Sunita Narain, a tremendous voice in India who's calling for her country to be part of a global solution.

[1] To **hasten** means to speed something up.
[2] If you **galvanize** people, you motivate them to take action.

> **"** Climate change is real, it is happening right now, it is the most urgent threat facing our entire species. **"**

Q: How can an issue like climate change attract more sustained attention?

DiCaprio: There is no issue this important—because the future of the planet is at stake.[3] We have no planet B. The energy we focus on solving climate change and the pressure we place on global leaders to lead on the question will help create a sustainable and livable environment for the long term.

Q: You traveled around the world for this film. What message do people have for Americans?

DiCaprio: We need to vote for leaders who understand the serious issues impacting our climate—and for leaders who believe in the undeniable truth of science. No nation or society is immune[4] to the symptoms of climate change. America is in many places already feeling the impacts of it: droughts in California, rising seas in Miami, more extreme storms in the Gulf of Mexico. We can still prevent these crises from becoming a widespread challenge in the future of our country. We have an opportunity to lead the world on one of the most crucial issues of all time.

[3] If something is **at stake,** it's at risk; it could be lost or be in danger.
[4] If a person or a thing is **immune,** it will not be affected by another person or thing.

SEVEN FACTS ABOUT CLIMATE CHANGE

1. The world is warming.

Earth's temperature goes up and down from year to year—but over the past half-century, it has gone up a lot (Fig. 1). The trend currently looks set to continue: the heat in 2016 broke the historic record set in 2015, which broke the one from 2014.

2. It's because of us.

Carbon dioxide warms the planet, and we've increased the amount in the air by nearly half, mostly since the 1960s (Fig. 2). Events such as El Niño—a climate cycle in the Pacific Ocean—also affect global temperatures. But no natural cause explains the half-century warming trend.

3. We're sure.

More than 9 out of 10 climate scientists agree: Carbon emissions cause global warming. A 2013 review

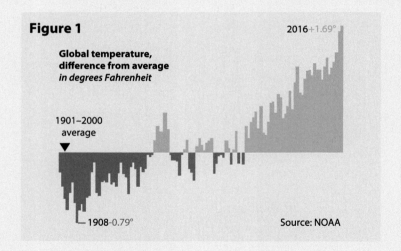

Figure 1

Global temperature, difference from average *in degrees Fahrenheit*

1901–2000 average

2016 +1.69°

1908 -0.79°

Source: NOAA

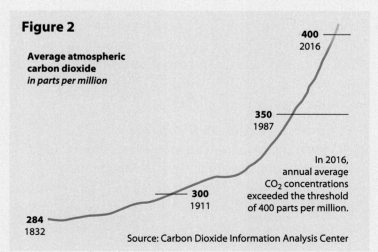

Figure 2

Average atmospheric carbon dioxide *in parts per million*

400
2016

350
1987

300
1911

284
1832

In 2016, annual average CO_2 concentrations exceeded the threshold of 400 parts per million.

Source: Carbon Dioxide Information Analysis Center

of more than 4,000 research papers found that 97 percent said humans cause global warming.

4. Ice is melting fast.

The Arctic has warmed more than the rest of the planet, and its sea ice is shrinking (Fig. 3). The ice loss speeds up global warming because more sunlight is absorbed by dark oceans instead of being reflected into space by the ice. Warming temperatures also mean the retreat of mountain glaciers worldwide. Together, these factors contribute to rising sea levels, which could rise by three feet by 2100—or maybe more.

5. Weather is getting intense.

Globally, the number of disasters related to climate has more than tripled since 1980 (Fig. 4). The extraordinary heat wave that killed some 70,000 people in Europe in 2003 should have been a once-in-500-years event; at the current level of global warming, it has become a once-in-40-years event. If global warming continues unchecked, by the end of this century, regions such as the Arabian Gulf may see days that are so hot that it will be unsafe to go outside.

6. Wildlife is already hurting.

Animals and plants are already vanishing from parts of their range that are now too hot. Extinctions come next. A 2016 study showed that of 976 species surveyed, 47 percent had vanished from areas on the warm edge of their range. The exceptional ocean warmth of the past few years has also devastated many of the world's coral reefs. Some species will adapt to the changing climate—but how many, and for how long?

7. We can do something about it.

The use of renewables—such as solar and wind energy—is projected to triple 1990 levels by 2040. Meanwhile, costs are falling, and are expected to decrease significantly from 2010

Figure 3

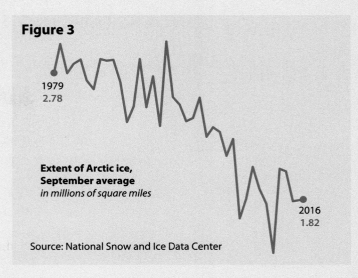

Extent of Arctic ice, September average
in millions of square miles

1979
2.78

2016
1.82

Source: National Snow and Ice Data Center

Figure 4

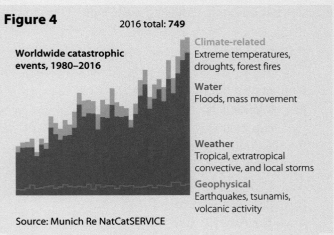

2016 total: **749**

Worldwide catastrophic events, 1980–2016

Climate-related
Extreme temperatures, droughts, forest fires

Water
Floods, mass movement

Weather
Tropical, extratropical convective, and local storms

Geophysical
Earthquakes, tsunamis, volcanic activity

Source: Munich Re NatCatSERVICE

Figure 5

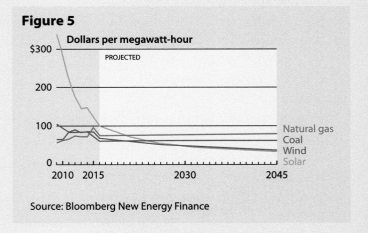

Dollars per megawatt-hour

PROJECTED

Natural gas
Coal
Wind
Solar

Source: Bloomberg New Energy Finance

levels (Fig. 5). By 2040, the cost of wind power is estimated to decrease by over 50 percent, and solar power prices may decrease by 500 percent. Carbon-free renewable sources may soon be cheaper than the fossil fuels that generate carbon, providing hope for a more sustainable future.

UNDERSTANDING THE READING

UNDERSTANDING
MAIN IDEAS

A Choose the best answer to the questions about the interview.

1. What was DiCaprio's main purpose for making *Before the Flood*?
   a. to explain in simple terms how the polar ice caps are melting
   b. to help people understand and want to solve the problem of climate change
   c. to raise money and global awareness for the Leonardo DiCaprio Foundation

2. When did DiCaprio first become interested in the issue of climate change?
   a. after a meeting with an influential politician
   b. after watching a documentary about the issue
   c. after speaking with people in areas affected by rising seas

3. What is special about the people that DiCaprio interviewed?
   a. They were the first scientists to identify the issue of global warming.
   b. They have all invented technologies for dealing with rising sea levels.
   c. They are individuals who can motivate people to fight climate change.

UNDERSTANDING
MAIN IDEAS

B Complete the sentences about the main ideas of the section "Seven Facts about Climate Change." Write no more than two words in each space.

1. The Earth's temperature is increasing, especially in the last _____.

2. Climate change is mostly caused by _____ activities, not _____ events.

3. Most _____ agree that climate change is caused by _____ emissions.

4. Loss of sea ice in the Arctic is _____ global warming.

5. Global warming is causing extreme _____ events to happen more _____ .

6. Wildlife species are _____ due to warming temperatures.

7. There are solutions to the problem. Renewable energy is likely to become _____ than fossil fuels in the future.

UNDERSTANDING
DETAILS

C Read the statements (1–7). For each statement, circle T for true, F for false, or NG if the information is not given.

1. The Earth's temperature in 2016 was hotter than in 2014.   **T   F   NG**
2. Atmospheric carbon dioxide levels have doubled since the 1990s.   **T   F   NG**
3. Factory emissions are the biggest contributor to global warming. **T   F   NG**
4. Sea levels could rise three feet by 2100.   **T   F   NG**

5. Major heat waves are becoming more common in the United States.   **T   F   NG**

6. Nearly half of species in a 2016 study had disappeared   **T   F   NG**
   from warmer edges of their range.

7. Solar power is expected to be 50% cheaper by 2040.   **T   F   NG**

D Match the graphs from the reading passage (Figures 1–5) with the descriptions (a–g). Two descriptions are extra.

INTERPRETING VISUAL INFORMATION

_____ a. decrease in the amount of ice in the Arctic in the last few decades

_____ b. comparison of future costs of energy sources

_____ c. main causes of global temperature changes

_____ d. rise in carbon dioxide in the atmosphere in the last two centuries

_____ e. increase in serious events caused by changing climates

_____ f. changes in different types of energy usage over time

_____ g. changes in global temperatures over 115 years

CRITICAL THINKING   To **infer** a person's **attitude**, look for words and expressions that show what they think about a topic, such as *important, awful, great, terrible, hope, hopeless,* etc. Also, look for modals such as *may, might, should, can, must, have to,* or *need to.* These can show attitudes such as urgency, optimism, or seriousness.

E Which of the following (a–c) best describes DiCaprio's attitude toward the problem? Underline examples in the passage that support your answer.

CRITICAL THINKING: INFERRING ATTITUDE

a. He believes that we are in an extremely dangerous situation and is frustrated that we have left it too late.
b. It is a very urgent problem, but if enough people work together, he is optimistic that a solution is possible.
c. He believes that changes in government policies are the best way to handle this problem.

F DiCaprio says that climate change is "the most urgent threat facing our entire species." Do you agree with his view? Why or why not? Note your ideas and discuss with a partner.

CRITICAL THINKING: EVALUATING

I **agree** / **disagree** with DiCaprio's view because _____

_____

_____ .

DEVELOPING READING SKILLS

> ### READING SKILL Understanding Appositives
>
> Look at the sentence below.
>
> NOUN   APPOSITIVE
> *Now <u>DiCaprio</u>, **a UN Messenger of Peace,** has produced a documentary.*
>
> The **appositive** "a UN Messenger of Peace" describes the noun "DiCaprio." It gives more information about the noun that it is describing.
>
> Appositives take the form of a noun or a noun phrase. They explain, define, or give more information about another noun or noun phrase that is close to them. Appositives can come before or after the noun they describe.
>
> Writers can use commas, dashes, parentheses, or colons to separate appositives from the nouns or noun phrases that they describe.
>
> NOUN PHRASE   APPOSITIVE
> *The documentary is about <u>a very real concern</u>: **climate change**.*

UNDERSTANDING
APPOSITIVES

A Read each sentence from the passage. Underline the appositive and circle the noun or noun phrase that it refers to.

1. Oscar-winning actor Leonardo DiCaprio likes to say that he makes his living in made-up worlds.

2. DiCaprio became a climate activist after a 1998 meeting with former U.S. Vice President Al Gore, ...

3. For the film we interviewed inspiring figures … like Sunita Narain, a tremendous voice in India who's calling for her country to be part of a global solution.

4. Events such as El Niño—a climate cycle in the Pacific Ocean—also affect global temperatures.

UNDERSTANDING
APPOSITIVES

B Match each appositive (a–d) to the noun or noun phrase it refers to.

a. an American director and producer

b. one of the oldest entertainment awards ceremonies in the world

c. ones that are fitted with filters

d. located on the East Coast of the United States

1. The Oscars, _____, takes place every year.

2. *Jurassic Park* is one of the most famous movies that Steven Spielberg, _____, is known for.

3. New York University, _____, has produced famous filmmakers such as Martin Scorsese and Ang Lee.

4. People have to put on special glasses—_____—in order to view a movie in 3-D.

APPLYING

C Scan for and write two examples of appositives in the Explore the Theme section. Share your answers with a partner.

1. _____

2. _____

Video

billy barr has lived alone in Gothic, Colorado, for more than 40 years.

THE SNOW GUARDIAN

BEFORE VIEWING

A Read the caption and title of the video. What do you think the video is about?

PREDICTING

B Read the information about a town in Colorado and answer the questions.

LEARNING ABOUT THE TOPIC

Gothic, Colorado, used to be a ghost town—a once-successful town that was later abandoned. For almost twenty years in the late 19th century, Gothic had a silver mine and almost 1,000 people lived and worked there. By the end of the 19th century, the silver was gone, and almost everyone had left.

In 1928, a scientist bought the town and started a research facility called Rocky Mountain Biological Laboratory. Today, about 160 scientists, professors, and students live and work in Gothic during the summers, studying local animals and climate change. One resident, billy barr (who doesn't capitalize his name), has lived in Gothic since 1972 and works as an accountant for the lab.

1. Why did most people leave Gothic?

   _____

2. What brought people back to Gothic?

   _____

3. Why do you think Gothic is a suitable place for doing scientific research?

   _____

   _____

C The words in **bold** below are used in the video. Read the sentences. Then match each word to its definition.

> Scientists keep **meticulous** records of their experiments. If they don't take careful and accurate notes, other people won't be able to duplicate their experiments.
>
> Children often have a great sense of **curiosity** and ask many questions about how things work.
>
> Some people think we might be able to **reverse** climate change if we reduce the amount of greenhouse gas emissions into the air.

1. _____ (n) a feeling of wanting to know or learn about things

2. _____ (adj) extremely thorough and with a lot of care for details

3. _____ (v) to change something to be the opposite of what it is

WHILE VIEWING

A ▶ Watch the video. Circle the correct options to answer the questions.

1. Why did billy barr first start recording data on snow?
   a. He was bored and wanted something to do.
   b. He was a researcher for a university.
   c. He wanted to gather evidence of climate change.

2. Which is the most suitable description of barr's attitude toward the problem?
   a. He feels confident that we can still reverse the situation if we put in more effort.
   b. He is seeing some signs of improvement after years of studying the snow.
   c. He thinks the problem is serious and is not sure how the situation can be fixed.

B ▶ Watch the video again. Complete the sentences about the trends that barr has observed.

1. The permanent _____ comes later than it used to.

2. The ground becomes _____ sooner than it used to.

3. There are usually _____ record high temperatures in a typical winter, but barr once recorded _____.

4. Snow is melting faster than before because of more _____ covering the snow.

AFTER VIEWING

A Would you like to conduct scientific research in a place like Gothic, Colorado? What are some of the location's advantages or disadvantages? Discuss with a partner.

B Work with a partner. What might be some limitations to billy barr's data? Do you think his data is a reliable indicator of climate change? Why or why not?

Reading 2

PREPARING TO READ

BUILDING VOCABULARY

A The words and phrases in blue below are used in Reading 2. Read the sentences. Then circle the correct options to complete the definitions.

> By recycling paper and plastic, we can **cut down on** the amount of garbage we produce.
>
> Car engines **emit** carbon dioxide (CO_2), which is a **major** contributor to global warming. Some countries have created laws to **regulate** the emissions from vehicles on the road.
>
> The world's oil supplies are **limited**, and with current rates of usage, we are in danger of **exhausting** them. Some scientists think we will **consume** all of the world's oil supplies by 2070.
>
> Solar panels **convert** the heat of the sun into energy that can be used to power homes.
>
> Installing solar panels can help homeowners get a **reduction** in their electricity bills. More homeowners now **invest** in solar panels and put them on their roofs.

1. To *regulate* something means to **control / advertise** something.
2. When a factory *emits* a gas, it **releases / contains** it.
3. When you *convert* something, you **increase / change** it.
4. If you *exhaust* something, you **use it often / use it up completely**.
5. If you *consume* something, such as a resource, you **use it up / give it away**.
6. A *major* factor is something that plays **a specific / an important** role.
7. A *reduction* is **an increase / a decrease** in size, amount, or degree.
8. If you *cut down on* something, you **use less of it / divide it up**.
9. If something is *limited* in quantity, there is **a lot / not a lot** of it.
10. If you *invest* in something, such as a business, you **get money from / put money into** it.

USING VOCABULARY

B Work with a partner. What do you **consume** a lot of? What would you like to **cut down on**?

PREDICTING

C Reading 2 is about eight ways we can create a sustainable future. What steps do you think people can take to achieve this? Discuss with a partner. Then check your ideas as you read.

Salish Kootenai Dam in Montana, U.S.A., generates enough electricity to power more than 100,000 homes.

EIGHT STEPS TO A SUSTAINABLE FUTURE

⌒ 2.04

A We humans have unlimited appetites,[1] but we live on a planet with limited resources. We already use more of Earth's renewable resources—such as forests, clean air, and fresh water—than nature can restore each year. And when the rate of consumption of a resource is greater than the rate at which it is replaced, the resource may become exhausted.

B Today, Earth's population stands at around seven billion, and it is still growing fast. By 2050, there may be nine billion people living on the planet. As a result, the imbalance between what nature replaces and what humans consume will probably continue to grow. So how will so many more people live on Earth without exhausting the planet?

C The key is sustainability—finding new and efficient ways of conserving resources so that we do not use them all up. Here are eight steps to sustainability from around the world.

1. SUSTAINABLE COMMUNITIES

D Sustainable cities and towns encourage residents to reduce their impact on both the local and global environments. Residents in Mbam, Senegal, for example, use solar ovens to cook food. By using energy from the sun instead of burning wood, people are saving trees for future generations. Communities in other places are using improved public transportation systems so that people do not use cars as much. In Curitiba, Brazil, city buses are frequent, convenient, and efficient, so 70 percent of the city's commuters use them. As a result, the city has little traffic congestion[2] and cleaner air.

2. SAFER PRODUCTION

E As meat consumption grows, the environmental and health effects of producing meat grow as well. For example, the animal waste that results from raising animals for food can cause water pollution. In addition, farms that are close to

[1] People's **appetites** for things are their strong desires for them.

[2] **Traffic congestion** occurs when there are a lot of vehicles on the road, making movement slower.

city centers can increase the risk of dangerous diseases—such as avian flu[3]—spreading. Some governments are using tax breaks to solve this problem. The government of Thailand placed a high tax on poultry farms that were within 62 miles (100 kilometers) of its capital city, Bangkok. As a result, many poultry producers moved away from the city center.

3. CLEANER POWER

F

Sun and wind power are two energy sources that are renewable and that do not pollute the environment. Harvesting solar energy is an increasing trend. One method is via the use of photovoltaic cells (PVs), cells that convert solar energy to electricity. By 2017, PVs produced more than 300 gigawatts[4] of power worldwide. Major solar energy producers include Germany, China, and the United States. Global wind power production grew by about 2,000 percent in the 15 years

between 2001 and 2016, and it is still growing. As of 2016, China was the leader in wind power, producing over 168,000 megawatts of wind energy. The United States and Germany are also major wind power producers.

4. SOCIAL INVESTMENT

G

People who practice socially responsible investing (SRI) buy shares in companies that focus on practices that are good for the planet, like cutting down on landfill[5] waste and creating alternative energy. While SRI activity is most common in Europe and the United States, it is growing quickly in Canada and Australia, too. There is also an increasing number of people in South Korea, Brazil, Malaysia, and South Africa who are practicing SRI.

5. GREENER LIGHTBULBS

H

The popularity of LED (light emitting diode) lightbulbs has been growing quickly since 2001.

---

[3] **Avian flu,** or **bird flu,** is a virus transmitted from birds to humans.
[4] A watt is a unit of measurement of electrical power. A **gigawatt** is one billion watts.

[5] A **landfill** is an area where garbage is buried in the ground.

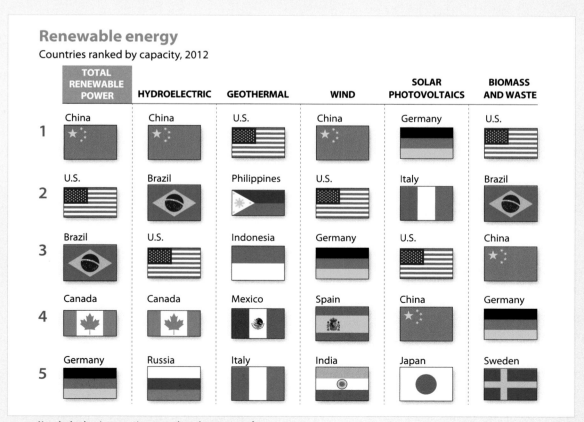

Renewable energy
Countries ranked by capacity, 2012

	TOTAL RENEWABLE POWER	HYDROELECTRIC	GEOTHERMAL	WIND	SOLAR PHOTOVOLTAICS	BIOMASS AND WASTE
1	China	China	U.S.	China	Germany	U.S.
2	U.S.	Brazil	Philippines	U.S.	Italy	Brazil
3	Brazil	U.S.	Indonesia	Germany	U.S.	China
4	Canada	Canada	Mexico	Spain	China	Germany
5	Germany	Russia	Italy	India	Japan	Sweden

Note: hydroelectric: generating power through movement of water
geothermal: heat energy from deep within Earth

This is because they use 75 percent less energy than traditional lightbulbs and last 25 times longer. Currently, about 16 percent of all lightbulbs sold are LEDs. However, by the year 2022, LEDs will make up 50 percent of the global market share.

6. CERTIFIED FORESTS

Logging—the cutting down of trees—has several negative effects on the environment. For example, it can lead to water pollution and destroy animal habitats. In an effort to cut down on these effects, several countries are creating certified forests. When a forest is certified, the logging is regulated and done in a sustainable way. In West Virginia (U.S.A.), for example, loggers must get special training. Roughly ten percent of the world's forests are certified. Canada has the largest areas, with about 410 million acres (166 million hectares) of certified forests.

7. GREEN EMPLOYMENT

About 10 million people around the world work in the renewable energy industry; this number has grown by almost 7 million in ten years. Sixty-two percent of these jobs are in Asia, but green jobs are growing in other countries, too. Denmark, for example, produces a large number of the world's wind turbines,[6] and the Kenyan government has invested more than one billion dollars jointly with private companies to build solar power plants across the country.

8. LOWER EMISSIONS

Carbon emissions continue to contribute to climate change. Since 1970, emissions from fossil fuels—such as coal, oil, and natural gas—have increased about 200 percent. However, some countries are committed to reversing this trend. Brazil, for example, has promised to emit 37 percent less CO_2 by 2025, compared to 2005 levels. In addition, India and Nigeria are planning major reductions by 2030.

[6] Wind turbines are machines that produce electricity, using large blades that are turned by the wind.

A worker testing one of the world's largest wind turbines in Denmark

UNDERSTANDING THE READING

A Complete the main ideas of the reading passage using the words below. One word can be used more than once.

UNDERSTANDING
MAIN IDEAS

> regulating investing making reducing motivating using increasing

Eight steps to sustainability:

1. _____ people to lower their impact on the environment and their cities

2. _____ the production of livestock safer

3. _____ more renewable energy sources

4. _____ in companies that try to protect the environment

5. _____ energy-efficient lightbulbs that are better for the environment

6. _____ logging by certifying forests

7. _____ the number of jobs in development and production of renewables

8. _____ carbon emissions

B Read the descriptions below and scan the passage to find the relevant sections. Then give an example for each description.

UNDERSTANDING
PROBLEMS AND
SOLUTIONS

1. how sustainable communities help the environment

   _____

2. how livestock production facilities harm the environment

   _____

3. the type of activity that a socially responsible company might engage in

   _____

4. one problem logging causes

   _____

5. an industry that provides green employment

   _____

6. a country that is trying to cut down on CO_2 emissions

   _____

C Answer these questions about the infographic in the reading passage.

1. What does the infographic show?
   a. the world leaders in renewable energy around the world
   b. the amount of money spent on renewable energy
   c. the best places in the world to invest in renewable energy

2. Which of the eight steps in the reading does the infographic relate to? _____

3. Which two countries are world leaders in more than one energy type?
   _____

4. Which country is in the top five for all the energy types?
   _____

5. Overall, which country has the highest capacity for renewable power?
   _____

D Find and underline the following words and phrases in **bold** in the reading passage. Use context to identify their meanings. Write your own definitions and share them with a partner.

1. **tax break** (paragraph E):

   _____

2. **harvesting** (paragraph F):

   _____

3. **market share** (paragraph H):

   _____

4. **jointly** (paragraph J):

   _____

E Scan paragraphs F and I for examples of appositives. Underline the appositive and circle the noun or noun phrase that it refers to.

F Work in groups. In your opinion, which three steps in the passage are the most important? List them and share your reasons with your group.

1. _____   2. _____   3. _____

I think … is the most important step as …

   That's true, but I think … will have a greater impact because …

Writing

EXPLORING WRITTEN ENGLISH

A Read the sentences below. In which sentence does the underlined part just give extra information—information that is not essential for the sentence? Discuss your answer with a partner.

NOTICING

1. We need to vote for leaders <u>who understand the serious issues impacting our climate</u>.

2. Together, these factors contribute to rising sea levels, <u>which could rise by three feet by 2100</u>.

3. Animals and plants are already vanishing from parts of their range <u>that are now too hot</u>.

LANGUAGE FOR WRITING Using Adjective Clauses

Adjective clauses give additional information about nouns in sentences. They can be either restrictive or nonrestrictive.

Restrictive adjective clauses give essential information about a noun. If you delete the adjective clause, you don't know which specific person or thing the sentence is about. These adjective clauses can begin with the relative pronouns *who* (for people) and *that* (for things and people). Do not use commas with restrictive clauses.

> *The man **who** wrote the article is an environmentalist.* (The restrictive clause tells us which man.)

> *One source of energy **that** China uses is wind power.* (The restrictive clause gives essential information.)

Nonrestrictive adjective clauses give extra information about a noun—information that isn't necessary or essential to identify the noun. Using nonrestrictive adjective clauses is a good way to add details to your sentences and make your writing more interesting. These adjective clauses can begin with the relative pronouns *who* (for people) and *which* (for things). Use commas with nonrestrictive adjective clauses.

> *Metal ores, **which** we use to manufacture goods, are nonrenewable resources.* (The nonrestrictive clause gives more details about metal ores.)

> *It's time for investors, **who** do not always consider the effects of their investments, to become more environmentally conscious.* (The nonrestrictive clause gives more details about the investors.)

B Combine the sentences using restrictive adjective clauses.

Example: Companies had to pay a fine. The companies dumped waste into a nearby lake.

   Companies that dumped waste into a nearby lake had to pay a fine.

1. Farms can increase the risk of dangerous diseases—such as avian flu—spreading. The farms are close to city centers.

   _____

   _____

2. The Thai government placed a high tax on poultry farms. The poultry farms were within 100 kilometers of Bangkok.

   _____

   _____

3. Sun and wind power are two energy sources. Sun and wind power are renewable.

   _____

C Use nonrestrictive adjective clauses to add extra information to the sentences.

1. Beef production contributes to climate change. It requires a lot of water.

   _____

2. The city of Curitiba has very little traffic congestion. Curitiba has an efficient bus system.

   _____

   _____

3. Leonardo DiCaprio has produced a documentary on climate change. He is a UN Messenger of Peace.

   _____

   _____

WRITING SKILL Writing an Opinion Essay

When you write an opinion essay, you express your feelings about an issue and give reasons to explain your opinion.

The thesis statement states your opinion and your reasons. You can include an opinion expression in your thesis statement, such as *In my opinion, I think, I believe, From my point of view,* and *From my perspective.*

> *In my opinion, two effective ways to minimize the effects of climate change are to reduce carbon emissions from factories and to make people aware of the problem.*

Each body paragraph includes a topic sentence that gives a reason. It also includes details, examples, and facts that explain the reason.

D Look at the outline for an opinion essay. Note answers to the questions below and discuss with a partner.

1. What issue is the writer expressing an opinion about?

_____

2. What is the writer's opinion?

_____

3. What are the two main reasons the writer gives for their opinion?

_____

4. What are some ways the writer will explain the first reason? The second reason?

_____

_____

Introductory Paragraph

Hook / Background Information	*overconsumption of resources; need to change habits*
Thesis Statement	*In my opinion, becoming a vegetarian is the best way to preserve our resources and slow down global warming because it saves water and cuts down on carbon emissions.*

Body Paragraphs

Topic Sentence 1	*One reason that vegetarianism is a good way to reduce our use of resources is that it saves large amounts of water.*
Details	*• meat production uses a lot of water; e.g., beef production: 1 kg of beef = 16,000L*
	• plant production uses much less; e.g., 1 kg of rice = 3,400L; 1 kg of corn = 833L
Topic Sentence 2	*Another reason that becoming a vegetarian is good for the planet is that it helps to slow down global warming.*
Details	*• meat production ⟶ greenhouse gases ⟶ more than cars*
	• meat production uses a lot of fossil fuels (to run production facilities; to transport, process, and refrigerate meat)

Concluding Paragraph

Summary Statement	*Not eating meat is a good way to ensure a sustainable future because it uses less water and it doesn't contribute as much to greenhouse gases.*
Final Thought	*veg diet ⟶ healthy planet, healthy people*

WRITING TASK

GOAL You are going to write an opinion essay on the following topic:

In your opinion, what is the most important thing that individuals, businesses, or governments can do to ensure a sustainable future? Give two reasons why this is the best thing to do.

BRAINSTORMING **A** Make a list of things that individuals, businesses, or governments can do to ensure a sustainable future. Use the ideas from the reading passages or your own ideas.

PLANNING **B** Follow these steps to make notes for your essay.

Step 1 Choose the one most important action that can lead to a sustainable future.

Step 2 Think of two reasons to support your opinion. Write a thesis statement and a topic sentence for each of your body paragraphs in the outline.

Step 3 Add two examples or details to explain each reason.

Step 4 Note some ideas for your introductory paragraph.

Step 5 Write a summary statement and add a final thought.

OUTLINE

Introductory Paragraph

Hook / Background Information: _____

Thesis Statement: _____

_____

Body Paragraphs

Topic Sentence 1: _____

_____

Details: _____

Topic Sentence 2: _____

_____

Details: _____

Concluding Paragraph

Summary Statement: _____

_____

Final Thought: _____

FIRST DRAFT **C** Use the information in your outline to write a first draft of your essay.

REVISING PRACTICE

The draft below is similar to the one you are going to write. Follow the steps to create a better second draft.

1. Add these sentences (a–c) in paragraphs **B–D** to provide extra information.

    a. One reason that vegetarianism is a good way to reduce our use of resources is that it saves large amounts of water.

    b. Besides being good for the planet, vegetarianism has some additional benefits.

    c. In fact, according to a United Nations report, raising animals for food produces more greenhouse gases than cars.

2. Now fix the following problems (d–f) in the essay.

    d. Add this restrictive clause to paragraph A: *that heat up the planet*

    e. Add this nonrestrictive clause to paragraph A: , *which all living things need to survive,*

    f. Cross out a sentence that doesn't belong in paragraph B.

A

It's a fact that we're using more of Earth's resources than nature can replenish. For example, fresh water _____ is becoming scarce. In addition, lifestyle habits _____ are causing climate change. What's the answer? In my opinion, becoming a vegetarian is the best way to preserve our resources and slow down global warming because it saves water and cuts down on carbon emissions.

B

_____ Meat production, which involves raising animals and processing them to turn them into edible products, is very water intensive. For example, it takes 16,000 liters of water to produce just one kilogram of beef. By comparison, it takes only 3,400 liters of water to produce a kilogram of rice, and a mere 833 liters to produce the same amount of corn. Producing biofuels from corn and other plants also uses large amounts of water.

C

Another reason that becoming a vegetarian is good for the planet is that it helps to slow down global warming. Meat production emits greenhouse gases such as CO_2. Trees, which absorb CO_2, are often cut down to make room for grazing animals. In addition, meat production uses a lot of fossil fuels to run production facilities and to transport meat products. These fossil fuels contribute to greenhouse gases. _____ By not eating meat, we might be able to slow down climate change.

D

Not eating meat is a good way to ensure a sustainable future because it uses less water, and it also reduces greenhouse gas emissions. _____ Studies show that a vegetarian diet, which tends to be low in fat, leads to a lower risk of heart disease. It also reduces the risk of other serious diseases such as cancer. By becoming vegetarians, we will ensure the health of the planet and our own health at the same time.

D Now use the questions below to revise your essay.

REVISED DRAFT

☐ Does your thesis statement express your opinion and mention your reasons?

☐ Do your body paragraphs include enough details to support your reasons?

☐ Do all your sentences relate to the thesis statement?

☐ Did you include a summary statement and a final thought in your concluding paragraph?

EDITING PRACTICE

Read the information below.

In sentences with adjective clauses, remember to:
- use commas before and after a nonrestrictive adjective clause if it is in the middle of the sentence.
- use *who* for people and *which* for things in nonrestrictive adjective clauses.
- use *who* for people and *that* for people or things in restrictive clauses.

Correct one mistake with adjective clauses in each of the sentences (1–6).

1. Vegetarianism which means not eating meat, is one way to reduce greenhouse gas emissions.

2. CFLs, that are popular in countries like Japan, use 75 percent less energy than traditional lightbulbs.

3. Logging which is done without regulation causes many types of environmental harm.

4. Costa Rica, which already generates 80 percent of its energy through renewable sources has promised to have zero net carbon emissions by 2030.

5. DiCaprio, which is the founder of the Leonardo DiCaprio Foundation, is working to make people aware of the effects of climate change.

6. DiCaprio made a film, that gave people a sense of urgency.

FINAL DRAFT   **E**   Follow these steps to write a final draft.

1. Check your revised draft for mistakes with adjective clauses.
2. Now use the checklist on page 253 to write a final draft. Make any other necessary changes.

UNIT REVIEW
Answer the following questions.

1. Which of the ideas in the unit do you think is the best approach for achieving a sustainable future? Why?

_____

_____

_____

2. What is the difference between restrictive and nonrestrictive adjective clauses?

_____

_____

_____

3. Do you remember the meanings of these words? Check (✓) the ones you know. Look back at the unit and review the ones you don't know.

Reading 1:

☐ crucial AWL   ☐ currently   ☐ exceptional

☐ focus on AWL   ☐ generate AWL   ☐ practical

☐ related to   ☐ shrink   ☐ vanish

☐ worldwide

Reading 2:

☐ consume AWL   ☐ convert AWL   ☐ cut down on

☐ emit   ☐ exhaust   ☐ invest AWL

☐ limited   ☐ major AWL   ☐ reduction

☐ regulate AWL

MEDICAL INNOVATIONS

**A drone delivers medical supplies
to a clinic in Virginia, U.S.A.**

THINK AND DISCUSS

1 In what ways have medical treatments
   changed over the past century?
2 What kinds of medical innovations do you
   hope will happen in the next century?

A Look at the information on these pages and answer the questions.

1. Read the information in the timeline. Which of these medical firsts do you think was the most important? Why?

2. What is one other medical innovation that you can add to the timeline?

B Match the correct form of the words in blue to their definitions.

_____ (n) a way of doing something

_____ (v) to be able to do something that is challenging

_____ (n) a person who leads the way in a new area of knowledge

400 B.C.
First scientific study of medicine

The Greek physician Hippocrates first recognized that disease is caused by a patient's environment, diet, and/or daily habits. This discovery is regarded as the beginning of modern medicine.

4th Century A.D.
First hospitals

The earliest hospitals with trained doctors appeared in what is now Turkey. By the ninth century, hospitals were common in Islamic cities such as Baghdad and Cairo.

1628
First theory of blood circulation

English physician William Harvey proved that the beating heart drives the body's blood circulation.

1846
First use of anesthesia

American dentist William Morton developed a method for anesthetizing patients using a gas called ether. The patient fell asleep and felt no pain as Morton took out his rotten tooth.

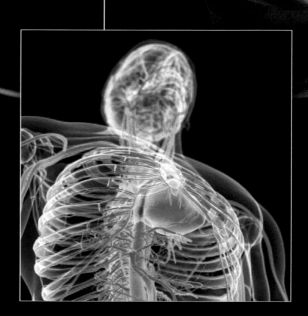

MEDICAL FIRSTS

1859
First theory of germs and disease
French chemist Louis Pasteur was a pioneer in microbiology. He revealed how germs can infect people and make them sick.

1928
First use of penicillin
The Scottish biologist Alexander Fleming discovered the effect of penicillin on bacteria. Penicillin is still used today as an antibiotic to fight infection.

1983
First discovery of HIV virus
A team of French scientists managed to solve one of the biggest mysteries of modern disease when it discovered that the cause of AIDS was the human immunodeficiency virus (HIV).

2015
First bionic eye
A medical technology company—Second Sight—developed an implant that helps blind people see light.

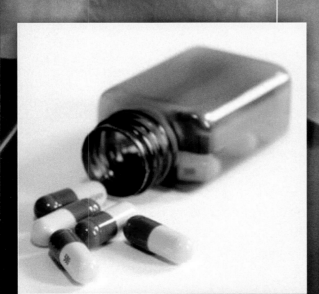

Reading 1

PREPARING TO READ

BUILDING
VOCABULARY

A The words in blue below are used in Reading 1. Read the sentences. Then match the correct form of each word to its definition.

> It is important to improve **existing** hospitals as well as build new ones.
>
> Medical students study **general** topics before choosing a specific area to specialize in.
>
> The ancient Greek and Roman **civilizations** developed their own medical tools and techniques.
>
> People should stay home when they have the flu so that they don't **spread** it to other people.
>
> The *Merck* **Manual** *of Diagnosis and Therapy* is one of the oldest medical textbooks in English.
>
> Persian physician Ibn Sina **compiled** his medical knowledge in *The Canon of Medicine*, which includes basic **concepts** about the human body and the uses of medical substances.

1. _____ (adj) available at the time

2. _____ (n) an idea about something

3. _____ (adj) not relating to a particular area

4. _____ (v) to reach more people or a larger area

5. _____ (v) to gather information to create a book or a report

6. _____ (n) a group of people with its own culture and way of life

7. _____ (n) a book that includes instructions on how to do something

USING
VOCABULARY

B Discuss these questions with a partner.

1. When you buy something new, such as a smartphone, do you prefer to read the **manual** or figure out how to use it on your own? Why?

2. How do you remember new **concepts** you learn in class? What **methods** do you use?

BRAINSTORMING

C How do you think medical knowledge has been passed down over the centuries? Discuss with a partner.

PREDICTING

D Look at the photos and read the title of the reading passage. What do you think the passage is about? Check your idea as you read.

a. a medical innovator who lived in Spain many years ago

b. the man who built the first hospital in Europe

c. a doctor who found a cure for a common disease

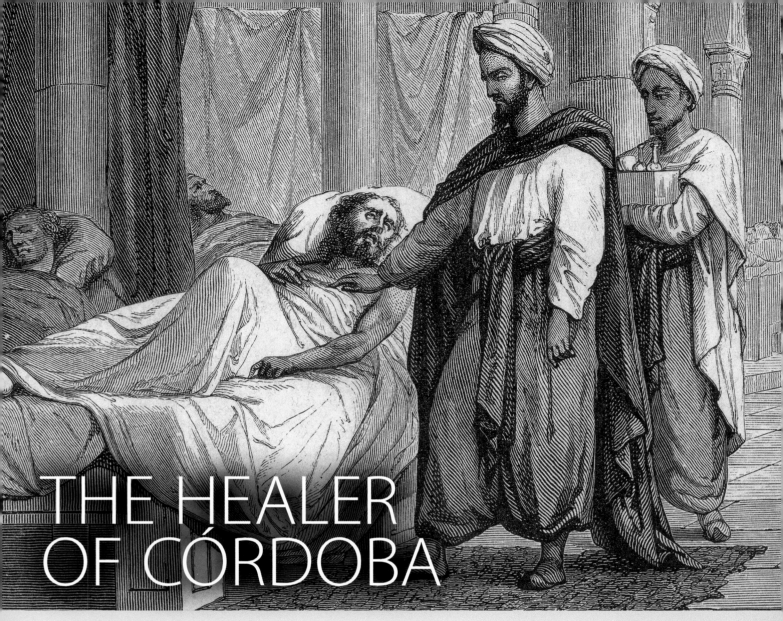

THE HEALER OF CÓRDOBA

🎧 2.05

An illustration of Al-Zahrawi treating a patient

A It is the year 1005. In the Andalusian[1] city of Medina Azahara, a woman is giving birth. Through the window of the delivery room, she can see the city's elaborate[2] columns, fountains, and finely polished marble terraces.[3] Her heart is pounding because she fears this is the last time she will see them. However, she has great faith in her doctor.

B The doctor's name is Al-Zahrawi, and, in later years, he will be known as Abulcasis, one of the great pioneers of surgery. At the moment, all of Al-Zahrawi's attention is focused on the difficult birth. He sees that the baby must be turned before it can pass through the birth canal. From his medical bag, he takes out a tool that he made himself—a pair of forceps with a semicircular end designed to pull the fetus from the mother. In fact, he pioneered the use of forceps about 50 years earlier, when he was just starting his medical career.

[1] **Andalusia** is a region of southern Spain.
[2] If something is **elaborate**, it is richly decorated with a lot of detail.
[3] A **terrace** is a flat area of stone or grass next to a building.

"Will my baby live?" the desperate mother manages to ask between contractions.[4] "Almost certainly," the doctor answers. "You have a healthy boy. But this next moment is going to be painful." The mother is happy to hear that her baby will live, but as the doctor warned, the pain is terrible. It is so strong that she loses consciousness for a few moments, but soon she is awakened by her baby's healthy cry.

C

THE METHOD OF MEDICINE

The forceps are just one of 200 surgical instruments that Al-Zahrawi described in his work *Al-Tasrif,* or *The Method of Medicine.* Many of the instruments and techniques described in its pages were invented by Al-Zahrawi himself. Born in Córdoba in 936, Al-Zahrawi was a doctor for the Spanish royal court at the height of Muslim civilization in Spain. During his long career, he compiled huge amounts of medical knowledge based on existing texts and his own experience.

D

Al-Zahrawi brought all his knowledge together in *Al-Tasrif.* This work was a 30-volume collection of all medical knowledge available at the time. The collection begins with basic concepts. Then it moves on from these general ideas to describe hundreds of topics including food and nutrition, skin diseases, and poisons. The final—and longest—volume deals with surgery. It includes treatments for head and spinal injuries, as well as techniques for amputating[5] a limb without killing the patient.

E

The ruins of Medina Azahara Palace, near Córdoba, Spain

[4] **Contractions** are the tightening of the muscles of the uterus during childbirth.
[5] **Amputating** a person's arm or leg means cutting all or part of it off in an operation.

The work also includes the world's first illustrations of surgical instruments, such as knives, scissors, and forceps. Many of the instruments look very familiar today. Al-Zahrawi's tools were helpful for treating conditions such as bone diseases, bladder[6] stones, and wounds. They were also useful in childbirth. One of Al-Zahrawi's most important inventions was the use of catgut[7] for sewing up a patient internally after surgery. Catgut is a strong substance that can dissolve[8] naturally in the body. It is still sometimes used in surgeries today.

Al-Zahrawi wrote about his instruments and methods to share his knowledge with others, including doctors who came after him. However, he surely could not have predicted how his work would educate and inform surgeons centuries after his death. There was only a single handwritten copy of *Al-Tasrif*. It was almost lost during an attack on the area in 1010, when many buildings and documents were destroyed. Fortunately, the work was saved. Over the next several decades, it was passed from person to person. Eventually, *Al-Tasrif* was translated into Latin from its original Arabic. More than four centuries after they were written, parts of the work were finally printed in 1471.

The printed translation spread Al-Zahrawi's knowledge throughout Europe. There, it had an enormous influence on medicine and surgery. *The Method of Medicine* was used as a manual for surgery in medical schools for centuries. Al-Zahrawi's legacy[9] can still be seen in many of the techniques and tools used in modern hospitals. He continues to be regarded as the "father of modern surgery."

---

[6] Your **bladder** is the part of your body where urine is stored.

[7] **Catgut** is a strong cord or thread made from the intestines of animals, usually sheep.

[8] To **dissolve** is to melt away or disappear.

[9] A person's **legacy** is something that they do or create that will continue to exist after they are dead.

UNDERSTANDING THE READING

SUMMARIZING

A Complete the summary of the passage. Write no more than two words in each space.

Al-Zahrawi was a medical innovator who lived in ¹_____ during the 11th century. He worked as a doctor for the Spanish ²_____ . Al-Zahrawi was a(n) ³_____ in the use of various surgical tools and techniques. He compiled all of his ⁴_____ in his work called *Al-Tasrif*. A translation of his writings—*The Method of Medicine*—was used to teach ⁵_____ in European medical schools for hundreds of years. Many of his inventions and methods are still in use today.

IDENTIFYING MAIN IDEAS

B Match each section from the passage to its main idea.

_____ 1. Paragraphs A–C   a. Al-Zahrawi's writings were almost destroyed, but they were saved and then translated.

_____ 2. Paragraph D   b. Al-Zahrawi's writings contain detailed information about medical treatments and tools.

_____ 3. Paragraphs E–F   c. Al-Zahrawi's work helped doctors for centuries, and continues to influence medicine today.

_____ 4. Paragraph G   d. Al-Zahrawi helps a woman through a difficult birth using a medical tool he designed.

_____ 5. Paragraph H   e. Al-Zahrawi developed numerous medical techniques during his career.

CRITICAL THINKING   Based on information the writer provides and their use of language, you can **infer**, or guess, the **writer's purpose**. What does the writer want to do: entertain, inform, or persuade? How does the writer use language to achieve their purpose?

CRITICAL THINKING: INFERRING PURPOSE

C Answer the questions and discuss your answers with a partner.

1. How does the reading passage begin?
   a. with a factual description of Al-Zahrawi's later career
   b. with a story about how Al-Zahrawi helped a patient
   c. with an opinion about Al-Zahrawi's skills as a doctor

2. Skim the verbs in paragraphs A–C. What form are most of them in?
   a. past tense
   b. present tense
   c. future tense

3. Why do you think the writer started the passage this way?
   a. to describe an important moment in Al-Zahrawi's career
   b. to explain Al-Zahrawi's reasons for becoming a doctor
   c. to make readers interested in Al-Zahrawi

D Put the events about Al-Zahrawi's life and achievements (a–f) on the timeline.   SEQUENCING

a. Al-Zahrawi was born.
b. The translated version of *Al-Tasrif* was printed.
c. *Al-Tasrif* was passed on through different people.
d. The original copy of *Al-Tasrif* was nearly lost.
e. Medical schools in Europe began using *The Method of Medicine* as a textbook.
f. Al-Zahrawi wrote about his knowledge and inventions in a 30-volume collection.

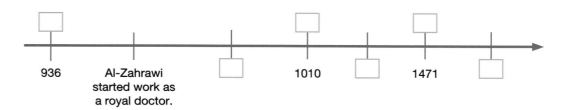

936   Al-Zahrawi   1010   1471
             started work as
             a royal doctor.

E Write short answers to these questions about Al-Zahrawi's work *Al-Tasrif*.   UNDERSTANDING DETAILS

1. What are two things described in the last volume of *Al-Tasrif*?

   _____

2. What aspect of *Al-Tasrif* was unique at the time?

   _____

3. Al-Zahrawi described the use of catgut in *Al-Tasrif*. How was this invention useful?

   _____

4. How was *Al-Tasrif* nearly destroyed in 1010?

   _____

5. How did *Al-Tasrif* become more widely known after Al-Zahrawi's death?

   _____

F Write short answers to the questions below. Then discuss with a partner.   CRITICAL THINKING: REFLECTING

1. Imagine that *Al-Tasrif* had been destroyed in 1010. Would modern medicine be any different today? Why or why not?

   _____

   _____

2. Can you think of any other book or books that had a major impact on science or society? Why were they significant?

   _____

   _____

DEVELOPING READING SKILLS

READING SKILL Understanding Passive Sentences

Sentences can be active or passive. An active sentence focuses on the agent of an action (the subject is performing the action). A passive sentence, on the other hand, focuses on the recipient of an action (the subject is being "acted upon").

> *Fortunately, <u>someone</u> **saved** the work.*   (active)
> *Fortunately, <u>the work</u> **was saved**.*   (passive)

Writers often use passive sentences:
- when the agent is unknown.
- when the agent is obvious to the reader.

When writers state the agent in a passive sentence, they include it in a phrase starting with *by*.

> *<u>Al-Tasrif</u> was written **by** <u>Al-Zahrawi</u>.*

However, the main focus of the sentence is still on the recipient (*Al-Tasrif*) of the action and not the agent (Al-Zahrawi).

IDENTIFYING
PASSIVE SENTENCES

A Read the sentences from the reading passage. Write P if the underlined verb is passive and A if it is active.

_____ 1. He sees that the baby must <u>be turned</u> before it can pass through the birth canal.

_____ 2. Al-Zahrawi <u>brought</u> all his knowledge together in *Al-Tasrif*.

_____ 3. It <u>is</u> still <u>used</u> in surgeries today.

_____ 4. In fact, he <u>pioneered</u> the use of forceps about 50 years earlier, when he was just starting his medical career.

UNDERSTANDING
PASSIVE SENTENCES

B Read the sentences (a–c) below. Then match each description (1–4) to one or more of the sentences.

a. Eventually, *Al-Tasrif* was translated into Latin from its original Arabic.

b. Many of the instruments and techniques were invented by Al-Zahrawi himself.

c. *The Method of Medicine* was used as a manual for surgery in medical schools for centuries.

_____ 1. The sentence has an agent.

_____ 2. The sentence doesn't have an agent.

_____ 3. The agent is not mentioned because it is obvious.

_____ 4. The agent is not mentioned because it is unknown.

Video

HEALTHCARE INNOVATOR

National Geographic Explorer Aydogan Ozcan uses cell phone technology to test people for infectious diseases.

BEFORE VIEWING

A Read the caption of the photo. How do you think a cell phone might be used for testing people's health? Discuss with a partner.

PREDICTING

B Read the information about infectious diseases. Note two reasons why they are a problem in developing areas. Then discuss with a partner.

LEARNING ABOUT THE TOPIC

Infectious diseases can be spread from one person to another. Two common infectious diseases are malaria and tuberculosis. In 2015, there were over two hundred million malaria cases worldwide—90 percent of which occurred in Africa. Tuberculosis is a lung infection caused by bacteria. In 2015, about ten million people suffered from the disease, and almost two million died from it. More than half of tuberculosis cases occurred in six countries, such as India, Indonesia, and Nigeria. Many infectious diseases like these are treatable. However, lack of access to proper medical care makes it difficult to cure these diseases globally.

_____

_____

C The words in **bold** below are used in the video. Read the sentences. Then match each word to its definition.

> Doctors can use X-rays to **diagnose** medical problems, but sometimes they can determine patients' illnesses with just a physical examination.
>
> After a patient takes a blood test, lab technicians **process** the blood sample.
>
> Doctors use various machines to **monitor** a patient's blood pressure and heart rate.

1. _____ (v) to regularly check the progress of something

2. _____ (v) to identify (an illness or a disease)

3. _____ (v) to take in and analyze for information

WHILE VIEWING

A ▶ Watch the video. Why is the cell phone a suitable device to use as a diagnostic tool? Check (✓) the reasons.

☐ 1. Many people in developing countries own cell phones.

☐ 2. The diagnosis is more accurate than traditional test kits.

☐ 3. It provides almost instant test results.

☐ 4. It allows regional health information to be collected and studied.

B ▶ Watch the video again. Complete the steps for using the cell phone as a diagnostic tool.

1. Insert the _____ onto the back of the phone.

2. Select _____ on the menu.

3. An image of the _____ appears on-screen.

4. The _____ taps on the image of the diagnostic test.

5. The app _____ the image and produces the result.

6. The _____ is sent to a central server for healthcare workers to use.

AFTER VIEWING

A How else might cell phones be used for monitoring health or providing healthcare services? List two ideas and discuss with a partner.

_____

_____

B How do you think Ozcan's data could be used? Who would it be useful for? Discuss with a partner.

Reading 2

PREPARING TO READ

A The words and phrases in blue below are used in Reading 2. Read the paragraph. Then match the correct form of each word or phrase to its definition.

BUILDING VOCABULARY

Major advances are **taking place** in the field of prosthetics—**artificial** limbs made for people who have lost their arms or legs. Scientists have moved beyond **replacement** limbs made of plastic and metal. Instead, they are **seeking** to create robotic limbs that are more lifelike. For example, they are working to make limbs that allow the wearer to have a sense of touch. These limbs are in the **experimental** stages now, but if this **inventive** idea becomes a reality, it will be a **breakthrough** in medical technology. Users will have replacement limbs that look, feel, and operate almost exactly like real limbs.

1. _____ (v) to look to find

2. _____ (v) to happen or occur

3. _____ (adj) creative, innovative

4. _____ (adj) still being tested

5. _____ (adj) made by humans and not by nature

6. _____ (n) a person or thing that takes the place of another

7. _____ (n) a sudden improvement in knowledge or technology

B Read the sentences in the box. Then match each word in blue to its definition.

BUILDING VOCABULARY

> Effective testing and early diagnosis have caused a **decline** in death rates of certain cancer types.
>
> **Survival** rates for cancer patients are much higher than they were 50 years ago; today, people with some types of cancer can live long lives.
>
> If you need blood and receive the wrong blood type, your body will **reject** it.

1. _____ (n) the continuation of life

2. _____ (n) a reduction in quality, amount, or number

3. _____ (v) to refuse to accept

C What recent medical breakthroughs do you know of? Discuss with a partner.

USING VOCABULARY

D Look at the title, headings, and photos in the reading passage. What is the passage about? Check your idea as you read.

PREDICTING

a. two recent advances in medical technology

b. the main challenges of medical transplants

c. the history of biotechnology

MEDICAL FRONTIERS

⌒ 2.06

A For centuries, medical pioneers have refined a variety of methods and medicines to treat sickness, injury, and disability, enabling people to live longer and healthier lives. Two of the most exciting breakthroughs in medical science today are regenerative medicine and nanotechnology.

GROWING BODY PARTS

B "A salamander[1] can grow back its leg. Why can't a human do the same?" asked Peruvian-born surgeon Dr. Anthony Atala. The question, a reference to work aiming to grow new limbs for wounded soldiers, captures the inventive spirit of regenerative medicine. This innovative field seeks to provide patients with replacement body parts. These parts are not made of steel; they are the real thing—living cells, tissue, and even organs.

C Regenerative medicine is still mostly experimental and limited to procedures such as growing sheets of skin on burn wounds. One of its most significant advances took place in 1999. A research group at North Carolina's Wake Forest Institute for Regenerative Medicine successfully replaced a bladder with one grown in a lab. Since then, the team—led by Dr. Atala—has created a variety of other tissues and organs, from kidneys to ears.

D The field of regenerative medicine is based on the first successful donor tissue and bone transplants done in the early 20th century. However, donor organs are not always the best option. First of all, they are in short supply. In the United States alone, more than 100,000 people are waiting for organ transplants—many people die while waiting for an available organ. Secondly, a patient's body may reject the donor organ. With regenerative medicine, however, tissues are grown from a patient's own cells and will not be rejected.

[1] A **salamander** is a small lizard-like animal that lives on land and in water.

E Today, several labs are working to create artificial body parts that are made from a patient's own cells. Scientists at Columbia University and Yale University have grown a jawbone and a lung. At the University of Minnesota, Dr. Doris Taylor has created a beating bioartificial rat heart. Dr. Atala's team has had long-term success with bioengineered bladders for young patients with spina bifida.[2] And at the University of Michigan, Dr. H. David Humes has created an artificial kidney.

F So far, the kidney procedure has only been used successfully with sheep. However, there is hope that one day it will be possible to implant a similar kidney in a human patient. The continuing research of scientists such as these may eventually make donor organs unnecessary. As a result, individuals may have significantly increased chances of survival.

[2] **Spina bifida** is a birth defect that involves the incomplete development of the spinal cord.

An artificial human nose created by Dr. Atala and his team

How to (Re)grow a Kidney

More people are waiting for a kidney than any other organ, but it's one of the hardest to grow. Here is the strategy being followed by the research group at Wake Forest in its search to create the first transplantable bioartificial human kidney.

1
Sample a tiny bit of the patient's kidney.

2
Sort kidney tissue cells from those of blood vessels running through it.

Vessel cells   Kidney cells

3
Multiply both types of cells in lab cultures.

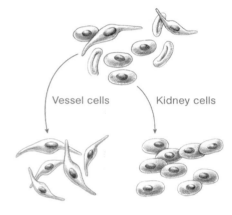

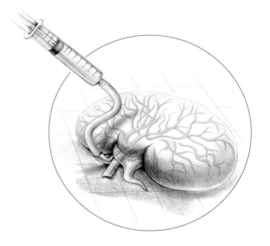

4
Inject the cultured cells of the patient into a scaffold,[3] which is made by washing a pig kidney with mild detergent[4] until the pig cells are gone and only the tough collagen remains.

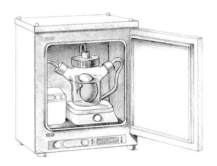

5
Incubate[5] at 98.6°F (37°C) in a bioreactor that delivers oxygen and nutrients to the growing tissue.

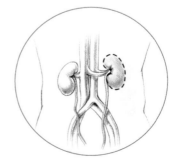

6
Implant a functioning human organ into the patient.

[3] A **scaffold** is a supporting structure.
[4] **Detergent** is a type of soap.
[5] To **incubate** something is to put it in an environment with a specific temperature for it to develop or grow.

A mouse injected with nanoparticles glows under ultraviolet light.

USING NANOTECHNOLOGY

The main thing to know about nanotechnology is that it is small—really small. *Nano-* is a prefix that means "dwarf"[6] in Greek. It is short for *nanometer*—one-billionth of a meter. To get an idea

G of how small a nanometer is, a comma (,) consists of about half a million nanometers. The nail on your little finger is about ten million nanometers across. To put it another way, a nanometer is the amount a man's beard grows in the time it takes him to lift a razor to his face.

How can nanotechnology be applied to medicine? One of the potential applications is as an aid in surgery. Scientists at Rice University have used a solution of tiny silica[7] balls covered with gold to reconnect two pieces of animal

H tissue. These balls are called nanoshells. Someday soon, surgeons may be able to use a nanoshell treatment like this to reconnect blood vessels that have been cut during surgery. "One of the hardest things a doctor has to do during a kidney or heart transplant is reattach cut arteries," says

André Gobin, a graduate student at Rice. "They have to sew the ends [of cut arteries] together with tiny stitches. Leaks are a big problem." The nanoshells will enable a surgeon to make a clean join between the two ends of a cut artery, preventing blood from leaking out.

Nanotechnology may also help cancer patients. Traditional cancer treatments are severe and may cause a decline in the patient's health. However, nanotechnology promises treatment without the risks or side effects. Researchers at Rice University have engineered nanoshells that are about 120 nanometers wide—about 170 times smaller

I than a cancer cell. When they are injected into the bloodstream, they can enter tumors.[8] When an infrared laser is focused on the tumor, the light passes through healthy tissue but heats up the nanoshells. In laboratory tests using mice, the treatment killed cancer cells while leaving healthy tissue unharmed. The technique has the potential one day to be applied to human cancer patients.

[6] The word **dwarf** is used to describe something small.

[7] **Silica** is a material used for making glass and ceramics. It often exists in sand.

[8] A **tumor** is a mass of diseased or abnormal cells that has grown inside a person's or an animal's body.

UNDERSTANDING THE READING

A Complete the summary of the passage. Write no more than two words in each space.   SUMMARIZING

Growing Body Parts

The field of regenerative medicine involves using a patient's ¹ _____

to grow replacement body parts. This is possibly a more effective way to treat patients who

require ² _____ . Although the procedure is still mostly

³ _____ , scientists hope to successfully grow organs such as kidneys

for ⁴ _____ patients in the future.

Using Nanotechnology

Nanotechnology in medicine involves using very small particles to treat patients. For

example, some scientists have created tiny balls covered in gold called

⁵ _____ . These could help prevent blood from

⁶ _____ when doctors are sewing up a patient during surgery. They

could also help ⁷ _____ patients by reducing the risks and

⁸ _____ of treatment.

B According to the passage, what are some benefits of regenerative medicine? Check (✓)   UNDERSTANDING
the ones mentioned.   DETAILS

☐ 1. shorter waiting time for an available organ

☐ 2. longer lasting than a donor organ

☐ 3. higher chance of patient's body accepting the new organ

☐ 4. cheaper than organ transplant surgeries

C Match each innovation in regenerative medicine to a scientist or group of scientists (a–e).   UNDERSTANDING
Then complete the notes about the innovations using information from the passage.   DETAILS

a. Dr. Atala and team   d. Researchers at Rice University
b. Dr. Doris Taylor   e. Scientists at Columbia University and Yale University
c. Dr. H. David Humes

Scientist(s)	Innovation
	Bioengineered jawbone and lung
	Bioartificial rat heart
	Bioengineered bladder • _____ success with young patients with spinal problems
	Artificial kidney • Has been successfully used in _____ • May be possible to _____ a kidney in humans one day
	Nanoshell treatment • Could be used to reconnect _____ during surgery • Could be used to kill cancer cells without harming _____

D Put the steps for growing a kidney in order (1–6).

_____ a. Place the kidney into the patient.

_____ b. Take some cells from the patient's kidney.

_____ c. Allow the cells to increase in number in a culture.

_____ d. Separate the kidney cells from blood vessel cells.

_____ e. Keep the growing kidney tissue at body temperature.

_____ f. Place the cells in an animal kidney that has been cleaned and treated.

INFERRING MEANING **E** Find and underline the following words and phrases in **bold** in the reading passage. Use context to identify their meanings. Then complete the definitions with your own words.

1. Paragraph A: If someone has **refined** something, they have _____ it by making small changes.

2. Paragraph D: If something is **in short supply**, there _____ of it available.

3. Paragraph G: "To **put it another way**" means to _____.

4. Paragraph H: If you **reattach** two things, you _____.

UNDERSTANDING REFERENCING **F** Read the sentences from the reading passage. For each item, circle the noun that the **bold** pronoun refers to.

1. These parts are not made of steel; **they** are the real thing—living cells, tissue, and even organs.

2. However, donor organs are not always the best option. First of all, **they** are in short supply.

3. "One of the hardest things doctors have to do during a kidney or heart transplant is reattach cut arteries," says André Gobin, a graduate student at Rice. "**They** have to sew the ends [of cut arteries] together with tiny stitches."

4. Researchers at Rice University have engineered nanoshells that are about 120 nanometers wide—about 170 times smaller than a cancer cell. When **they** are injected into the bloodstream, they can enter tumors.

CRITICAL THINKING: SYNTHESIZING **G** How is Al-Zahrawi's use of catgut and Rice University's use of nanoshells similar? Write an answer and then discuss your idea with a partner.

Both catgut and nanoshells can be used _____

_____

Writing

EXPLORING WRITTEN ENGLISH

Most essays require some research so that your ideas are supported by facts and evidence. When you are doing research online, it is important to evaluate the quality of the information that you find. Here are some things to think about when evaluating information online.

Purpose/Point of View: Is the purpose of the website to deliver information in a factual or objective way? If it is trying to promote or sell something, or to persuade readers, then the information on the site may not be completely objective or accurate.

Authority: Who is the author? Are they an expert on the topic? If the website is a news or magazine site, is it a trustworthy source—that is, does it present facts and balanced arguments? Note that URLs ending in *.gov* or *.edu* are usually reliable sources: *.gov* indicates a government site and *.edu* is a school site.

Accuracy: Is the information correct? Are you able to check it against other sources?

Currency: When was the content written? Is the information still accurate or is it outdated? If the article or post is not dated, skim the text for time references.

Coverage: Is the information thorough? Is important information left out? For example, are facts or arguments missing because they do not fit the author's purpose or point of view?

A Imagine you are researching a newly discovered plant that may have health benefits. Read the descriptions of five websites and rank them according to their usefulness (1 = most useful; 5 = least useful). Then share your ideas with a partner.

CRITICAL THINKING: EVALUATING SOURCES

_____ a. A newspaper website. The newspaper is owned and operated by a political group. The information is updated every day. The site's URL ends in *.com*.

_____ b. A blog whose URL ends in *.com*. The blogger is a doctor and has worked as a professional nutritionist for 20 years. She writes a new post every day.

_____ c. A *.gov* website that focuses on nutrition. There is a lot of information on the site. The latest information is two years old.

_____ d. A *.org* website that focuses on nutrition. The contributors are doctors and researchers. The information is updated weekly.

_____ e. A *.com* site that sells diet and nutrition pills. It contains a lot of information about a newly discovered plant and is offering a diet pill made from the plant.

When writing an essay, you can sometimes include a quote to support your argument. The quote can help explain something or give important factual information. When you include a direct quote, you have to use the exact same language that is in the source. You also need to provide a **citation** that shows where the information comes from.

There are different styles for quoting and citing sources. Below are some rules for quoting websites based on the American Psychological Association (APA) Style.

- Make sure that your quote fits grammatically into your sentence. For example:

  Al-Zahrawi's work continues to be relevant today as his "legacy can still be seen in many of the techniques and tools used in modern hospitals." (correct)

  Al-Zahrawi's work continues to be relevant today as "legacy can still be seen in many of the techniques and tools used in modern hospitals." (incorrect)

- Include an **in-text citation** (a short citation within your essay) along with the quote. See below for guidelines on in-text citations for online sources.

- Include the full citation (in alphabetical order) in a **References** section at the end of the essay.

Example of an in-text citation:

  According to Morris (2017), surgeons have been using robotic hearts "to break the last taboo of heart surgery—operating on an unborn child" (para. 22).

Example of a reference entry:

  Morris, T. (2017, May 23). Robot hearts: medicine's new frontier. *The Guardian*. Retrieved from https://www.theguardian.com/science/2017/may/23/robot-hearts-medicines-new-frontier

APA In-Text Citation Guideline (for citing website/webpage sources)	
When you have . . .	**Examples**
author, date, and title of article	Smith (2017) says "language … in humans" (para. 3). Research has shown that "language … in humans" (Smith, 2017, para. 3).
no date (= n.d.)	Smith (n.d.) says "language … in humans" (para. 3). Research has shown that "language … in humans" (Smith, n.d., para. 3).
no author	According to *Medical Innovations* (2017), "language … in humans" (para. 3). A study showed that "language … in humans" (*Medical Innovations*, 2017, para. 3).
no author and no date	According to *Medical Innovations* (n.d.), "language … in humans" (para. 3). A study showed that "language … in humans" (*Medical Innovations*, n.d., para. 3).

Note: Only the year (not the full date) needs to be included in an in-text citation.

B Choose the quote that fits grammatically into the sentence.

1. Martin (2017) points out that most of us will deal with health professionals virtually, …
   a. making "face-to-face doctor's appointments a thing of the past" (para. 4).
   b. and "face-to-face doctor's appointments a thing of the past" (para. 4).

2. According to *GenomicsToday* (n.d.), advances in genetic research will lead to personalized medicine and …
   a. "revolutionary way to cure and prevent diseases" (para. 1).
   b. "a revolutionary way to cure and prevent diseases" (para. 1).

3. According to Park (2017), a single organ donor can …
   a. save "the lives of eight people" (para. 6).
   b. "saving the lives of eight people" (para. 6).

C Read the sentence parts below. Then complete each sentence by underlining a suitable part of the quote.

1. Economist Kyung-Hwan Kim believes that it isn't possible to …
   "You can't understand urbanization in isolation from economic development."

2. Urban planner Richard Wurman thinks that people are attracted to cities as there are many …
   "People flock to cities because of the possibilities for doing things that interest them."

3. According to researcher Dr. Rachel Grant, rats may be the most sensitive animals to earthquakes as they …
   "What was interesting was that the rodents were the first to disappear."

D Compare the in-text citations with the references below. The reference entries have been created for this exercise. Correct one mistake in each citation.

1. As Lampl explains, advances in 3-D printers "have allowed us to create artificial limbs quickly and economically" (para. 5).

2. According to *The Future of Diagnosis* (n.d.), someday doctors will be able to "use smartphones to diagnose patients in remote areas quickly and accurately" (para. 2).

3. Thanks to the wealth of online health sites, patients today come to office visits "with a great deal of information about their condition" (Maple, para. 10, 2018).

References

Lampl, N. (n.d.). The new age of medicine. Retrieved from http://www.sharpu.edu/blog/thenewageofmedicine/505/33

Maple, S. (2018, April 2). Trends in healthcare. Retrieved from http://www.todaynurse.com/patient-care/trends/2134

The Future of Diagnosis. (2016, March 12). Retrieved from http://www.FNN.com/thefutureofdiagnosis/news/march2016/fijydj

WRITING TASK

GOAL You are going to write a research-based essay on the following topic:

Research a current innovation in the field of medicine, science, or technology. Explain why this innovation is important or significant.

BRAINSTORMING **A** Make a list of medical innovations that you are aware of. You can list innovations from this unit and other ones you know or have heard about. If possible, find out who was responsible for each innovation.

PLANNING **B** Follow these steps to make notes for your essay.

Step 1 Choose one innovation from your brainstorming notes. Note it in the outline.

Step 2 Think of two reasons why this innovation is important. For each body paragraph, write a topic sentence that expresses a reason.

Step 3 Write a thesis statement that states your innovation and mentions the reasons for its importance.

Step 4 Add details to support each reason. Include at least two quotes.

Step 5 Write a summary statement and add a final thought for the concluding paragraph.

OUTLINE

Innovation (+ innovator): _____

Thesis Statement: _____

_____

Body Paragraphs

Topic Sentence 1: _____

_____

Details: _____

Topic Sentence 2: _____

_____

Details: _____

Concluding Paragraph

Summary Statement: _____

Final Thought: _____

FIRST DRAFT **C** Use your outline to write a first draft of your essay. Include in-text citations with your quotes.

REVISING PRACTICE

The draft below is similar to the one you are going to write. Follow the steps to create a better second draft.

1. Add the sentences (a–c) in the most suitable spaces.
    a. The computer will then interpret the photo, diagnose the disease in the blood, and send a diagnosis back in a few minutes.
    b. He and his research team have developed a way to turn regular cell phones into diagnostic tools.
    c. It is fairly inexpensive to modify a cell phone for use as a diagnostic tool.

2. Now fix the following problems (d–e) in the essay.
    d. Correct one sentence in paragraph B to make the quote fit grammatically.
    e. Correct a mistake with an in-text citation in paragraph C.

A

Imagine that you are in a remote village somewhere with no access to medical treatment. You become very sick, but you have to wait until a mobile medical unit arrives to help you. The doctors examine you and take blood samples, but they won't be able to help you until they test the samples back at the hospital. Even though you may only have a simple infection, you might die because of the delay. Thanks to one man, many people may never be in this situation. Aydogan Ozcan, an electrical engineer at UCLA, has made an important contribution with a new medical innovation. _____

B

Ozcan's invention is important because it is very accurate and easy to use. As healthcare workers in remote areas may not always be properly trained, they may not be able to use microscopes and other tools to make diagnoses accurately. With Ozcan's cell phone technology, mobile health workers can take a photo of a blood sample and send it over the Internet to a central computer at a hospital. _____ This turns the cell phone into "mobile medical lab with the capability to test and diagnose diseases" (Ward, 2012).

C

Another reason that Ozcan's invention is important is that it is inexpensive. His technology only requires a modified cell phone and an Internet connection. _____ As Eisenberg (n.d.) points out, Ozcan was able to do it using "about $10 worth of off-the-shelf hardware" (para. 2). In the future, cell phones will be able to do much more than they do today.

D

By making use of existing technology—cell phones—Ozcan and his team have invented a medical tool that is accurate and easy to use. Ozcan's simple tool might one day save the lives of millions of people all over the world.

References

Eisenberg, A. (2009, Nov. 7). Far from a lab? Turn a cell phone into a microscope. *The New York Times*. Retrieved from http://www.nytimes.com/2009/11/08/business/08novel.html

Ward, Lauren. 2012, August 14. Closer Look: Turning Mobile Phones Into Mobile Medical Labs. Retrieved from https://voices.nationalgeographic.org/2012/08/14/closer-look-turning-mobile-phones-into-mobile-medical-labs/

D Now use the questions below to revise your essay.

- ☐ Did you include a clear thesis statement?
- ☐ Do your body paragraphs include enough details to fully explain your ideas?
- ☐ Did you use quotes and include in-text citations?
- ☐ Does your concluding paragraph have a summary statement and a final thought?

EDITING PRACTICE

Read the information below.

When you quote from original sources, remember that quotes must fit grammatically into your sentences.

Correct each of the sentences (1–4) so that the quotes fit grammatically.

1. Lampl (2017) points out that a 3-D-printed hand costs 40 pounds, or about "same price as an adult ticket for a ride on the London Eye" (para. 10).

2. Root (2018) believes that health workers need to calm down patients who has "read too much about medical conditions online" (para. 4).

3. Science blogger Anna Chung (2018) says that regenerative medicine can "completely changed the game" when it comes to organ transplantation (para. 7).

4. According to *What's New in Medicine* (n.d.), research shows that "even though about 99.9 percent of the DNA between two individuals is identical" (para. 1).

FINAL DRAFT **E** Follow these steps to write a final draft.

1. Check your revised draft for mistakes with in-text citations.
2. Now use the checklist on page 253 to write a final draft. Make any other necessary changes.

UNIT REVIEW
Answer the following questions.

1. What is one ancient medical innovation and one modern one?

_____

_____

_____

2. What are two things to consider when you are evaluating an online source?

_____

_____

_____

3. Do you remember the meanings of these words? Check (✔) the ones you know. Look back at the unit and review the ones you don't know.

Reading 1:

☐ civilization	☐ compile **AWL**	☐ concept **AWL**
☐ existing	☐ general	☐ manage to
☐ manual **AWL**	☐ method **AWL**	☐ pioneer
☐ spread		

Reading 2:

☐ artificial	☐ breakthrough	☐ decline **AWL**
☐ experimental	☐ inventive	☐ reject **AWL**
☐ replacement	☐ seek	☐ survival
☐ take place		

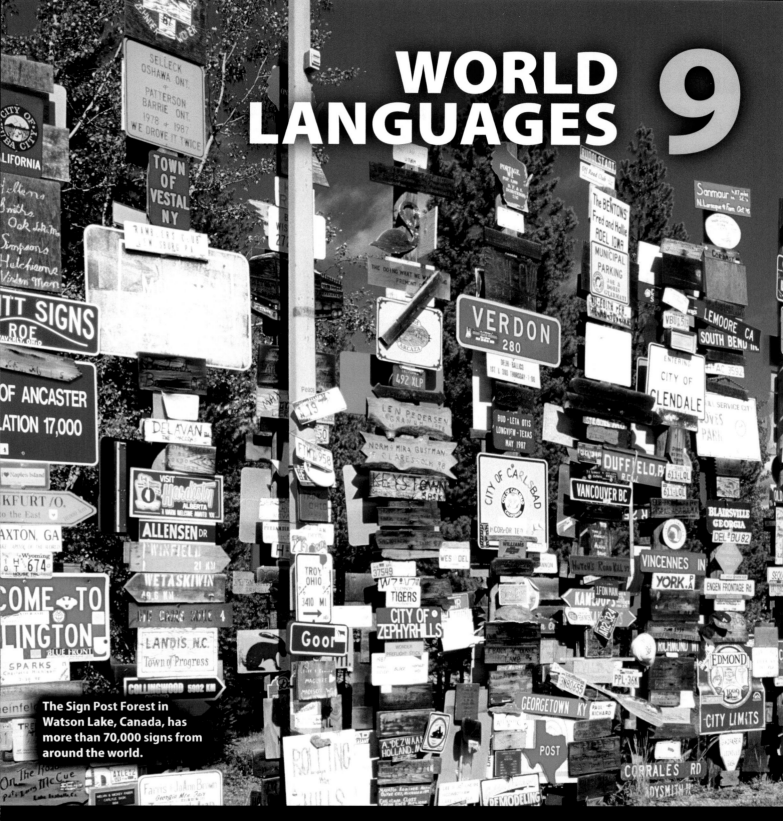

WORLD LANGUAGES 9

The Sign Post Forest in Watson Lake, Canada, has more than 70,000 signs from around the world.

THINK AND DISCUSS

1 How many languages do you speak? How well do you speak them?

2 What are the most common languages in your country?

A Look at the information on these pages and answer the questions.

1. Which language family is the largest? What are some of the regions and countries where people speak the languages in this family?

2. What can we infer about the areas listed as "other" in the map?

3. Why do you think the number of languages has decreased? Do you think this is a positive or a negative trend? Why?

B Match the words in blue to their definitions.

_____ (adv) having a large degree of something

_____ (adj) relating to languages

_____ (v) to make up parts of a whole

Major Language Families Today

- Afro-Asiatic
- Altaic
- Austro-Asiatic
- Austronesian
- Dravidian
- Indo-European
- Japanese/Korean
- Kam-Tai
- Niger-Congo
- Nilo-Saharan
- Sino-Tibetan
- Uralic
- Other

Disappearing Languages

Even though Earth's population is increasing fast, the number of languages people speak is decreasing. Linguists fear that by 2100, over half of the 7,000 languages spoken today will disappear.

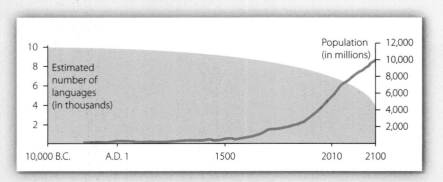

WORLD LANGUAGES

Languages are grouped into families according to word origin and structure. The three main **linguistic** families are Indo-European, Afro-Asiatic, and Sino-Tibetan. Indo-European, which includes English, German, Spanish, and Hindi, is the world's largest language family. Over 400 languages **constitute** the Indo-European family, which has approximately three billion speakers. Sino-Tibetan languages are spoken by over a billion people. One of these languages, Mandarin Chinese, has more native speakers than any other language. The Afro-Asiatic family includes about 370 languages, but has **considerably** fewer speakers—about 350 million people. The largest language in this family is Arabic, with more than 300 million speakers worldwide.

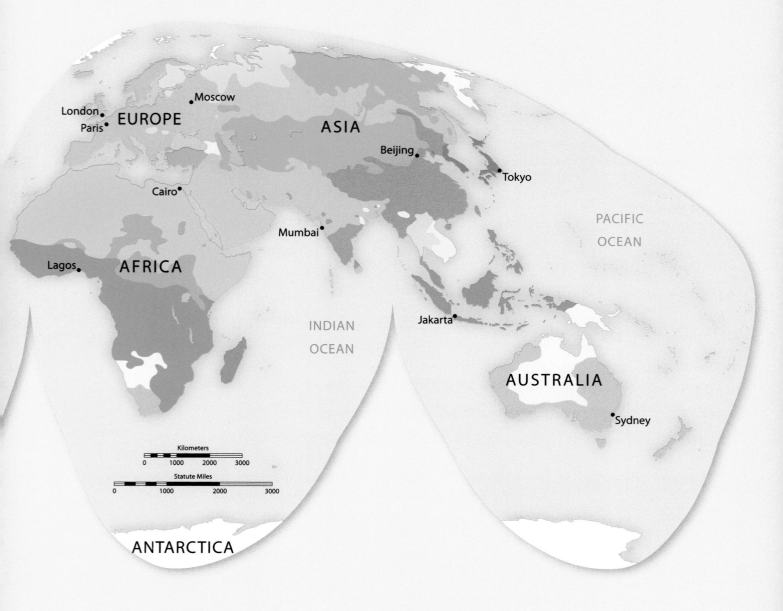

Reading 1

PREPARING TO READ

A The words and phrases in blue below are used in Reading 1. Read the paragraph. Then match the correct form of each word or phrase to its definition.

Why should you learn a second language? **Acquiring** another language can **lead to** many opportunities in life, both professional and personal. For example, many employers regard **competence** in a second language as a desirable quality in job seekers, and experts **anticipate** this trend to continue to grow. People who speak only their **native** language may be seen as less valuable. In addition, international travel can be more rewarding for people who can speak the languages of the places they are visiting, as it allows them to have conversations with locals and to make new friends. **Furthermore**, speaking more than one language can **expand** a person's cognitive abilities. For example, research shows that multilingual people have better memories and better problem-solving skills.

1. _____ (v) to result in

2. _____ (v) to get something

3. _____ (adv) in addition

4. _____ (n) the ability to do something well

5. _____ (v) to make larger in size or scale

6. _____ (v) to foresee or expect something

7. _____ (adj) connected to a person's place of birth

B Discuss these questions with a partner.

1. What do you think are the best ways to **acquire** a new language?

2. What other opportunities can learning a second language **lead to**?

C Work with a partner. Discuss your answers to these questions.

1. Why do you think English is so commonly used today?

2. Do you think English will be as important in 50 years? Why or why not?

D Read the title and subheadings, and look at the photos in the reading passage. What do you think it is about? Check your idea as you read.

a. the role of English and other languages in the future
b. evidence that English will be less commonly spoken in the future
c. reasons why English has become a global language for communication

THE FUTURE OF ENGLISH

▲ Over a billion people worldwide are learning English.

🎧 2.07

A   The world's language system is at a crossroads, and a new linguistic order is about to emerge. That is the conclusion of a study authored by David Graddol, a researcher on the future of language. He argues that this transformation is partly due to demographics. The world's population rose quickly during the second half of the 20th century, and much of this increase took place in developing countries. This has had an impact on the world's top languages.

B   In his study, Graddol points out that there has been a relative decline in the use of English as a first language. In the mid-20th century, people who spoke English as a first language constituted about 9 percent of the world's population. By 2050, the figure is expected to be just 5 percent. Currently, English still has the third largest number of native speakers, with Arabic and Hindi lagging considerably behind in fourth and fifth places. However, these two languages are expected to catch up by around 2050. Even so, they are not the fastest growing languages; some other languages such as Bengali (spoken in Bangladesh and India), Tamil (spoken in Sri Lanka and India), and Malay (spoken in parts of Southeast Asia) are experiencing even faster growth.

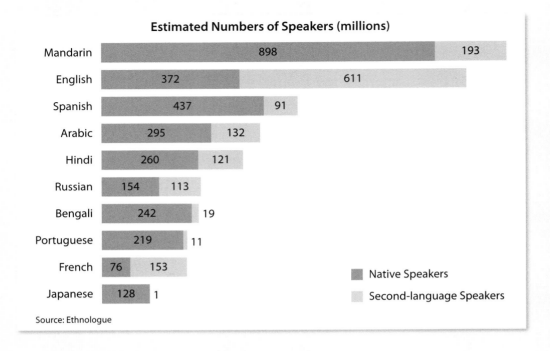

Estimated Numbers of Speakers (millions)

Language	Native Speakers	Second-language Speakers
Mandarin	898	193
English	372	611
Spanish	437	91
Arabic	295	132
Hindi	260	121
Russian	154	113
Bengali	242	19
Portuguese	219	11
French	76	153
Japanese	128	1

Source: Ethnologue

C   When ESL (English as a Second Language) and other non-native speakers are included, English is the most spoken language globally, and can be regarded as a "world language." However, according to Graddol, it is unlikely that one language will dominate in the near future. Although linguists expect that English will continue to be important, other languages will challenge its position. For example, Mandarin Chinese will probably be the next must-learn language, especially in Asia. As a result of these trends, Graddol says, "the status of English as a global language may peak[1] soon."

ENGLISH FOR SCIENCE

D   However, just as the relative number of native speakers of English is decreasing, a separate study shows that English is expanding its influence in the world of science. The dominance of one language allows for more international collaboration and research, making it possible to publish scientific articles to broader audiences.

E   Science writer Scott Montgomery, author of *The Chicago Guide to Communicating Science,* describes how science is creating new words and expressions in English. "Because of its scale and dynamism,"[2] he says, "science has become the most active and dynamic creator of new language in the world today. And most of this creation is occurring in English, the *lingua franca*[3] of scientific effort." Montgomery expects that in the future, English will continue to expand its role in science, especially in international settings. More than 90 percent of journal literature in some scientific fields is already published in English. He predicts that more and more scientists who do not speak English will have to learn the language.

[1] When something **peaks,** it reaches its highest value or level.
[2] If something has **dynamism,** it is full of energy or full of new and exciting ideas.
[3] A *lingua franca* is a language used between people who do not speak each another's native language.

RISE OF MULTILINGUALISM

F   Graddol notes that in many parts of the world, acquiring a second language is considered a basic skill, like computer competence. This will lead to the creation of "new generations of bilingual and multilingual speakers around the world." At the same time, he notes, international businesses will increasingly look for multilingual employees. Businesses whose employees speak only one language will find themselves at a disadvantage. And English may not be the only language of business. With China's growing economy, more companies—especially those doing business in Asia—will look to hire workers who can speak Mandarin.

G   Linguists anticipate that in the future, the majority of the world's population will speak more than one language. Furthermore, it's likely that speakers will switch between languages for routine tasks. As a result, people who speak only one language may have a difficult time in a multilingual society. According to Graddol, some monolingual speakers—especially native English speakers—"have been too complacent about […] the need to learn other languages."

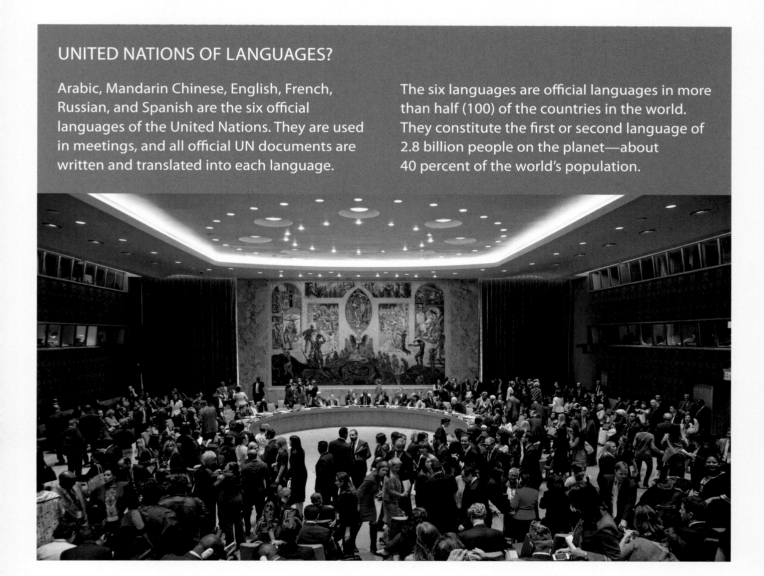

UNITED NATIONS OF LANGUAGES?

Arabic, Mandarin Chinese, English, French, Russian, and Spanish are the six official languages of the United Nations. They are used in meetings, and all official UN documents are written and translated into each language.

The six languages are official languages in more than half (100) of the countries in the world. They constitute the first or second language of 2.8 billion people on the planet—about 40 percent of the world's population.

UNDERSTANDING THE READING

A Match the paragraphs (A–G) to their main ideas.

_____ 1. As the world becomes increasingly multilingual, monolinguals will need to learn to adapt.

_____ 2. The use of English is growing in the world of science.

_____ 3. Knowledge of multiple languages will be an essential skill in future workplaces.

_____ 4. Population changes are having an important effect on the world's language system.

_____ 5. Other languages besides English will become equally widespread, but there may not be a single global language.

_____ 6. English for science will expand because the field is contributing new words and expressions to the language.

_____ 7. The number of native English speakers is decreasing, while the number of native speakers of other languages is growing.

B Scan the passage to find answers to the questions below.

1. Where did the world's population increase the most in the second half of the 20th century?

   _____

2. What are three of the most rapidly growing languages?

   _____

3. Why is the dominance of one language useful in science?

   _____

4. What language is increasingly becoming an important business language? Why?

   _____

C Find and underline the following words and expressions in **bold** in the reading passage. Use context to identify their meanings. Then complete the definitions.

1. Paragraph A: **Demographics** relates to the characteristics of _____.
   a. human populations
   b. language change

2. Paragraph B: If something is **lagging** behind, it is _____.
   a. getting close
   b. moving slowly

3. Paragraph B: If a person or thing **catches up**, they _____.
   a. take something away from someone or something else
   b. reach the same point as someone or something else

4. Paragraph C: If something **dominates** in an area, it is the most _____.
   a. well-known
   b. common or important

D Look back at the graph in the reading passage. Note answers to these questions and discuss with a partner.

INTERPRETING VISUAL INFORMATION

1. Which language has the greatest number of first-language speakers? Which has the second greatest number of native speakers?

   _____

2. Which language has the greatest number of second-language speakers?

   _____

3. Which two languages have more non-native speakers than native speakers? What does this show about these languages?

   _____

   _____

CRITICAL THINKING   **Applying an idea to a real-world situation** means comparing situations that you read about to experiences in your own life. Ask yourself: How do the ideas in the text relate to my experience—are they similar or different? Do I agree or disagree with what the author is saying? Do the ideas in the text change my opinions about anything?

E Think about the ideas in the reading passage and discuss these questions with a partner.

CRITICAL THINKING: APPLYING IDEAS

1. What is the main reason you are studying English? Is your reason similar to or different from the reasons described in the reading passage?

   _____

   _____

2. Do you think that it is important for people in your country to learn more than one second language? Why or why not? Note two reasons.

   _____

   _____

DEVELOPING READING SKILLS

READING SKILL Understanding Predictions

In Unit 2, you learned that there are different words and phrases that show the level of certainty, such as *definitely* and *maybe*. Similarly, when you read about a prediction, look for words and expressions that express the writer's degree of certainty. Ask yourself: Which predictions does the writer feel certain about? Which ones do they feel less certain about?

Writers use the modal *will* to make predictions that they are most certain about.
> In the near future, students **will** study Mandarin as a second language.

They use words such as *expect*, *anticipate*, *believe*, and *likely* to make predictions that they are reasonably certain about.
> Educators **expect** that the number of students learning English will decline.
> We **anticipate** that there will be fewer students next semester.

When writers are less certain about a prediction, they use words such as *seem* and *probably*. The modals *may, might,* and *could* indicate even less certainty.
> English will **probably** continue to be an important language in business.
> Mandarin **might** replace English as the most popular second language in my school.

IDENTIFYING
PREDICTIONS

A Find an example of these predictions in the passage. Then write the word that the author uses to express a level of certainty.

1. an example of a reasonably certain prediction in paragraph E _____

2. an example of a less certain prediction in paragraph F _____

ANALYZING
PREDICTIONS

B Answer these questions about other predictions in the passage.

1. Look for and underline the four predictions described below in the reading passage.

   a. which language dominates in the future _____

   b. when English as a global language reaches its peak _____

   c. businesses whose employees speak only one language _____

   d. monolinguals in a multilingual society _____

2. How certain does the author feel about each prediction above? Rate them (1 = less certain, 2 = reasonably certain, 3 = certain) and discuss your answers with a partner.

3. Do you disagree with any of the predictions above? Why? Note your ideas and discuss with a partner.

_____

_____

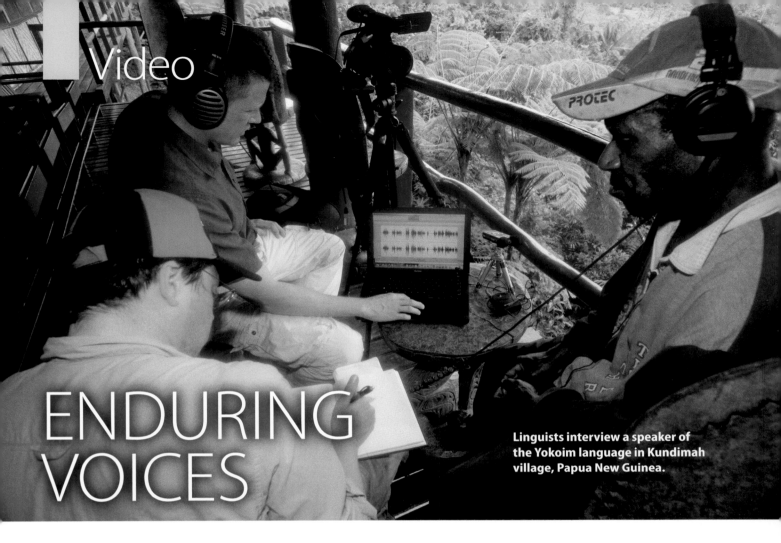

Video

ENDURING VOICES

Linguists interview a speaker of the Yokoim language in Kundimah village, Papua New Guinea.

BEFORE VIEWING

A Look at the photo and read the caption. What are the researchers doing? Why do you think they are doing this? Discuss with a partner.

PREDICTING

B Read the information about the Living Tongues Institute. Then answer the questions.

LEARNING ABOUT THE TOPIC

Half of the world's 7,000 languages may disappear in the next few decades, but linguists from the Living Tongues Institute are working hard to save them and the important historical and cultural information they contain. In one town in India, researchers observed that the younger generation was not speaking the traditional language of their parents. Young people tend to use global languages such as English or Hindi.

1. Why is the Living Tongues Institute trying to save dying languages?

_____

2. Why do you think the younger generation in that Indian town is no longer speaking the traditional language?

_____

C The words in **bold** below are used in the video. Read the sentences. Then match the correct form of each word to its definition.

> Young people are **abandoning** the languages of their parents and speaking more dominant languages.
>
> When people no longer use a language, language **extinction** occurs.
>
> India has great linguistic **diversity**—it has more than 22 official languages.
>
> If people **neglect** their native languages, the languages will eventually be forgotten.

1. _____ (n) a variety

2. _____ (v) to not give attention to

3. _____ (v) to give up something completely

4. _____ (n) a situation in which something no longer exists

WHILE VIEWING

A ▶ Watch the video. Complete the summary with suitable words.

The Enduring Voices project was created to bring attention to the issue of language loss around the world. In [1]_____ , linguists on the team spoke with a man who is probably [2]_____ of his language. The team then went to the village of Hong in northeast India, where it collected information on Apatani—a language now mostly used by [3]_____ . The team hopes that by creating a [4]_____ of these dying languages, it is able to keep them alive.

B ▶ Watch the video again. Circle T for true, F for false, or NG if the information is not given.

1. Northeast India is a language hot spot.   T F NG

2. Younger people in Hong prefer to speak in English and Hindi   T F NG
   because they want to move out of the village.

3. Only one speaker of Apatani is left in the village of Hong.   T F NG

4. The team taught the villagers how to use the technology kit   T F NG
   so they can continue to keep a record of their traditional language.

AFTER VIEWING

A Do you think recording the words and phrases of a language is enough to keep it alive? Why or why not? Discuss with a partner.

B Does the language trend shown in the video support the predictions about language in Reading 1? Why or why not? Discuss with a partner.

Reading 2

PREPARING TO READ

A The words and phrases in blue below are used in Reading 2. Complete the sentences with the correct words and phrases. Use a dictionary to help you.

BUILDING VOCABULARY

combined	critically	died out	express	rate
roughly	highly	political	rapidly	perspective

1. The total number of native speakers of Mandarin Chinese currently exceeds the _____ number of native English speakers and Arabic speakers.

2. According to a 2015 study, the current _____ of species extinction is _____ 100 times higher than in the past; within this century, at least a dozen species have _____ completely.

3. Conservationists are working to preserve the last Sumatran tigers as there are fewer than 700 left in the wild. The species is _____ endangered.

4. According to a 2014 study, the ability to _____ yourself in French will become a _____ valued skill for anyone doing business in Africa. This is because the population of French-speaking people in sub-Saharan Africa is expected to grow _____ in the coming decades.

5. From one _____ , it is an advantage if everyone in the world speaks the same language; another viewpoint is that it will reduce cultural diversity.

6. The status of languages can be influenced by _____ decisions, such as when governments choose to promote or ban minority languages in schools.

B Discuss these questions with a partner.

USING VOCABULARY

1. Aside from speaking and writing, how else do people **express** themselves?
2. If you want to learn a new language **rapidly**, what should you do?

C Look at the questions in the three headings of the reading passage. Note some possible answers for each one and share with a partner. Then check your ideas as you read.

PREDICTING

_____

_____

_____

VANISHING VOICES

Johnny Hill, Jr. is one of the last speakers of Chemehuevi, an endangered Native American language.

🎧 2.08

A   The Earth's population of seven billion people speaks roughly 7,000 languages. However, there is a very unequal distribution in the number of people who speak these languages. In fact, just 85 of them are spoken by 78 percent of the world's population. And the least common 3,500 languages are spoken by fewer than 9 million people combined. For example, there are only 235,000 speakers of Tuvan, the native language of the Republic of Tuva in the Russian Federation. And there are fewer than 2,000 known speakers of Aka, a language from Arunachal Pradesh in northeastern India.

B   Many of these smaller languages are disappearing rapidly. More than 1,000 are listed as critically or severely endangered. In fact, it is estimated that a language "dies" every 14 days. According to linguists, within the next century, nearly half of the world's current languages will disappear as communities abandon native tongues in favor of English, Mandarin, or Spanish. But should we be concerned about language extinction? And what can we do to prevent it?

HOW DO LANGUAGES DIE?

C   Since humans first started to communicate with each other, languages have come and gone. The languages of powerful groups have spread, while the languages of smaller cultures have disappeared. Today, languages dominate not only because they are spoken by powerful groups, but also because of how they are used. For example, languages like English are commonly used on television, on the Internet, and in international business.

In an increasingly globalized age, languages spoken in remote places are no longer protected from dominant world languages. Languages such as Mandarin, English, Russian, Hindi, Spanish, and Arabic reach into tiny communities and compete with smaller languages. When one language dominates, children from nondominant language groups tend to lose their native languages as they grow up,
D go to school, and get jobs. Sometimes they don't want to speak the less dominant languages, partly because they think that speaking these languages makes it difficult to succeed. These attitudes, along with the strong desire to fit in, threaten the survival of native languages. Political pressure can also affect the survival of smaller languages. Governments sometimes pass laws that require people to use dominant languages at school, at work, and in the media.

WHY SHOULD WE BE CONCERNED?

Why is the extinction of a language with a small number of speakers a concern? Different languages express unique perspectives on the world. For example, languages can show us how a culture experiences basic concepts such as time, numbers, and colors. The Pirahã, an Amazonian tribe, appear to have no words
E for numbers. Instead, they get by with quantity words such as *few* and *many*. This suggests that numbers may be an invention of culture, and not an idea that humans are born with. The way that people think of colors also depends on their language. For example, the Candoshi language in Peru uses one word to describe shades of green, blue, and purple. However, it has a separate word for dark green.

The loss of a language also means the loss of knowledge, similar to the possibility of losing a future miracle drug[1] if a species dies out. For example, the Seri in the Sonoran Desert of Mexico have terms for more than 300 desert plants.
F By studying their language, scientists learned about a highly nutritious[2] food source similar to wheat, called *eelgrass*. Scientists have also learned a lot about the habitats and behaviors of local animals. There are only 650 to 1,000 Seri speakers left, so by losing the language we might lose important scientific knowledge.

[1] A **miracle drug** is a treatment for a disease that is surprisingly effective and safe.
[2] Something that is **nutritious** is healthy.

Language Hot Spots

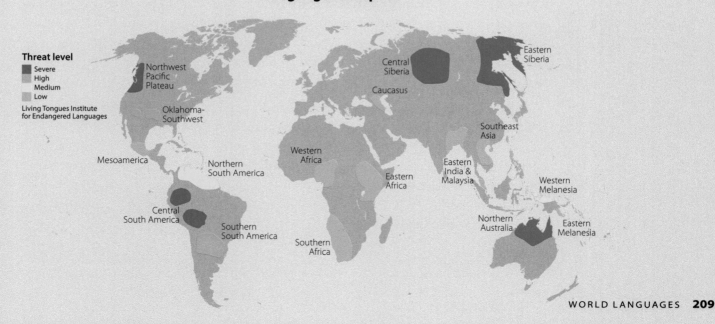

The Seri have more than 50 terms for family relationships, such as between two cousins.

If languages continue to vanish at today's rapid rate, we may lose knowledge about plants that could someday lead to useful drugs. We may also lose information about the history and skills of many of the world's cultures. In Micronesia, for example, some sailors can find their way across miles of ocean without using any maps or modern equipment. Sadly, their skills and knowledge are encoded in languages that are at risk of disappearing.

HOW CAN WE SAVE DYING LANGUAGES?

Fortunately, groups around the world are working to bring threatened languages back to life. These groups are giving people more opportunity to use these threatened languages, and are changing the attitudes that caused people to stop using them. One group that is helping to preserve disappearing languages is the Enduring Voices Project. This project works to identify language hot spots—places with languages that are both unique and at risk of disappearing. The Enduring Voices Project has two goals: to accurately document the languages of these places and to record the cultural information they contain.

Projects such as these are very important to the survival of endangered languages. The work of these groups will allow us to pass on a wealth of historical, cultural, and scientific knowledge to future generations. As Enduring Voices team member K. David Harrison says, it would be wrong for us to think that "we have nothing to learn from people who just a generation ago were hunter-gatherers[3] ... What they know—which we've forgotten or never knew—may someday save us."

[3] **Hunter-gatherers** are people who live by hunting and collecting food rather than by farming.

UNDERSTANDING THE READING

A Choose the main idea of each section in the reading passage.

UNDERSTANDING MAIN IDEAS

1. **How Do Languages Die?**
   a. It's difficult for less dominant languages to spread and grow because their speakers often live in areas that are more remote.
   b. A greater number of people today are choosing to speak widely used languages such as English and Mandarin over their native languages.

2. **Why Should We Be Concerned?**
   a. When a language disappears, we lose knowledge and culture that is specific to that language.
   b. Scientists believe that information from speakers of smaller languages can help them find a miracle drug.

3. **How Can We Save Dying Languages?**
   a. Some groups are encouraging the use of minority languages and recording them.
   b. Some groups are building centers that teach minority languages to younger generations of speakers.

B Look back at the reading passage to find answers to the questions below.

UNDERSTANDING DETAILS

1. What do linguists predict will happen to the world's languages in the next 100 years? Why?

   _____

2. What are three factors that contribute to the death of languages?

   _____

   _____

3. Why is the work done by the Enduring Voices Project important? Give one reason.

   _____

C Look at the map in the reading passage and answer the questions.

INTERPRETING VISUAL INFORMATION

1. What does the map show?
   a. how many languages are disappearing
   b. the areas where languages are at risk of disappearing
   c. the places the Enduring Voices team is working

2. Which areas in the world have languages that are under severe threat?

   _____

   _____

3. Why do you think languages in these areas are facing the greatest threat? Discuss with a partner.

D Complete the concept map about the effects of language loss according to the reading passage.

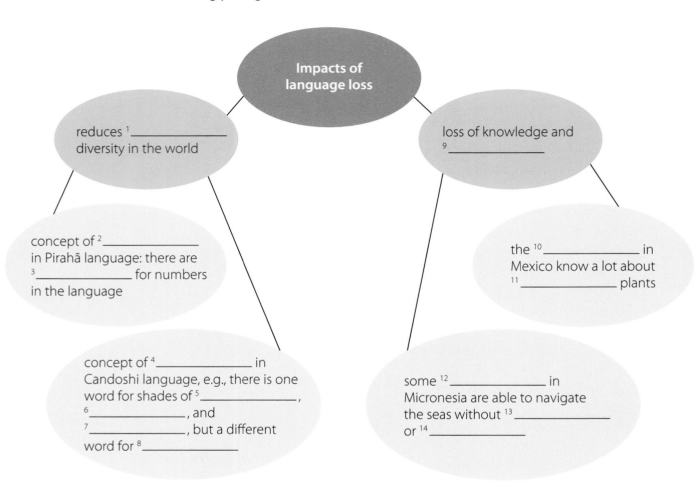

Impacts of language loss

reduces ¹_____ diversity in the world

concept of ²_____ in Pirahã language: there are ³_____ for numbers in the language

concept of ⁴_____ in Candoshi language, e.g., there is one word for shades of ⁵_____, ⁶_____, and ⁷_____, but a different word for ⁸_____

loss of knowledge and ⁹_____

the ¹⁰_____ in Mexico know a lot about ¹¹_____ plants

some ¹²_____ in Micronesia are able to navigate the seas without ¹³_____ or ¹⁴_____

E Find and underline the predictions in paragraphs B, F, and G. Then write the word that the author uses to express the level of certainty of each one.

1. a certain prediction in paragraph B   _____
2. a less certain prediction in paragraph F   _____
3. a less certain prediction in paragraph G   _____

F The writer makes an argument in favor of saving disappearing languages. Which of the counterarguments below are the most convincing? Can you think of any other counterarguments? Discuss with a partner.

☐ 1. Children will be at a disadvantage if they do not learn the dominant language of their region.

☐ 2. Groups of people in a region who speak different languages might have difficulty cooperating politically and economically. This could lead to misunderstanding or conflict.

☐ 3. Traveling around the world to record speakers of disappearing languages is expensive. The money for this should be used for more important purposes, such as protecting an animal species.

Writing

EXPLORING WRITTEN ENGLISH

WRITING SKILL Planning an Essay Using a T-Chart

Using a T-chart can help you plan a persuasive essay. List and organize the supporting information for your arguments on both sides of the chart. Your chart should include the main arguments as well as supporting details for each argument. For a persuasive essay, include relevant facts and examples from expert sources as part of your supporting details. Take notes—don't write in complete sentences.

Example:

Pros	Cons
• Idea 1	• Idea 1
○ Fact	○ Example
• Idea 2	• Idea 2
○ Quote (source)	○ Detail

Once you have completed your T-chart, you can choose arguments (and counterarguments) that support your position on an issue.

A Complete the T-chart with the notes below. Then add one more pro and con based on what you have learned in this unit.

COMPLETING A T-CHART

- 898 mil. native Mandarin speakers; Eng. only 372 mil.
- Eng. as 1st lang. will be spoken by only 5% of pop. in 2050 (Graddol)
- 90% of scientific lit. is in Eng. (Montgomery)
- Important in media
- Mandarin becoming more important
- Over 500 mil. English Internet users (Internet World Stats)
- English declining as 1st language
- Important in science

Issue: Everyone should learn English.	
Pros	**Cons**
•	•
○	○
•	•
○	○
•	•

B Work with a partner. Think of both sides of the issue below. Write at least two pros and two cons. Then choose the side that you think is stronger.

Issue: Everyone should start learning a second language at the age of three.	
Pros	**Cons**
•	•
•	•

C Read the sentence from a persuasive essay and answer the questions.

Although it may be difficult for immigrant children to maintain both their native language and the dominant language of their new country, their parents should encourage them to be bilingual.

1. What are the two sides of the argument the writer presents?

   Argument 1: _____

   Argument 2: _____

2. Which is the writer's main argument?

   _____

LANGUAGE FOR WRITING Presenting Counterarguments

Arguments in a persuasive essay are more convincing and balanced when writers present and then refute the counterarguments—the arguments on the other side of the issue. Writers introduce counterarguments using **concession words and phrases** such as *while, even though*, and *although*.

COUNTERARGUMENT

While *flying around the world to record speakers of disappearing languages may be expensive, protecting the valuable knowledge these languages contain is worth it.*

WRITER'S ARGUMENT

In addition, writers often use modals such as *may, might,* and *could* when presenting counterarguments to show that these arguments are weaker—less likely or certain—than their own arguments. Writers sometimes also present their own arguments with modals such as *must, have to,* and *should* to show that their arguments are stronger.

WEAKER

*While saving endangered languages **may** preserve some cultural or scientific information, we **must not** discourage children from learning the dominant language of their region.* STRONGER

D Look back at the arguments in exercise C and answer the questions below.

ANALYZING ARGUMENTS

1. Which word introduces the counterargument? _____

2. Which modal introduces the writer's main argument? _____

E Combine the sentences (1–3) using concession words. Add modals to the underlined verbs in the counterarguments.

PRESENTING COUNTERARGUMENTS

Example: Argument: Not everyone can be effectively multilingual.

Counterargument: Being multilingual <u>is</u> an important skill today.

Although being multilingual may be an important skill today, not everyone can be effectively multilingual.

1. Argument: Most children should learn Mandarin as a second language.

Counterargument: English <u>is</u> useful in some situations.

_____

_____

2. Argument: Mandarin is useful in the world of business.

Counterargument: Mandarin <u>is</u> difficult to learn.

_____

_____

3. Argument: We must preserve smaller languages because of the important knowledge they contain.

Counterargument: Language diversity <u>leads to</u> misunderstanding or conflict.

_____

_____

F Choose a point (pro or con) in exercise B and a related counterargument. Combine them into a sentence using concession words and modals.

WRITING A COUNTERARGUMENT

_____

_____

_____

WRITING TASK

GOAL You are going to write a persuasive essay on the following topic:
Everyone in the world should speak the same language. Do you agree or disagree?

BRAINSTORMING **A** Think of arguments for both sides of the essay topic. Use a T-chart to make notes.

PLANNING **B** Follow these steps to plan your essay.

Step 1 Choose the side of the issue that you want to defend in your essay. Research information that strengthens your position.

Step 2 Choose arguments to support your position and use them to write your thesis statement in the outline.

Step 3 Write a topic sentence for each body paragraph.

Step 4 Use your research notes to write one or two supporting details for each argument.

Step 5 Use information from your T-chart to add counterarguments.

Step 6 Write a summary statement and add a final thought.

OUTLINE

Introductory Paragraph

Thesis Statement: _____

_____

Body Paragraphs

Topic Sentence 1: _____

_____

Details: _____

_____

Counterargument 1: _____

Topic Sentence 2: _____

_____

Details: _____

_____

Counterargument 2: _____

Concluding Paragraph

Summary Statement: _____

_____

Final Thought: _____

FIRST DRAFT **C** Use the information in the outline to write a first draft of your essay.

REVISING PRACTICE

The draft below is a persuasive essay about whether companies should employ multilingual workers or train existing workers to be multilingual. Follow the steps to create a better second draft.

1. Add the sentences (a–c) in the most suitable spaces.
   a. Another reason is that language learning is far too time-consuming.
   b. If businesses hire people who are fluent in more than one language, they won't only save time and money, they will also have a diverse workforce with many points of view.
   c. While it may be possible to become fluent in a second language as an adult, experts believe that age greatly affects our language learning ability.

2. Now fix the following problems (d–f) in the essay.
   d. Add a modal to weaken a counterargument in paragraph B.
   e. Cross out a sentence that doesn't belong in paragraph B.
   f. Add a missing concession word in paragraph C.

A

Speaking a second language is an important skill in today's global economy. An employee who can do business in more than one language is a valuable asset to most companies. However, companies should hire employees who are already bi- or trilingual rather than train them. Corporations should not pay for their employees to learn a second language because some people may not have the ability to learn another language, and the process takes too much time.

B

One reason companies should not pay for their employees to learn a second language is that some people may not be capable of learning an extra language. _____ According to the Ets-Hokin Center for Language Acquisition, research shows that "people's ability to learn a foreign language deteriorates as they age." Studies also show that people have a harder time learning to play an instrument when they are older. In addition, memorization is an important part of language learning. Even though an employee performs their job well, it does not mean that they have a good enough memory to retain information needed to learn a second language.

C

_____ Some language programs promise fluency in a short period of time, the average language learner needs constant and long-term exposure to a second language in order to become even somewhat fluent. For example, according to the article "How Long Does It Take to Learn a New Language?," a typical employee taking two hours off work each day to study a language would take several years to become even relatively fluent. From a financial perspective, it is more cost-effective to have that employee do their job for those two hours a day.

D

The fact that language learning is time-consuming and that there is a risk that some learners will fail in their attempt indicate that it isn't a good idea for companies to invest in language training. Rather, it is more cost-effective to hire employees who are already bi- or trilingual. _____

D Now use the questions below to revise your essay.

- ☐ Does your introduction have a clear thesis statement?
- ☐ Did you include a counterargument for each argument?
- ☐ Do all your sentences relate to your overall argument?
- ☐ Does your concluding paragraph have a summary statement and a final thought?

EDITING PRACTICE

Read the information below.

In sentences with concession words and modals, remember to use:
- a comma after the concession clause.
- a subject and a verb in both clauses.
- the base form of a verb after a modal.
- a weaker modal to present counterarguments, and stronger ones for the main arguments.

Correct one mistake with concession words and modals in each sentence (1–3).

1. While language instruction may being expensive, it is important that children learn a second language in order to compete in the global economy.

2. Even though Mandarin may soon become an important world language, probably will be challenging for learners to learn its writing system.

3. Although French was an important language in the past it shouldn't be an official UN language; there are just too few native speakers.

FINAL DRAFT **E** Follow these steps to write a final draft.

1. Check your revised draft for mistakes with words and expressions that present counterarguments.
2. Now use the checklist on page 253 to write a final draft. Make any other necessary changes.

UNIT REVIEW
Answer the following questions.

1. Do you think we should save dying languages? Why or why not?

_____

_____

_____

2. What are some examples of concession words?

_____

_____

_____

3. Do you remember the meanings of these words? Check (✔) the ones you know. Look back at the unit and review the ones you don't know.

Reading 1:
- ☐ acquire **AWL**
- ☐ anticipate **AWL**
- ☐ competence
- ☐ considerably **AWL**
- ☐ constitute **AWL**
- ☐ expand **AWL**
- ☐ furthermore **AWL**
- ☐ lead to
- ☐ linguistic
- ☐ native

Reading 2:
- ☐ combine
- ☐ critically
- ☐ die out
- ☐ express
- ☐ highly
- ☐ perspective **AWL**
- ☐ political
- ☐ rapidly
- ☐ rate
- ☐ roughly

SURVIVAL INSTINCT

10

According to Yellowstone National Park, the chances of a park visitor being injured by a grizzly bear are 1 in 2.7 million.

ACADEMIC SKILLS

READING	Identifying adverbial phrases
WRITING	Writing a descriptive narrative essay
GRAMMAR	Using past forms for narratives
CRITICAL THINKING	Interpreting figurative language

THINK AND DISCUSS

1. Do you know of anyone who has experienced a dangerous situation? What happened?
2. What kind of people do you think are most likely to survive dangerous situations?

A Look at the information on these pages and answer the questions.

1. What makes K2 difficult to climb?
2. What do you think is significant about the Pakistani side of the mountain?
3. Why do you think K2 is called the "savage mountain"?

B Match the correct form of the words in blue to their definitions.

_____ (n) a trip made for a specific purpose

_____ (n) a surface that is at an angle

_____ (n) the top of a mountain

THE SAVAGE MOUNTAIN

K2 is unique in high-altitude mountaineering. Although shorter than Mount Everest (Mount Qomolangma) by about 240 meters, it has long been known as "the mountaineer's mountain." Its distinctive shape—a towering, triangular silhouette with steep slopes—makes it the classic image of a mountain. But it also makes K2 one of the most difficult and dangerous to climb.

By 2010, Everest had been climbed more than 5,000 times; in contrast, K2 had been successfully climbed just over 300 times. For every four climbers who've succeeded, one K2 climber has died. Charles Houston and Robert Bates titled the account of their failed 1953 expedition *K2: The Savage Mountain*. A year later, K2 was finally "conquered" by an Italian expedition that put two men on the top via the Pakistani side of the mountain.

The diagram on these pages shows the route taken by the 2011 K2 North Pillar Expedition. Most attempts to reach the summit of K2 come from the Pakistani side; the approach via the north side is even more challenging, and rarely attempted.

K2 North Glacier

N

To Advanced Base Camp
Altitude 4,650 m

SUMMIT
8,611 meters (28,251 ft)

Japanese Couloir

Bivouac site
8,300 m
August 22

CAMP IV
7,950 m
August 21

Tent site
7,900 m

CAMP III
7,250 m
August 20

Tent site
7,300 m

CAMP II
6,600 m
August 19

Shoulder Depot Camp
6,250 m
August 18

Middle Camp
5,950 m

North Ridge

Northwest Ridge

CAMP I
5,300 m
Summit push: August 16-17

Reading 1

PREPARING TO READ

BUILDING VOCABULARY

A The words in **blue** below are used in Reading 1. Read the paragraphs about a climbing expedition. Then match the correct form of each word to its definition.

On November 8, 2014, three climbers set out to reach the summit of one of the highest peaks in Southeast Asia: Myanmar's Hkakabo Razi. To travel as lightly as possible on their final day, they left their food and **gear** behind at their camp. It was a decision that would determine the **fate** of the expedition.

Their final **task** was to complete the last few kilometers to the summit. But after four hours of climbing, they were still not close enough. Climber Cory Richards still **recalls** his **sensation** of fear as the team neared the peak: "I think we should turn around now." If the team carried on, he realized, they would have to spend a **terrifying** night on the mountain with no tents, sleeping bags, or food. The team agreed to end its expedition and to **descend** Hkakabo Razi the next day.

Climber Renan Ozturk feels they made the right choice: "The decision is, do you want to push hard enough to lose your toes, your fingers, or your life? That's always the trick with Himalayan climbing. You have to be good enough to know [when] to turn around."

1. _____ (v) to go down

2. _____ (v) to remember

3. _____ (n) a feeling or emotional state

4. _____ (adj) extremely frightening

5. _____ (n) an assignment; a job to be performed

6. _____ (n) equipment; usually used with outdoor activities

7. _____ (n) a result or an outcome that is beyond your control

USING VOCABULARY

B Discuss these questions with a partner.

1. What aspect of climbing a high-altitude mountain might be most **terrifying**?

2. What **gear** would be needed for climbing a mountain like Hkakabo Razi or K2?

SKIMMING

C Skim the reading passage. What kind of reading is it? Discuss your idea with a partner. Then check your answer as you read.

a. a work of fiction   b. a scientific article   c. a true story

The expedition members climb a steep edge of K2's North Ridge.

DEADLY SUMMIT

🎧 2.09

A   During the summer of 2011, a team of climbers attempted to climb the world's second highest peak—K2. Their goal was to climb the North Ridge on the Chinese side of the mountain without bottled oxygen or high-altitude porters.[1]

B   The team included two Kazakh climbers, an Argentinian photographer, and a videographer from Poland. All four had attempted K2 climbs before, but none had yet reached the peak. The fifth member, Gerlinde Kaltenbrunner, was a 40-year-old former nurse from Austria. If she succeeded, she would be the first woman in history to climb all of the world's tallest peaks without supplemental oxygen. Gerlinde was leading the **expedition** with her husband, Ralf Dujmovits, 49, who had previously reached the **summit** of K2 from the Pakistani side.

C   Starting on July 5, the six climbers established a series of camps, connected by thousands of feet of rope. These would give the expedition members places to rest during their ascent. To establish the route, they had to cope with vertical rock walls, avalanches,[2] and **slopes** covered in chest-deep snow.

D   On August 16, the team started the actual climb to the summit. Two days later, at around 6:30 a.m., Ralf stopped. The snow conditions were becoming dangerous, and he could no longer ignore his gut instinct.[3] "Gerlinde, I am going back," he said.

E   On their first climb together, Gerlinde and Ralf had made an agreement: neither would stand in the other's way if one wanted to continue and the other did not. Gerlinde had never been to the top of K2, so she was willing to take risks that Ralf was not. She coped with fear differently, too. Ralf liked

[1]A **porter** is someone who helps carry your bags or equipment.

[2]An **avalanche** is a mass of snow, ice, and rocks that falls down a mountainside.

[3]**Gut instinct** is a feeling you have that you can't explain logically.

how the sensation of fear in his stomach acted as a warning, compelling him to pay attention. Gerlinde strove to block out fear with a quiet calm. If she kept herself completely focused on the task at hand,[4] she didn't feel scared.

But now Ralf begged his wife to come down with him. "Ralf was yelling that the route is very, very avalanche prone. He was shouting desperately," recalled Maxut Zhumayev, one of the Kazakh climbers. "Gerlinde shouted in return that now is the moment when the fate of the climb will be decided." She was concerned that if they turned around now, they would miss the period of good weather.

"I was really afraid I would never see her again," Ralf explained later.

Gerlinde watched as Ralf descended into the mist. Then she focused on the task ahead. "It's not that I was indifferent to the risk," she said afterward. "But my gut feeling was good."

As Ralf had feared, the snow was becoming loose. Later that day, a small avalanche hit Tommy Heinrich, the Argentinian, who was climbing below the others; it knocked him upside down and stuffed[5] his nose and mouth. Only the fixed rope kept him from being swept off the mountain. He eventually dug himself out, but decided that he, too, would turn back.

So now they were four: Gerlinde, Maxut and Vassiliy (the two Kazakh climbers), and the videographer, Dariusz. The team spent a miserable night crammed into a two-person tent. Two days later, on August 20, they reached Camp III, exhausted and chilled to the bone. They drank coffee with honey and warmed their hands and feet over their gas stoves. All night the frosted tent walls snapped in the wind.

The weather improved on Sunday, August 21, helping to carry the team to Camp IV. They were now at nearly 8,000 meters, in the so-called death zone. Here the body struggles to deal with the oxygen-thin air. Cognition is affected, and even simple tasks seem to take forever. The team checked their gear and melted snow for water. Below them, a terrifying void[6] plunged nearly two miles to the glacier below. Two thousand feet above was the glistening white summit.

"There was a moment when we all started to get nervous, in a good way," Gerlinde said later. "We touched each other's hands and looked at each other in the eyes and said, 'OK, tomorrow is our day.'"

On August 22, they were greeted by a cloudless day, the weather like a gift. The gales were gone, and the sky ran blue and cloudless. But with only a third of the oxygen at sea level, snow up to their chests in places, and stinging blasts of icy wind, the climbers made painfully slow progress. By 1 p.m., they had gained less than 180 meters.

From Advanced Base Camp, Ralf guided them by phone and watched as their figures, no bigger than commas on a piece of paper, edged toward the peak. After climbing for 12 hours, they were just 300 meters below the summit. On the radio, Ralf urged Gerlinde to return to Camp IV for the night now that they had broken the trail and knew the way.

"You cannot sleep there, you cannot relax," he said.

"Ralf," said Gerlinde, "we are here. We don't want to go back."

With the sun low in the west, the team stopped to put up a tiny tent on the edge of a crevasse.[7] After an hour of hacking at the ice, they had a platform four feet wide. They secured the tent with ice axes, and by 8:15 they were sitting inside, a stove hanging from the ceiling with a pot of melting snow. The temperature was minus 25 Celsius. They would rest until morning, then resume the push for the prize, now so close.

---

[4]If something is **at hand**, it is in front of you or is the thing you are now dealing with.

[5]To **stuff** something is to fill or block it up.

[6]A **void** is an empty space.

[7]A **crevasse** is a deep crack, especially in ice or a snow-covered mountain.

They set out around 7 a.m. as another clear morning dawned. By mid-afternoon, they reached the base of a ramp beneath the summit ridge. For the first 20 meters, the snow only covered their shins. But soon the snow became chest deep. "Oh no," Gerlinde thought, "it's not possible that we've come so far up and will have to turn back…" With a surge of energy and hope, she finally crawled out of the ramp and onto the ridge. It was 4:35 p.m. She could see the summit dome.

"You can make it!" Ralf cried over the radio. "You can make it! But you are late! Take care!"

She sipped from her water bottle. Her throat was cracked; it hurt to swallow. It was too cold to sweat, and she was dehydrated just from panting for air.

And then she walked the final steps to the apex of K2, reaching the summit at 6:18 p.m.

She wanted to share the moment with Ralf, but when she opened the radio, she couldn't speak. There were mountains in every direction. Mountains she had climbed. Mountains that had stolen the lives of friends and nearly claimed hers, too. Alone, with the world at her feet, she turned from one point of the compass to another.

Fifteen minutes later, Maxut and Vassiliy arrived, shoulder to shoulder, followed by Dariusz. Everyone embraced. It was 7 p.m. Dariusz filmed Gerlinde as she tried to explain what it meant to be there at that moment. She began to cry, then composed herself. "It was very, very hard, … and now it's just amazing." She gestured to the sea of peaks in all directions, as a golden light began to burnish[8] the world. "You see all this—I think everybody can understand why we do this."

[8] When you **burnish** something, such as metal, you rub it or polish it to make it shiny.

Members of the 2011 K2 expedition team take their final steps toward the summit.

UNDERSTANDING THE READING

SUMMARIZING **A** Complete the summary of the reading passage. Write no more than two words in each space.

In the summer of [1]_____, a team of mountain climbers attempted to climb [2]_____. The team consisted of [3]_____ climbers, including one woman, Gerlinde Kaltenbrunner. First, they set up a number of [4]_____ along a ridge on the north side of the mountain. Then they began their ascent. The climb soon became dangerous, and [5]_____ climbers eventually decided to turn back, including Gerlinde's [6]_____, Ralf Dujmovits. After a few days, the [7]_____ improved, allowing the climbers to reach an altitude known as the [8]_____. They pushed on and finally reached the summit on August 23. Gerlinde became the [9]_____ to climb all of the world's highest peaks without using extra [10]_____.

UNDERSTANDING
MAIN IDEAS **B** How did the climbers respond to fear during the climb? Check (✓) four statements that best summarize the information in paragraphs D–H.

☐ 1. Gerlinde and Ralf reacted differently to their fears.

☐ 2. Most of the climbers were concerned and wanted to turn back.

☐ 3. Ralf felt fear and knew he should return to base camp.

☐ 4. Gerlinde blocked out her fear and focused on climbing.

☐ 5. Ralf was keen that the other team members continue.

☐ 6. Gerlinde was prepared to take risks that Ralf would not.

SEQUENCING **C** Put the events (a–h) of the climb in order on the timeline.

a. The team members get to Camp III.

b. The team members enter the "death zone."

c. The team starts the climb to the summit.

d. The weather turns bad, and Ralf quits the climb.

e. The team begins setting up camps along the route.

f. The team members get within 300 meters of the summit.

g. Gerlinde and other team members reach the summit.

h. An avalanche hits Tommy Heinrich, and he decides to drop out.

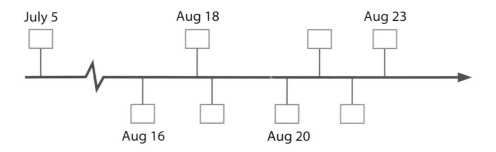

D Find and underline the following words in **bold** in the reading passage. Use context to identify their meanings. Then match each word to its definition. INFERRING MEANING

_____ 1. **supplemental** (paragraph B)   a. sloped downward at a steep angle

_____ 2. **indifferent** (paragraph H)   b. the top or summit

_____ 3. **crammed** (paragraph J)   c. additional

_____ 4. **plunged** (paragraph K)   d. not feeling concerned

_____ 5. **apex** (paragraph U)   e. put in with too many other people or things in a space that is too small

---

CRITICAL THINKING   If a sentence or phrase doesn't make sense literally, it might be an example of **figurative language**. For example, in paragraph E, Gerlinde and Ralf agreed not to "stand in each other's way." This means that they agreed not to stop each other from doing what they wanted. You can look for clues in the context of a sentence to help you understand the meaning of figurative language.

E Think about the meaning of the underlined parts of these excerpts. Then discuss your answers to the questions with a partner. CRITICAL THINKING: INTERPRETING FIGURATIVE LANGUAGE

1. "On August 22, they were greeted by a cloudless day, the weather <u>like a gift</u>."

   Why did the good weather feel like a gift to the climbers?

   _____

   _____

2. "Ralf guided them by phone and watched as their figures, <u>no bigger than commas on a piece of paper</u>, edged toward the peak."

   Why does the writer compare the human figures with commas on paper?

   _____

   _____

3. "<u>Mountains that had stolen the lives of friends</u> and nearly claimed hers, too."

   What happened to some of Gerlinde's friends? How might this have affected her feelings toward these mountains?

   _____

   _____

F Look back at Gerlinde's quote in the final paragraph. Do you think the reward that mountaineers get is worth the risk? Why or why not? CRITICAL THINKING: REFLECTING

I don't think the risk is worth it because …

I think it's worth the risk. Mountain climbing …

DEVELOPING READING SKILLS

> **READING SKILL** Identifying Adverbial Phrases
>
> Adverbs (e.g., *quickly*, *today*) give more information about an action or event, such as *when*, *why*, *where*, or *how* something happens. An **adverbial phrase** is a group of words that acts like an adverb. It can modify verbs, adjectives, adverbs, clauses, and even entire sentences. However, it is different from a clause because it does not contain a subject and a verb.
>
> Reason (why):
>
>   *The team stopped <u>to put up a tiny tent</u>.*
>
> Note: The infinitive phrase is used as an adverbial phrase instead of an object of the verb in this example. To differentiate between the two uses, replace the infinitive phrase with *in order to*. An infinitive phrase functioning as an adverbial can be replaced with *in order to*.
>
>   *The team stopped in order to put up a tiny tent.* (adverbial phrase)
>
>   *The team decided to put up a tent.* (object)
>
> Manner (how):
>
>   *They secured the tent <u>with ice axes</u>.*
>
> Time (when):
>
>   *<u>By 8:15</u>, they were sitting inside …*

IDENTIFYING
ADVERBIAL PHRASES

A Underline the adverbial phrases in these excerpts from the reading passage.

1. During the summer of 2011, a team of climbers attempted to climb the world's second highest peak. _____

2. Their goal was to climb the North Ridge on the Chinese side of the mountain. _____

3. To establish the route, they had to cope with vertical rock walls, avalanches, … _____

4. If she succeeded, she would be the first woman in history to climb all of the world's tallest peaks without supplemental oxygen. _____

5. On their first climb together, Gerlinde and Ralf had made an agreement. _____

6. Below them, a terrifying void plunged to the glacier below. _____

7. But … the climbers made painfully slow progress. _____

8. They would rest until morning, then resume the push for the prize. _____

9. With a surge of energy and hope, she finally crawled onto the ridge. _____

10. Fifteen minutes later, Maxut and Vassiliy arrived, … _____

IDENTIFYING
ADVERBIAL PHRASES

B Look at each adverbial phrase that you underlined in exercise A. Identify the purpose of each phrase. Write *when*, *why*, *where*, or *how* on the lines.

APPLYING

C Find three more examples of adverbial phrases in the reading passage and note the kinds of information they provide.

Video

Although shark attacks can be dangerous, they rarely occur.

SURVIVAL LESSONS

BEFORE VIEWING

A What do you think you should do in these situations? Discuss your ideas with a partner.   PREDICTING

1. If a shark attacks you, you should _____ .

   a. splash violently   b. attack its eyes   c. pretend to be dead

2. If an elephant is charging toward you, you should _____ .

   a. run between its legs   b. turn and run   c. scream and yell

B Read the information below. Then answer the questions with a partner.   LEARNING ABOUT THE TOPIC

Animal	Number of People Killed (annually)
mosquitoes	725,000
snakes	50,000
crocodiles	1,000
elephants	500
deer	120
bees	53
sharks	10

1. Why do you think mosquitoes kill so many more people than sharks?

   _____

2. Which of these animals are you most worried about? Why?

   _____

VOCABULARY
IN CONTEXT

C Below are some quotes from the video. Match each **bold** phrase to its definition.

"The probability of getting killed is much lower if you **stand your ground** than if you run."

"[…] if he really wants to, he can **catch up** to you, and you don't want to run away."

"A limp body tells the shark it's time to **tuck in** for a big meal."

1. _____ (v) to eat and enjoy
2. _____ (v) to stay where you are and refuse to move
3. _____ (v) to move faster in order to reach someone or something

WHILE VIEWING

UNDERSTANDING
MAIN IDEAS

A ▶ Watch the video. What is the main idea?

a. that sharks and elephants are usually scared of people

b. how to survive if you encounter shark and elephant attacks

c. that shark and elephant attacks are becoming less common

UNDERSTANDING
DETAILS

B ▶ Watch the video again. For each statement, circle T for true or F for false.

1.	Most species of shark are man-eaters.	T	F
2.	Sharks usually bite because they are hungry.	T	F
3.	A shark may swim away if you hit its gills.	T	F
4.	Elephants show their ears to give a warning.	T	F
5.	You should not show your back to an elephant.	T	F
6.	Elephants can run faster than humans.	T	F

AFTER VIEWING

REACTING TO
THE VIDEO

A Look back at your answers to exercise A in Before Viewing. Did you choose the same options as the advice in the video? Did you find the answers surprising? Discuss with a partner.

_____

_____

REFLECTING

B Do you know any other survival tips for encounters with wild animals? Discuss with a partner.

_____

_____

Reading 2

PREPARING TO READ

A The words and phrases in **blue** below are used in Reading 2. Complete each sentence with the correct word or phrase. Use a dictionary to help you.

BUILDING VOCABULARY

alter	assume	consciously	crisis	demonstrate
determination	instantly	separate	take over	version

1. A _____ of something is one form of it.

2. When you _____ something, you change it.

3. A _____ is a very serious or dangerous situation.

4. When you _____ a situation, you gain control of it.

5. If something happens _____, it happens immediately.

6. If you _____ two things, you keep them away from each other.

7. When you _____ how something works, you show how it works.

8. If you do something _____, you notice or realize that you are doing it.

9. If you _____ something, you believe it is true based on available facts.

10. If you have _____ to do something, you will not let anything stop you.

B Discuss these questions with a partner.

USING VOCABULARY

1. What kinds of jobs do you think require a lot of **determination**?

2. What characteristics can help a person deal well with a **crisis**?

3. What kinds of experiences can **alter** a person's life?

C When you feel scared, what do you do to calm down? Note your answers and discuss with a partner.

BRAINSTORMING

_____

_____

D Skim the reading passage. What do you think it will be about? Complete the statement below. Then check your idea as you read.

PREDICTING

I think the reading will be about _____ and about a

woman who _____.

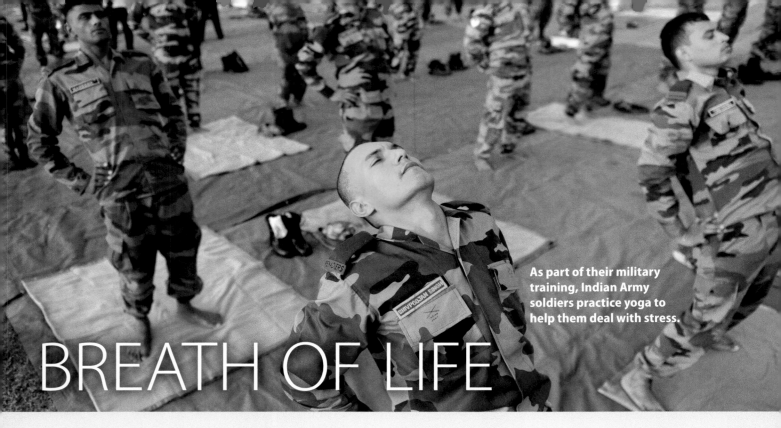

As part of their military training, Indian Army soldiers practice yoga to help them deal with stress.

BREATH OF LIFE

🎧 2.10

A When we encounter a stressful or frightening situation, our heart rate increases, our breath quickens, and our muscles become tense—these all happen naturally. In fact, for most of history, we have assumed that there is a line separating our natural, basic instinct and our learned behavior. But recent brain research has proved that our brain can change in structure and function throughout our life, depending on our experiences. So would it be possible to train our brain to control our "natural responses," such as to fear?

B One of the most surprising ways to control our fear response is breathing. Combat trainers, for example, use "tactical breathing" techniques to prepare FBI agents for crisis situations. These are basically the same concepts taught in yoga classes. One version that police officers learn works like this: Breathe in for four counts; hold for four counts; breathe out for four counts; hold for four; start again. How could something so simple be so powerful?

C The breath is one of the few actions that reside in both our somatic nervous system (which we can consciously control) and our autonomic system (which includes our heartbeat and other actions we cannot easily access). So the breath is a bridge between the two. By consciously slowing down the breath, we can slow down the primal fear response that otherwise takes over.

D One scientific study demonstrated how rhythmic breathing can actually alter the brain. Sara Lazar, an instructor at Harvard Medical School, scanned the brains of 20 people who meditate for 40 minutes a day. When she compared their brain images with those of nonmeditating people of similar ages and backgrounds, she found a significant difference. The meditators had 5 percent thicker brain tissue in the parts of the brain that are used during meditation—that is, the parts that handle emotion regulation, attention, and working memory, all of which help control stress.

E Studies such as those conducted at Harvard suggest that meditators—like deep-breathing police officers—may have found a way for us to evolve past the basic human fear response. With training, it may be possible to become better prepared for a life-or-death situation.

A SURVIVOR'S STORY

F In January 2000, photographer Alison Wright, 45, was riding a bus in Laos when it was struck by a logging truck. According to medical professionals, she should have died that day. Wright's **determination** to live—combined with her ability to regulate her fear response—enabled her to defy the odds.

G "When the truck hit, I slammed my head hard. I know it sounds cliché,[1] but all I could see was a bright white light—I had to ask myself if I'd died. The impact **instantly** broke my back [and] ribs; my left arm plunged through the window and was shredded to the bone; … my diaphragm[2] and lungs were punctured; my heart, stomach, and intestines tore loose and actually lodged in my shoulder.

H When I came to,[3] I looked around the bus, which was on its side, and the endorphins[4] kicked in. I pushed apart the seats that pinned me down and managed to pull myself out of the bus and crawl out onto the road. Then I realized how difficult it was to breathe, and I started to think about my situation in very matter-of-fact terms. Like, I remember not wanting to cry and waste any water with my tears, and I checked to make sure I had my wallet so that if I died, people could ID me.

[1] If an idea or a phrase is **cliché**, it has been used so much that it is no longer interesting.

[2] Your **diaphragm** is a muscle between your lungs and stomach that is used for breathing.

[3] When you **come to**, you regain consciousness.

[4] **Endorphins** are chemicals that occur naturally in the brain and that can block the feeling of pain.

"I knew that if I was going to survive, I had to calm myself down and get my breathing under control."

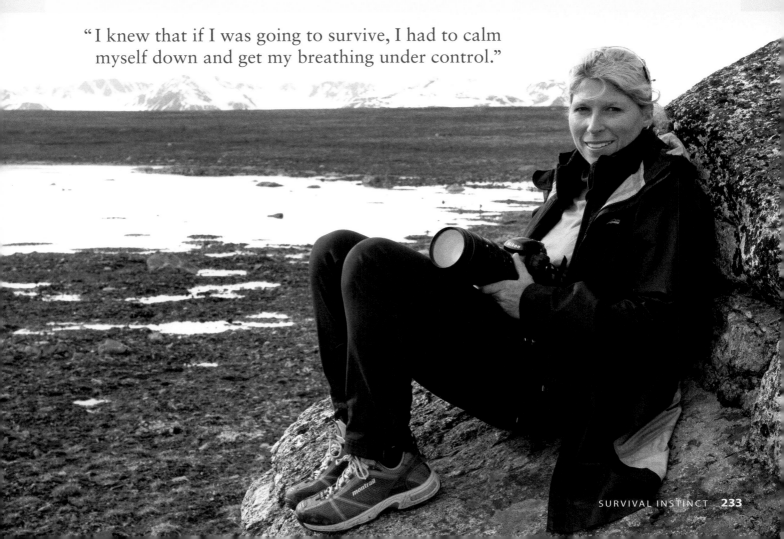

I knew that if I was going to survive, I had to calm myself down and get my breathing under control. I'd studied meditation and yoga for years, both of which focus on breathing techniques. I was able to call on that experience to calm my breathing and, as a result, calm myself. I remember looking at the bamboo moving in the wind around me, and waiting for help, just focusing on my breaths.

I was eventually rescued that day by a passing aid worker, who drove me seven hours to a hospital. Back home in San Francisco, though, I faced new challenges. Physically, I had to totally rebuild my muscles, which had atrophied[5] after four months in bed. Doctors told me I should accept the fact that my life would never be the same. Obviously, they didn't know me. When one told me I'd never have abdominal muscles[6] again, I worked toward doing sit-ups. I eventually did a thousand a day. Every morning I'd wake up and put my feet on the ground and feel gratitude.

I set the goal of climbing Mount Kilimanjaro, which I did in 2004. For years, I suffered from post-traumatic stress disorder[7] and had horrible nightmares about the accident. But in 2005, I traveled back to Laos and rode the same bus route again. I realized then what a gift it was to be thrown into adversity[8] and come out on the other end. "

[5] If a part of the body has **atrophied,** it has weakened because of disease, bad nutrition, or injury.

[6] **Abdominal muscles** are the muscles in the stomach area.

[7] **Post-traumatic stress disorder,** or PTSD, is a psychological condition that can occur after a frightening or stressful experience.

[8] **Adversity** is a very difficult situation.

POSTSCRIPT

Following her rehabilitation, Alison Wright recorded her experiences in her memoir, *Learning to Breathe: One Woman's Journey of Spirit and Survival*. Wright's accident inspired her to set up a charity—the Faces of Hope Fund—that aims to "give back in some small way to the communities" that she photographs. Her first activity as the founder of Faces of Hope was to return with five doctors and $10,000 worth of medical supplies to the village and people in Laos that saved her life.

Wright visiting an earthquake victim in Haiti in 2010

UNDERSTANDING THE READING

A Match each paragraph from the first part of the passage (A–E) to its main idea.

_____ 1. Learning breathing techniques is one way to control our fear response.

_____ 2. We have long believed that there is a clear divide between our instincts and our learned actions, but this may not be the case.

_____ 3. Researchers have found that some breathing techniques are able to improve areas of the brain that help control stress.

_____ 4. Consciously controlling our breathing can affect other actions that we have less control over.

_____ 5. We may be able to train our brain to better deal with life-threatening situations.

B Complete the timeline of events from "A Survivor's Story."

a. She gets out of the bus.

b. She crawls to the road.

c. She hits her head and loses consciousness.

d. She uses breathing techniques to calm down.

e. She checks for her wallet.

f. She comes to inside the bus.

g. She notices that it is difficult to breathe.

A truck hits the bus Wright is riding in. — An aid worker spots her.

C Write short answers using information from the reading passage.

1. How did Alison Wright learn the breathing techniques that helped save her life?

_____

2. How was her recovery difficult? List two ways.

_____

_____

3. What did Wright achieve after recovering from her accident? List three things.

_____

_____

_____

D Which ideas from paragraphs A–E does Alison Wright's story illustrate? Check (✓) the two best answers.

☐ 1. People who meditate 40 minutes a day may have better memories than people who do not meditate.

☐ 2. Using yoga breathing techniques can help people control their fear response.

☐ 3. Rhythmic breathing can change the features of the brain.

☐ 4. Rhythmic breathing can help people control stress.

☐ 5. Breathing is part of both the somatic and autonomic systems.

E For each sentence below, underline the adverbial phrase and write *when*, *how*, or *why*.

1. _____ Combat trainers, for example, use "tactical breathing" techniques to prepare FBI agents for crisis situations.

2. _____ By consciously slowing down the breath, we can slow down the primal fear response that otherwise takes over.

3. _____ With training, it may be possible to become better prepared for a life-or-death situation.

4. _____ I was able to call on that experience to calm my breathing and, as a result, calm myself.

5. _____ Every morning I'd wake up and put my feet on the ground and feel gratitude.

F Read the quote by Alison Wright. Note your answers to the questions. Then discuss them with a partner.

"I realized then what a gift it was to be thrown into adversity and come out on the other end."

1. What does Alison Wright mean by being "thrown into adversity"? What does it mean to "come out on the other end"?

   _____

   _____

2. In what ways do you think she might feel her experience was "a gift"?

   _____

   _____

G How were Gerlinde Kaltenbrunner's and Alison Wright's responses to fear similar? Note two ideas. Then discuss with a partner.

_____

_____

Writing

EXPLORING WRITTEN ENGLISH

NOTICING

A Read the sentences and notice the underlined verbs. What action does each one describe? Match each sentence to a description.

a. Many people <u>had attempted</u> to reach the summit of Mount Everest, but no one actually succeeded until 1953.

b. After the accident, Wright <u>did</u> a thousand sit-ups a day in order to rebuild her muscles.

c. The snow conditions <u>were becoming</u> dangerous, but the team decided to continue anyway.

_____ 1. a series of events that occurred before another event happened

_____ 2. an event that was ongoing when another event happened

_____ 3. a habit that someone regularly performed in the past

LANGUAGE FOR WRITING Using Past Forms for Narratives

When you are writing a narrative, use past forms to describe events that have already happened.

Use the **simple past** to describe a single past event, a series of past events, or a past habit.

> *Back home in San Francisco, though, I **faced** new challenges.*

Use the **past continuous** to describe an ongoing event in the past.

> *In January 2000, photographer Alison Wright, 45, **was riding** a bus in Laos when it was struck by a logging truck.*

Use the **past perfect** to describe an event or events that happened before another event or time in the past.

> *All four **had attempted** K2 climbs before, but none **had** yet **reached** the peak.*

Use the **past perfect continuous** to give background information about an ongoing event that happened before another event or time in the past.

> *Kaltenbrunner **had been hoping** to ascend all of the world's 8,000-meter peaks, and her dream finally came true in 2011.*

B Circle the correct options to complete the paragraph below.

On October 1, Walter Mitchell, a young emergency helicopter pilot, [1] **had just completed** / **just completed** three months of rescue training. He usually [2] **arrived** / **was arriving** at work at 6 a.m., but this morning he [3] **received** / **had received** his first emergency call at 5 a.m. Two men [4] **hiked** / **had been hiking** in the mountains and were lost. One of the men [5] **fell** / **had fallen** and was injured. The situation was dangerous, as it [6] **snowed** / **was snowing**. This was Mitchell's first real emergency, and he was afraid. The fear [7] **had been making** / **was making** it difficult for him to think clearly. When Mitchell got to the helicopter, he [8] **sat** / **had sat** down and [9] **got** / **was getting** ready to fly. During his training, he [10] **learned** / **had learned** a breathing technique to help overcome his fear. He breathed in slowly for four counts, held his breath for four counts, and then breathed out slowly for four counts. After doing this a few times, he felt ready to face the day's challenge.

C Complete each sentence with a suitable past tense form of the verbs in parentheses.

1. Gerlinde and Ralf _____ (climb) together for several years before they _____ (decide) to climb K2 together.

2. Gerlinde _____ (attempt) to climb K2 six times before she finally _____ (succeed) on August 23, 2011.

3. Tommy Heinrich _____ (climb) up the mountain when an avalanche _____ (hit) him.

4. Gerlinde _____ (wait) at the summit for 15 minutes when Maxut and Vassiliy _____ (get) to the top.

WRITING SKILL Writing a Descriptive Narrative Essay

A descriptive narrative is a real-life story about a person or a group of people. It should tell the events of the story in sequence—the order in which they happened. Like other essays, a descriptive narrative has a clear beginning, middle, and end. Use the following guidelines as you plan and write a narrative essay.

- The beginning, or the introductory paragraph, should introduce the **setting** (the time and place of the story), the **character** (person) that the narrative is about, and the **conflict** (the problem or challenge the person faced). The introductory paragraph should also include a **thesis statement**. The statement can show what the reader can learn from the story, what the person learned from the experience, or what helped the person get through the conflict. Here is an example:

  The story of Gerlinde Kaltenbrunner's ascent to the top of K2 in the face of many obstacles shows what a person can accomplish with grit and determination.

- The middle, or the body paragraphs, should contain the details of the story's events **in sequence**. You can use time words and expressions such as *before*, *after*, *earlier*, *later*, *meanwhile*, *during*, *suddenly*, *eventually*, *after a while*, *when*, and *as soon as* to indicate the sequence of events.
- The end, or the concluding paragraph, should contain the **resolution**, or the outcome of the story.

Note: If you are writing a narrative about yourself, write it in the first person (using *I*, *me*, *we*). If you are writing about someone else, write it in the third person (using *he*, *him*, *she*, *her*, *they*, *them*).

D Make notes about "A Survivor's Story" in Reading 2. Then discuss your answers with a partner.

1. Is the narrative in the first person or third person? _____

2. What do you think was the main "conflict"—or challenge—Alison Wright faced?

   _____

3. Complete the sentences about the events in the story.

   a. Alison Wright was traveling on a bus in _____ in 2000 when an accident occurred.

   b. She broke her _____ and injured her organs badly.

   c. When she woke up, she realized she had to _____ if she wanted to live.

   d. She was rescued by _____ who drove her for

   _____ to a hospital.

4. What was the "resolution" to Wright's story?

   _____

5. What are some examples of time words used in these paragraphs?

   Paragraph G: _____

   Paragraph H: _____

   Paragraph J: _____

E Choose the best thesis statement for the descriptive narrative of Alison Wright's story.

1. In January 2000, photographer Alison Wright, 45, was riding a bus in Laos when it was struck by a logging truck.

2. According to medical professionals, Alison Wright should have died when the truck hit her bus.

3. Alison Wright's will to live—combined with her ability to regulate her fear response— enabled her to defy the odds.

WRITING TASK

GOAL You are going to write a descriptive narrative essay on the following topic:

Describe the true story of a person who overcame adversity or survived a dangerous situation.

BRAINSTORMING **A** Think of possible challenges or dangerous situations people could face. Go online to research stories of people who overcame or survived these difficult situations. Choose the story that interests you the most and note the following details.

- the survivor's name and background
- the survivor's challenge

PLANNING **B** Follow these steps to make notes for your essay.

Step 1 Note details of the survivor, setting, and conflict in the outline. Write your thesis statement describing what the survivor learned from the challenge.

Step 2 Write topic sentences for the body paragraphs. Each one should introduce a main event in the story. Note details for each event in chronological order.

Step 3 Note the resolution and write a summary statement.

OUTLINE

Introductory Paragraph

Survivor: _____

Setting: _____

Conflict: _____

Thesis Statement: _____

_____

Body Paragraphs

Topic Sentence 1 / Details: _____

_____

_____

Topic Sentence 2 / Details: _____

_____

_____

Topic Sentence 3 / Details: _____

_____

_____

Concluding Paragraph

Resolution: _____

Summary Statement: _____

_____

FIRST DRAFT **C** Use the information in your outline to write a first draft of your essay.

REVISING PRACTICE

The draft below is similar to the one you are going to write. Follow the steps to create a better second draft.

1. Add the sentences (a–c) in the most suitable spaces.
   a. His situation seemed hopeless, but his calm decision-making would help save his life.
   b. He realized that it had stopped him from falling an additional 600 feet down a steep slope.
   c. Andereggen had learned that day that when you are in a desperate situation, simply doing the next right thing can save your life.

2. Now fix the following problems (d–f) in the essay.
   d. Delete an unrelated detail in paragraph B.
   e. Correct a past form in paragraph D.
   f. Correct a past form in paragraph E.

A

On June 6, 2006, Michael Andereggen, an experienced climber, was climbing Mount Temple in Canada's Banff National Park with his climbing partner, Kyle Smith. After 18 hours of climbing, he suddenly slipped and fell 400 feet. _____

B

Andereggen woke up to find himself alone in the snow. His face was bruised, and his eyes were almost swollen shut. He was so exhausted that he could barely move his legs. He could not climb back up the mountain to find his friend. Weather conditions on the mountain can change rapidly.

C

Andereggen saw that the rope he was climbing with was still wrapped around his upper body. _____ When he pulled on the rope, it came loose from the rock that it was stuck on and he slid about six feet. That was when he realized that the best thing he could do was stay very still.

D

Eventually, Andereggen fell asleep. When he woke up, he found himself in wet clothes, lying in melted snow. He had realized that he probably wouldn't survive another 24 hours in these conditions. So he just did what he could to survive for as long as possible. He crossed his arms over his chest to keep warm, and flexed his leg muscles to keep his blood flowing.

E

The next morning, Andereggen heard a faint noise in the distance. He couldn't see very well, but he waved his arm in the direction of the sound. Eventually, he was hearing someone ask, "Are you all right?" It was a park employee. Andereggen was so relieved that he began to sob. _____

D Now use the questions below to revise your essay.

☐ Did you include details about the survivor, setting, and conflict in your introduction?
☐ Did you include enough details to explain the main events in your body paragraphs?
☐ Did you use time words to indicate the sequence of events?
☐ Did you include a resolution in your conclusion?

EDITING PRACTICE

Read the information below.

When using past forms in a descriptive narrative, remember to use:
- the simple past to describe events or habits in the past.
- the past continuous to describe an ongoing event in the past.
- the past perfect to describe something that happened before another event or time in the past.
- the past perfect continuous to describe an ongoing event that happened before another event or time in the past.

Correct one mistake with past forms in each of the sentences (1–5).

1. Wright is traveling in Laos when she was involved in an accident.
2. After the climbers had setting up their camps, they began their ascent.
3. Ralf had been explaining later that he was afraid he'd never see Gerlinde again.
4. She planned the climb for many years, and finally got the chance to do it in 2011.
5. Suddenly, Andereggen had been falling 400 feet down the side of the mountain.

FINAL DRAFT **E** Follow these steps to write a final draft.

1. Check your revised draft for mistakes with past forms.
2. Now use the checklist on page 253 to write a final draft. Make any other necessary changes.

UNIT REVIEW
Answer the following questions.

1. Whose personal experience in this unit did you find the most interesting? Why?

_____

_____

_____

2. How is an adverbial phrase different from a clause?

_____

_____

_____

3. Do you remember the meanings of these words? Check (✔) the ones you know. Look back at the unit and review the ones you don't know.

Reading 1:

☐ descend   ☐ expedition   ☐ fate
☐ gear   ☐ recall   ☐ sensation
☐ slope   ☐ summit   ☐ task AWL
☐ terrifying

Reading 2:

☐ alter AWL   ☐ assume AWL   ☐ consciously
☐ crisis   ☐ demonstrate AWL ☐ determination
☐ instantly   ☐ separate   ☐ take over
☐ version AWL

VOCABULARY EXTENSION   UNIT 1

WORD LINK *pre-*

Words that begin with the prefix *pre-* mean "before in time." For example, *previously* means "before the time period that you are talking about." *Pre-* can be added to some common root words. For example, *preview* means "to see a part of something before watching the whole thing."

Complete each sentence with the words below. One word is extra.

| predict | prepare | preschool | prevent | preview | previous |

1. It is a good idea to _____ some slides before giving a presentation.

2. Scientists are developing apps that can _____ a person's behavior better than a human can. For example, the app can tell if a customer will buy a product again.

3. For many entry-level jobs, no _____ experience is required.

4. To _____ conflict in a workplace, try to avoid aggressive behavior with your co-workers.

5. Movie companies often upload a short video online to give people a _____ of an upcoming movie and get them excited about it.

VOCABULARY EXTENSION   UNIT 2

WORD LINK *-ist*

Some nouns that end in *-ist* can refer to someone who works in a specific academic or professional field. An *archaeologist*, for example, works in the field of archaeology. In general, for words ending in a vowel or *-y*, drop the vowel or *-y* and add *-ist*.

Complete each sentence with the correct noun form of the underlined word.

1. Someone who writes <u>novels</u> is a _____ .

2. Someone who produces <u>art</u> is an _____ .

3. Someone who looks at how the <u>economy</u> works is an _____ .

4. Someone who provides <u>therapy</u> to other people is a _____ .

5. Someone who plays the <u>piano</u> as a job is a _____ .

VOCABULARY EXTENSION   UNIT 3

Below are some common expressions with the word *income*.

annual income: the amount of money you earn in a year

source of income: where you get your money from, e.g., a salary, investments, etc.

income tax: a percentage the government takes from your income in the form of taxes

disposable income: the amount of money you have left after paying taxes

income inequality: a situation where there is a difference in income levels between the highest and lowest earners

Complete each sentence with the expressions from the box above.

1. Rent from people living in property you own can be an additional _____.

2. In the United States, the gap between top earners and low-wage earners is very large. This _____ concerns some economists.

3. If your _____ is $100,000 a year and you have to pay _____ of 20 percent, your _____ is $80,000.

VOCABULARY EXTENSION   UNIT 4

WORD FORMS Changing Nouns/Adjectives into Verbs with *-en*

Some nouns and adjectives can be made into verbs by adding *-en*. The suffix *-en* means "to cause to be or have." For example, *threaten* means "to cause threats."

Circle the correct form of the word to complete each sentence.

1. Hurricanes **threat** / **threaten** many parts of the world.

2. Hurricanes gain **strength** / **strengthen** over warm waters.

3. After hurricanes make landfall, they usually **weak** / **weaken**.

4. Hurricanes often produce a storm surge—extremely high waves of seawater that cause coastal flooding. The storm surge produced by Hurricane Sandy had a **height** / **heighten** of over four meters.

5. A hurricane brings extreme clouds and heavy rainfall. After the storm passes, the sky **lights** / **lightens** and residents can start cleaning up.

VOCABULARY EXTENSION UNIT 5

Most words ending in -ive are adjectives, though some can also be used as nouns. For instance, *alternative* can be used as an adjective (*There is an alternative plan.*) or a noun (*The alternative won't work.*).

Read the sentences below. Label each underlined word as N if it is a noun or A if it is an adjective.

1. The <u>distinctive</u> design of the Eiffel Tower makes it a well-known icon worldwide.

2. One of the <u>objectives</u> of sustainable tourism is to manage tourist destinations in a way that preserves their original state.

3. The Mayan are <u>native</u> people who live in modern-day Mexico, Honduras, and Guatemala.

4. Many companies hire sales <u>representatives</u> to sell their products to customers.

5. Companies with a strong online presence have a <u>relative</u> advantage over those companies that do not.

6. Solar power is one example of an <u>alternative</u> energy source.

VOCABULARY EXTENSION UNIT 6

The prefix *mis-* means "wrong or bad." For example, *mislead* means "to make someone think of something that is wrong or untrue."

Circle the correct words to complete the paragraph.

While most graphs accurately [1] **represent / misrepresent** data, some graphs can contain [2] **leading / misleading** information. One reason for this is that the designer of the graph simply made a [3] **calculation / miscalculation** with the numbers. Another reason is that the designer may have used an inappropriate scale. This can cause people to [4] **interpret / misinterpret** the significance of the information in the graph. A final reason is that the designer may have incorrectly compared two pieces of data. This is a [5] **use / misuse** of data because it shows a correlation that doesn't really exist.

VOCABULARY EXTENSION   UNIT 7

Many expressions with *cut* can be used in business settings. For example, you can use *cut back* to talk about reducing the number of employees or the amount of waste. Below are some other expressions with *cut*.

cut across: to affect many similar businesses, industries, or groups

cut through: to solve or deal with a problem quickly

a cut above: a product that is better than another similar product

cut one's losses: to stop losing money by getting out of a business situation

cut corners: to produce a product quickly or cheaply (often with bad results)

cut one's teeth on: to learn something useful at the start of a process or career

Complete each sentence with the correct word from the box below. One word is extra.

across	back	corners	losses	teeth	through

1. During the recession, many companies cut _____ on hiring new employees.

2. After a large number of complaints about the product, the company decided to cut its _____ and stop producing any more of it.

3. Environmental problems often cut _____ many cities and countries.

4. Young sales representatives can cut their _____ on becoming familiar with products and customers. They then have the skills to become successful managers.

5. Some businesses want to cut _____ regulations that they think are preventing them from growing faster.

VOCABULARY EXTENSION   UNIT 8

Antonyms are words that are opposite in meaning. For instance, the words *narrow* and *wide* are antonyms.

Match each word to its antonym. Use a dictionary to help you.

a. natural   b. specific   c. minimum   d. rise   e. accept

_____ 1. reject   _____ 2. decline   _____ 3. general   _____ 4. artificial   _____ 5. maximum

VOCABULARY EXTENSION   UNIT 9

Adding an adjective before the word *language* can provide more information about the kind of language you are talking about. Below are definitions of common collocations with *language*.

native language: the language you learn from birth

body language: communicating through gestures or facial expressions

official language: the language used legally in a country or organization

foreign language: a language used in a different country from your own

technical language: words and terms mainly understood in a particular professional field

Circle the correct word to complete each sentence.

1. The **native** / **body** language of Brazil is Portuguese.

2. Learning a **native** / **foreign** language when you are an adult can be much harder than when you are a child.

3. The two **official** / **technical** languages of the International Olympic Committee are English and French.

4. Sometimes you can tell how someone is feeling by looking at their **body** / **foreign** language.

5. Specialized fields, such as computer programming, often have their own **official** / **technical** language.

VOCABULARY EXTENSION   UNIT 10

Adjectives that end in *-ed* often describe someone's feelings, e.g., *scared*. Adjectives that end in *-ing* describe the characteristic of a person, thing, or situation. For example, something that is *terrifying* makes someone feel *terrified*. Below are more examples of adjectives that can end in *-ed* or *-ing*.

confused—confusing   *irritated—irritating*   *tired—tiring*

relaxed—relaxing   *shocked—shocking*   *surprised—surprising*

Circle the correct adjectives to complete the paragraph.

My most [1] **terrified** / **terrifying** experience was when I went trekking with my friends. Our map app didn't work because there was no cell phone service. This made me [2] **irritated** / **irritating** because I thought the phone would work fine. The signs along the trekking path were [3] **confused** / **confusing**, so we ended up getting lost. We were also [4] **shocked** / **shocking** to discover that we had forgotten our water bottles. Fortunately, we found a stream and drank some water. This made us feel [5] **relaxed** / **relaxing** again. Then my friend spotted a path near the stream. We were all relieved when the path took us back to our car.

Independent Student Handbook

TIPS FOR READING FLUENTLY

Reading slowly, one word at a time, makes it difficult to get an overall sense of the meaning of a text. As a result, reading becomes more challenging and less interesting. In general, it is a good idea to first skim a text for the gist, and then read it again more closely so that you can focus on the most relevant details. Use these strategies to improve your reading speed:

- Read groups of words rather than individual words.

- Keep your eyes moving forward. Read through to the end of each sentence or paragraph instead of going back to reread words or phrases.

- Skip functional words (articles, prepositions, etc.) and focus on words and phrases carrying meaning—the content words.

- Use clues in the text—such as **bold** words and words in *italics*—to help you know which parts might be important and worth focusing on.

- Use section headings, as well as the first and last lines of paragraphs, to help you understand how the text is organized.

- Use context clues, affixes, and parts of speech—instead of a dictionary—to guess the meaning of unfamiliar words and phrases.

TIPS FOR READING CRITICALLY

As you read, ask yourself questions about what the writer is saying, and how and why the writer is presenting the information at hand.

Important critical thinking skills for academic reading and writing:

- **Analyzing:** Examining a text in close detail in order to identify key points, similarities, and differences.

- **Applying:** Deciding how ideas or information might be relevant in a different context, e.g., applying possible solutions to problems.

- **Evaluating:** Using evidence to decide how relevant, important, or useful something is. This often involves looking at reasons for and against something.

- **Inferring:** "Reading between the lines"; in other words, identifying what a writer is saying indirectly, or *implicitly*, rather than directly, or *explicitly*.

- **Synthesizing:** Gathering appropriate information and ideas from more than one source and making a judgment, summary, or conclusion based on the evidence.

- **Reflecting:** Relating ideas and information in a text to your own personal experience and viewpoints.

TIPS FOR NOTE-TAKING

Taking notes will help you better understand the overall meaning and organization of a text. Note-taking also enables you to record the most important information for future uses— such as when you are preparing for an exam or completing a writing assignment. Use these techniques to make your note-taking more effective:

- As you read, underline or highlight important information such as dates, names, and places.

- Take notes in the margin. Note the main idea and supporting details next to each paragraph. Also note your own ideas or questions about the paragraph.

- On a separate piece of paper, write notes about the key points of the text in your own words. Include short headings, key words, page numbers, and quotations.

- Use a graphic organizer to summarize a text, particularly if it follows a pattern such as cause-effect, comparison-contrast, or chronological sequence. See page 108 for an example.

- Keep your notes brief by using these abbreviations and symbols. Don't write full sentences.

approx.	approximately	→	leads to / causes
e.g./ex.	example	↑	increases / increased
i.e.	that is / in other words	↓	decreases / decreased
etc.	and others / and the rest	& or +	and
Ch.	Chapter	*b/c*	because
p. (pp.)	page (pages)	*w/*	with
re:	regarding, concerning	*w/o*	without
incl.	including	=	is the same as
excl.	excluding	>	is more than
info	information	<	is less than
yrs.	years	~	is approximately / about
para.	paragraph	∴	therefore

TIPS FOR LEARNING VOCABULARY

You often need to use a word or phrase several times before it enters your long-term memory. Here are some strategies for successfully learning vocabulary:

- Use flash cards to test your knowledge of new vocabulary. Write the word you want to learn on one side of an index card. Write the definition and/or an example sentence that uses the word on the other side.

- Use a vocabulary notebook to note down a new word or phrase. Write a short definition of the word in English and the sentence where you found it. Write another sentence of your own that uses the word. Include any common collocations (see *Word Partners* in the Vocabulary Extensions).

- Make word webs or word maps.

- Use memory aids, or mnemonics, to remember a word or phrase. For example, if you want to learn the idiom *keep an eye on someone*, which means "to watch someone carefully," you might picture yourself putting your eyeball on someone's shoulder so that you can watch the person carefully. The stranger the picture is, the more likely you will remember it!

Prefix	Meaning	Example
com- / con-	with	compile
con-	together, with	constitute
em- / en-	making, putting	empower, endanger
ex-	away, from, out	explode
in-	not	independent
inter-	between	interact
pre-	before	preview
re-	back, again	restore
trans-	across	transfer
un-	not	unclear
vid- / vis-	seeing	video, vision

Suffix	Part of Speech	Example
-able	adjective	affordable
-al	adjective	traditional
-ate	verb	generate
-ed	adjective	involved
-ent / -ant	adjective	confident, significant
-er	noun	researcher
-ful	adjective	harmful
-ive	adjective	inventive
-ize	verb	criticize
-ly	adverb	definitely
-ment	noun	replacement
-tion	noun	determination

TIPS FOR ACADEMIC WRITING

There are many types of academic writing (descriptive, argumentative/persuasive, narrative, etc.), but most types share similar characteristics. Generally, in academic writing, you should:

- write in full sentences.
- use formal English. (Avoid slang or conversational expressions such as *kind of*.)
- be clear and coherent—keep to your main point; avoid technical words that the reader may not know.
- use signal words or phrases and conjunctions to connect your ideas. (See examples below.)
- have a clear point (main idea) for each paragraph.
- use a neutral point of view—avoid overuse of personal pronouns (*I*, *we*, *you*) and subjective language such as *nice* or *terrible*.
- use facts, examples, and expert opinions to support your argument.
- avoid using abbreviations or language used in texting. (Use *that is* rather than *i.e.*, and *in my opinion*, not *IMO*.)
- avoid using contractions. (Use *is not* rather than *isn't*.)
- avoid starting sentences with *or*, *and*, or *but*.

Signal Words and Phrases

Use signal words and phrases to connect ideas and to make your writing more academic.

Giving personal opinions	Giving details and examples	Linking ideas
In my opinion, …	An example of this is …	Furthermore, …
I (generally) agree that …	Specifically, …	Moreover, …
I think/feel (that) …	For instance, …	In addition, …
I believe (that) …		Additionally, …
		For one thing, …

Presenting similar ideas	Presenting contrasting views	Giving reasons
Similarly, …	On the other hand, …	This is because (of) …
Both … and …	In contrast, …	This is due to …
Like … , …	While it may be true that …	One reason (for this) is …
Likewise, …	Despite the fact that …	
	Even though …	

Describing causes and effects	Describing a process	Concluding
Therefore, …	First (of all), …	In conclusion, …
As a result, …	Then / Next / After that, …	In summary, …
Because of this, …	As soon as …	To conclude, …
If … , then …	Once …	To summarize, …
	Finally, …	

Writing Citations

Below are some examples of how to cite **print sources** according to the American Psychological Association Style (see also *Language for Writing* in Unit 8 for information on citing websites).

Guidelines	Reference entry	In-text citation
For an **article**, include: the author's name, year and month of publication, article title, the name of the magazine/journal, and page references.	White, M. (2011, June). Brimming pools. *National Geographic*, 100–115.	(White, 2011) White (2011) says …
For a **book**, include: the author's name, year of publication, title of the book, the location of the publisher (if known), and the name of the publisher.	Hawking, S. (1988). *A brief history of time*. New York, NY: Bantam.	(Hawking, 1988) Hawking (1988) says …
If there are **two authors**, use & to list their names.	Sherman, D., & Salisbury, J. (2008). *The west in the world: Renaissance to present*. New York, NY: McGraw-Hill.	(Sherman & Salisbury, 2008) Sherman and Salisbury (2008) say …
For a **book that is not the first edition**, include the edition number after the title.	Turnbull, C. M. (2009). *A history of modern Singapore, 1819–2005*, (3rd ed.). Singapore: NUS Press.	(Turnbull, 2009) According to Turnbull (2009), …

TIPS FOR EDITING

Capitalization and Punctuation

- Capitalize the content words in titles. Don't capitalize articles such as *the* or prepositions such as *in* and *on*, unless they are the first word of a title (e.g., *The Power of Creativity*).

- Avoid using exclamation marks (!) to indicate strong feelings such as surprise or joy. They are generally not used in academic writing.

- Use quotation marks (" ") to indicate the exact words used by someone else. (*"Our pleasures are really ancient," says psychologist Nancy Etcoff.*)

Other Proofreading Tips

- Print out your draft and read it out loud. Use a colored pen to make corrections so you can see them easily when you write your next draft.

- Have someone else read your draft and give you comments or ask you questions.

- When using a computer's spell-check function, make sure you agree with the correction before you accept the change.

- Keep a list of spelling and grammar mistakes that you commonly make so that you can be aware of them as you edit your draft.

- Check for frequently confused words:

  - *there*, *their*, and *they're*
  - *its* and *it's*
  - *your* and *you're*
  - *then* and *than*

  - *whose* and *who's*
  - *where*, *wear*, *we're*, and *were*
  - *affect* and *effect*

  - *quit*, *quiet*, and *quite*
  - *write* and *right*
  - *through*, *though*, and *thorough*

EDITING CHECKLIST

Use the checklist to find errors in the second draft of your writing task for each unit.

	Unit				
	1	2	3	4	5
1. Did you use capitalization correctly, e.g., for the first word of a sentence, for proper nouns, etc.?					
2. Do your subjects and verbs agree?					
3. Are commas used in the right places?					
4. Do all possessive nouns have an apostrophe?					
5. Is the spelling of places, people, and other proper nouns correct?					
6. Did you check for frequently confused words? (see examples in the *Tips for Editing* section)					
7. Did you use appropriate signal words and phrases to introduce and connect ideas? (see examples in the *Tips for Academic Writing* section)					
8. For essays that require research and the use of information from external sources, did you cite all sources properly? (see examples in the *Writing Citations* section)					

	Unit				
	6	7	8	9	10
1. Did you use capitalization correctly, e.g., for the first word of a sentence, for proper nouns, etc.?					
2. Do your subjects and verbs agree?					
3. Are commas used in the right places?					
4. Do all possessive nouns have an apostrophe?					
5. Is the spelling of places, people, and other proper nouns correct?					
6. Did you check for frequently confused words? (see examples in the *Tips for Editing* section)					
7. Did you use appropriate signal words and phrases to introduce and connect ideas? (see examples in the *Tips for Academic Writing* section)					
8. For essays that require research and the use of information from external sources, did you cite all sources properly? (see examples in the *Writing Citations* section)					

GRAMMAR REFERENCE

UNIT 3
Language for Writing: Using the Simple Past and the Present Perfect

Simple Past

- describes completed actions or events in the past
- often used with time expressions, e.g., *yesterday*, *last week*

> The scientists **gave** a presentation about the research paper **last year**.
> (The presentation was completed at a specific time in the past.)

Present Perfect

1. describes past actions or events where the specific time is unimportant or unknown

> The scientists **have made** some interesting discoveries.
> (The discoveries are more important than when they were made).

2. describes actions or events that happened in the past and that may continue into the future

> The scientists **have given** several presentations about the project this year.
> (The scientists may give more presentations before the end of the year).

3. can be used with time expressions such as *for*, *since*, and *in the* + [time period] to describe actions or events that started in the past and continue to the present

> The project **has generated** a lot of media interest **in the past month**.

Past Participle Forms of Commonly Used Irregular Verbs		
become—become	fall—fallen	read—read
begin—begun	find—found	say—said
bring—brought	get—gotten	see—seen
build—built	give—given	speak—spoken
buy—bought	have—had	take—taken
choose—chosen	hear—heard	tell—told
do—done	know—known	think—thought
eat—eaten	make—made	write—written

UNIT 7
Language for Writing: Using Adjective Clauses

Adjective clauses (also known as relative clauses) give more information about subject and object nouns in the main clauses of sentences. An adjective clause contains a subject, a verb, and a relative pronoun. The adjective clause functions in a similar way to an adjective—it gives descriptive information about a noun.

> One <u>resource</u> **that is disappearing** is fresh water.

> The <u>author</u> **who wrote the article** has strong feelings.

> The Leonardo DiCaprio Foundation works on <u>issues</u> **that concern our planet**, such as climate change and wildlife conservation.

We use different relative pronouns to introduce different kinds of information.

Relative pronoun	Used for ...
that	people, things
which	things
who	people
whose	someone's belongings

Restrictive and Nonrestrictive Adjective Clauses

Restrictive adjective clauses give essential information about the noun. Do not use commas with restrictive adjective clauses.

> I read an article **that** didn't really change my mind.

> I read the article **that** you told me about.

Nonrestrictive adjective clauses give extra, or nonessential, information about the noun. Commas always set off nonrestrictive adjective clauses.

> Petroleum, **which** is a nonrenewable resource, is getting harder to extract.

> The author, **who** is a noted environmentalist, gave a lecture at the university.

UNIT 8
Reading Skill: Understanding Passive Sentences

An active sentence focuses on the subject (or the agent) of an action where the subject performs that action.

> The city government built the hospital last year.
> (The focus is on the subject the city government.)

A passive sentence focuses on the object (or the recipient) of an action. Use passive sentences when the agent is unknown or when the agent is unimportant in the context.

> The hospital was built last year.
> (The focus is on the object the hospital. It is not important to know who built it.)

Add by + the agent to passive sentences to show who did the action.

> A bionic eye was developed by Second Sight.

Passive sentences always include a form of be + the past participle form of the verb.

	Active	Passive
Simple Present	People still **use** Al-Zahrawi's instruments today.	Al-Zahrawi's instruments **are** still **used** today.
Simple Past	Luckily, no one **destroyed** his books.	Luckily, his books **weren't destroyed**.
Present Continuous	Surgeons **are studying** Al-Zahrawi's books today.	Al-Zahrawi's books **are being studied** today.

VOCABULARY INDEX

Word	Unit	CEFR Level	Word	Unit	CEFR Level	Word	Unit	CEFR Level
accumulate*	4	C2	crucial*	7	B2	gear (n)	10	B2
acquire*	9	B2	currently	7	B2	gender*	1	B2
affordable	4	C1	cut down on	7	B2	general	8	B1
aggressive	1	B2				generally	1	B1
alert (v)	4	C1	deadly	4	B2	generate*	7	B2
alter* (v)	10	B2	decline* (n)	8	B2	gesture (n)	6	C1
alternative* (n)	5	B2	deliberately	6	B2	get out	4	B1
ambitious	1	B2	demonstrate*	10	B2	growth	3	B2
analysis*	2	B2	dense	3	B2			
anticipate*	9	C1	descend	10	B2	harmful	5	B2
archaeologist	2	C1	destruction	4	B2	have to do with	6	B2
artificial	8	B2	detective*	2	B1	hazard (n)	4	C1
aspect*	3	B2	determination	10	B2	heal	2	B2
assume*	10	B2	determine	2	C1	highly	9	B2
attempt (n)	3	B1	die out	9	B2			
awareness*	5	C1	disaster	4	B2	identity*	2	B2
			discipline (v)	1	B2	income*	3	B2
basically	3	B2	distinctive*	5	C1	increasingly	3	B2
behavior	1	B1	downside	6	C1	industrial	3	B2
breakthrough	8	B2				instantly	10	B2
			earn a living	5	B2	intense*	1	C1
care for	1	B2	ecological	5	B2	interact	1	B2
carry out	2	B1	economy*	5	B2	interpret*	6	B2
civilization	8	B2	effectively	4	B2	inventive	8	-
collapse* (v)	4	B2	emit	7	C2	invest*	7	B2
combination	2	B2	emphasize*	6	B2			
combine	9	B2	enhance*	3	C1	landmark	5	C1
comfort (n)	5	B2	enriching	5	C1	lead to	9	B2
commit*	2	B2	entire	4	B2	limited	7	B1
competence	9	C1	eruption	4	C2	linguistic	9	C1
compile*	8	C1	establish	1	B2			
concentration*	3	B2	examine	2	B2	maintain*	5	B2
concept*	8	B2	exceptional	7	B2	major* (adj)	7	B2
conflict (n)	1	B2	exhaust (v)	7	C1	majority*	3	B2
consciously	10	B2	existing	8	B1	manage to	8	B1
considerably*	9	B2	expand*	9	B2	manual* (n)	8	B2
constitute*	9	C1	expedition	10	B1	mention (v)	2	B1
consume*	7	B2	experimental	8	C2	method*	8	B1
consumption*	3	C1	explode	4	B1	misleading	6	B2
context*	6	B2	express (v)	9	B2	moreover	2	B2
continuous	4	B2	extended family	1	B2	motivation*	1	B2
convert* (v)	7	B2				mystery	2	B1
convey	6	C1	fate	10	B2			
crack (n)	4	B2	faulty	6	B2	native (adj)	9	B2
crisis	10	B2	focus on*	7	B2	necessary	5	B1
critically	9	B2	forecast (v)	4	B1	neutral*	6	C1
criticize	1	B2	furthermore*	9	B2	nevertheless*	6	B2

Word	Unit	CEFR Level	Word	Unit	CEFR Level	Word	Unit	CEFR Level
objective* (adj)	6	B2	replace	1	B1	tend to	3	B2
objective* (n)	5	B2	replacement	8	B2	terrifying	10	B2
observe	1	B2	reveal*	2	B2	threaten	4	B2
obtain*	2	B2	roughly	9	B2	throughout	4	B2
official (adj)	5	B2	safety	3	B2	treat (v)	1	B2
partnership*	5	B2	sample (n)	2	B2	unclear	2	B2
perspective*	9	C1	seek	8	B2	universal	6	B2
phenomenon*	3	C1	sensation	10	B2	urban	3	B2
pioneer (n)	8	C2	separate (v)	10	B1	vanish	7	B2
political	9	B1	shrink (v)	7	B2	varied*	3	B2
practical	7	B2	slope (n)	10	B2	vast	4	B2
preserve	5	B2	social structure	1	B2	version*	10	B2
pressure (n)	4	B2	spiritual (adj)	5	B2	vision	6	B2
previously	1	B1	spread (v)	8	B2	vital	5	B2
productive	3	B2	spread out (v)	3	B2	worldwide	7	B2
propose	6	B2	stand out	6	B2			
prove	2	B1	statistic*	6	C1			
publication*	6	B2	status	1	C1			
rapidly	9	B2	suburb	3	B2			
rate (n)	9	B2	suffer from	2	B1			
recall (v)	10	B2	summit (n)	10	C1			
reduction	7	B2	survival	8	B2			
regulate*	7	C1	suspect (n)	2	B2			
reject* (v)	8	B2	sustainable*	5	C1			
related to	7	C1	take over	10	B2			
reliance*	6	C2	take place	8	B1			
renewable	5	C1	task* (n)	10	B2			

*These words are on the Academic Word List (AWL). The AWL is a list of the 570 most frequent word families in academic texts. It does not include the most frequent 2,000 words of English.

ACKNOWLEDGMENTS

The Authors and Publisher would like to acknowledge the teachers around the world who participated in the development of the second edition of *Pathways*.

A special thanks to our Advisory Board for their valuable input during the development of this series.

ADVISORY BOARD

Mahmoud Al Hosni, Modern College of Business and Science, Oman; **Safaa Al-Salim**, Kuwait University; **Laila Al-Qadhi**, Kuwait University; **Julie Bird**, RMIT University Vietnam; **Elizabeth Bowles**, Virginia Tech Language and Culture Institute, Blacksburg, VA; **Rachel Bricker**, Arizona State University, Tempe, AZ; **James Broadbridge**, J.F. Oberlin University, Tokyo; **Marina Broeder**, Mission College, Santa Clara, CA; **Shawn Campbell**, Hangzhou High School; **Trevor Carty**, James Cook University, Singapore; **Jindarat De Vleeschauwer**, Chiang Mai University; **Wai-Si El Hassan**, Prince Mohammad Bin Fahd University, Saudi Arabia; **Jennifer Farnell**, University of Bridgeport, Bridgeport, CT; **Rasha Gazzaz**, King Abdulaziz University, Saudi Arabia; **Keith Graziadei**, Santa Monica College, Santa Monica, CA; **Janet Harclerode**, Santa Monica Community College, Santa Monica, CA; **Anna Hasper**, TeacherTrain, UAE; **Phoebe Kamel Yacob Hindi**, Abu Dhabi Vocational Education and Training Institute, UAE; **Kuei-ping Hsu**, National Tsing Hua University; **Greg Jewell**, Drexel University, Philadelphia, PA; **Adisra Katib**, Chulalongkorn University Language Institute, Bangkok; **Wayne Kennedy**, LaGuardia Community College, Long Island City, NY; **Beth Koo**, Central Piedmont Community College, Charlotte, NC; **Denise Kray**, Bridge School, Denver, CO; **Chantal Kruger**, ILA Vietnam; **William P. Kyzner**, Fuyang AP Center; **Becky Lawrence**, Massachusetts International Academy, Marlborough, MA; **Deborah McGraw**, Syracuse University, NY; **Mary Moore**, University of Puerto Rico; **Raymond Purdy**, ELS Language Centers, Princeton, NJ; **Anouchka Rachelson**, Miami Dade College, Miami, FL; **Fathimah Razman**, Universiti Utara Malaysia; **Phil Rice**, University of Delaware ELI, Newark, DE; **Scott Rousseau**, American University of Sharjah, UAE; **Verna Santos-Nafrada**, King Saud University, Saudi Arabia; **Eugene Sidwell**, American Intercon Institute, Phnom Penh; **Gemma Thorp**, Monash University English Language Centre, Australia; **Matt Thurston**, University of Central Lancashire, UK; **Christine Tierney**, Houston Community College, Houston, TX; **Jet Robredillo Tonogbanua**, FPT University, Hanoi.

GLOBAL REVIEWERS

ASIA

Antonia Cavcic, Asia University, Tokyo; **Soyhan Egitim**, Tokyo University of Science; **Caroline Handley**, Asia University, Tokyo; **Patrizia Hayashi**, Meikai University, Urayasu; **Greg Holloway**, University of Kitakyushu; **Anne C. Ihata**, Musashino University, Tokyo; **Kathryn Mabe**, Asia University, Tokyo; **Frederick Navarro Bacala**, Yokohama City University; **Tyson Rode**, Meikai University, Urayasu; **Scott Shelton-Strong**, Asia University, Tokyo; **Brooks Slaybaugh**, Yokohama City University; **Susanto Sugiharto**, Sutomo Senior High School, Medan; **Andrew Zitzmann**, University of Kitakyushu.

LATIN AMERICA AND THE CARIBBEAN

Raul Bilini, ProLingua, Dominican Republic; **Alejandro Garcia**, Colegio Marcelina, Mexico; **Humberto Guevara**, Tec de Monterrey, Campus Monterrey, Mexico; **Romina Olga Planas**, Centro Cultural Paraguayo Americano, Paraguay; **Carlos Rico-Troncoso**, Pontificia Universidad Javeriana, Colombia; **Ialê Schetty**, Enjoy English, Brazil; **Aline Simoes**, Way To Go Private English, Brazil; **Paulo Cezar Lira Torres**, APenglish, Brazil; **Rosa Enilda Vasquez**, Swisher Dominicana, Dominican Republic; **Terry Whitty**, LDN Language School, Brazil.

MIDDLE EAST AND NORTH AFRICA

Susan Daniels, Kuwait University, Kuwait; **Mahmoud Mohammadi Khomeini**, Sokhane Ashna Language School, Iran; **Müge Lenbet**, Koç University, Turkey; **Robert Anthony Lowman**, Prince Mohammad bin Fahd University, Saudi Arabia; **Simon Mackay**, Prince Mohammad bin Fahd University, Saudi Arabia.

USA AND CANADA

Frank Abbot, Houston Community College, Houston, TX; **Hossein Aksari**, Bilingual Education Institute and Houston Community College, Houston, TX; **Sudie Allen-Henn**, North Seattle College, Seattle, WA; **Sharon Allie**, Santa Monica Community College, Santa Monica, CA; **Jerry Archer**, Oregon State University, Corvallis, OR; **Nicole Ashton**, Central Piedmont Community College, Charlotte, NC; **Barbara Barrett**, University of Miami, Coral Gables, FL; **Maria Bazan-Myrick**, Houston Community College, Houston, TX; **Rebecca Beal**, Colleges of Marin, Kentfield, CA; **Marlene Beck**, Eastern Michigan University, Ypsilanti, MI; **Michelle Bell**, University of Southern California, Los Angeles, CA; **Linda Bolet**, Houston Community College, Houston, TX; **Jenna Bollinger**, Eastern Michigan University, Ypsilanti, MI; **Monica Boney**, Houston Community College, Houston, TX; **Nanette Bouvier**, Rutgers University – Newark, Newark, NJ; **Nancy Boyer**, Golden West College, Huntington Beach, CA; **Lia Brenneman**, University of Florida English Language Institute, Gainesville, FL; **Colleen Brice**, Grand Valley State University, Allendale, MI; **Kristen Brown**, Massachusetts International Academy, Marlborough, MA; **Philip Brown**, Houston Community College, Houston, TX; **Dongmei Cao**, San Jose City College, San Jose, CA; **Molly Cheney**, University of Washington, Seattle, WA; **Emily Clark**, The University of Kansas, Lawrence, KS; **Luke Coffelt**, International English Center, Boulder, CO; **William C. Cole-French**, MCPHS University,

Boston, MA; **Charles Colson**, English Language Institute at Sam Houston State University, Huntsville, TX; **Lucy Condon**, Bilingual Education Institute, Houston, TX; **Janice Crouch**, Internexus Indiana, Indianapolis, IN; **Charlene Dandrow**, Virginia Tech Language and Culture Institute, Blacksburg, VA; **Loretta Davis**, Coastline Community College, Westminster, CA; **Marta Dmytrenko-Ahrabian**, Wayne State University, Detroit, MI; **Bonnie Duhart**, Houston Community College, Houston, TX; **Karen Eichhorn**, International English Center, Boulder, CO; **Tracey Ellis**, Santa Monica Community College, Santa Monica, CA; **Jennifer Evans**, University of Washington, Seattle, WA; **Marla Ewart**, Bilingual Education Institute, Houston, TX; **Rhoda Fagerland**, St. Cloud State University, St. Cloud, MN; **Kelly Montijo Fink**, Kirkwood Community College, Cedar Rapids, IA; **Celeste Flowers**, University of Central Arkansas, Conway, AR; **Kurtis Foster**, Missouri State University, Springfield, MO; **Rachel Garcia**, Bilingual Education Institute, Houston, TX; **Thomas Germain**, University of Colorado Boulder, Boulder, CO; **Claire Gimble**, Virginia International University, Fairfax, VA; **Marilyn Glazer-Weisner**, Middlesex Community College, Lowell, MA; **Amber Goodall**, South Piedmont Community College, Charlotte, NC; **Katya Goussakova**, Seminole State College of Florida, Sanford, FL; **Jane Granado**, Texas State University, San Marcos, TX; **Therea Hampton**, Mercer County Community College, West Windsor Township, NJ; **Jane Hanson**, University of Nebraska – Lincoln, Lincoln, NE; **Lauren Heather**, University of Texas at San Antonio, San Antonio, TX; **Jannette Hermina**, Saginaw Valley State University, Saginaw, MI; **Gail Hernandez**, College of Staten Island, Staten Island, NY; **Beverly Hobbs**, Clark University, Worcester, MA; **Kristin Homuth**, Language Center International, Southfield, MI; **Tim Hooker**, Campbellsville University, Campbellsville, KY; **Raylene Houck**, Idaho State University, Pocatello, ID; **Karen L. Howling**, University of Bridgeport, Bridgeport, CT; **Sharon Jaffe**, Santa Monica Community College, Santa Monica, CA; **Andrea Kahn**, Santa Monica Community College, Santa Monica, CA; **Eden Bradshaw Kaiser**, Massachusetts International Academy, Marlborough, MA; **Mandy Kama**, Georgetown University, Washington, D.C.; **Andrea Kaminski**, University of Michigan – Dearborn, Dearborn, MI; **Eileen Kramer**, Boston University CELOP, Brookline, MA; **Rachel Lachance**, University of New Hampshire, Durham, NH; **Janet Langon**, Glendale Community College, Glendale, CA; **Frances Le Grand**, University of Houston, Houston, TX; **Esther Lee**, California State University, Fullerton, CA; **Helen S. Mays Lefal**, American Learning Institute, Dallas, TX; **Oranit Limmaneeprasert**, American River College, Sacramento, CA; **Dhammika Liyanage**, Bilingual Education Institute, Houston, TX; **Emily Lodmer**, Santa Monica Community College, Santa Monica, CA; **Ari Lopez**, American Learning Institute, Dallas, TX; **Nichole Lukas**, University of Dayton, Dayton, OH; **Undarmaa Maamuujav**, California State University, Los Angeles, CA; **Diane Mahin**, University of Miami, Coral Gables, FL; **Melanie Majeski**, Naugatuck Valley Community College, Waterbury, CT; **Judy Marasco**, Santa Monica Community College, Santa Monica, CA; **Murray McMahan**, University of Alberta, Edmonton, AB, Canada; **Deirdre McMurtry**, University of Nebraska Omaha, Omaha, NE; **Suzanne Meyer**, University of Pittsburgh, Pittsburgh, PA; **Cynthia Miller**, Richland College, Dallas, TX; **Sara Miller**, Houston Community College, Houston, TX; **Gwendolyn Miraglia**, Houston Community College, Houston, TX; **Katie Mitchell**, International English Center, Boulder, CO; **Ruth Williams Moore**, University of Colorado Boulder, Boulder, CO; **Kathy Najafi**, Houston Community College, Houston, TX; **Sandra Navarro**, Glendale Community College, Glendale, CA; **Stephanie Ngom**, Boston University, Boston, MA; **Barbara Niemczyk**, University of Bridgeport, Bridgeport, CT; **Melody Nightingale**, Santa Monica Community College, Santa Monica, CA; **Alissa Olgun**, California Language Academy, Los Angeles, CA; **Kimberly Oliver**, Austin Community College, Austin, TX; **Steven Olson**, International English Center, Boulder, CO; **Fernanda Ortiz**, University of Arizona, Tucson, AZ; **Joel Ozretich**, University of Washington, Seattle, WA; **Erin Pak**, Schoolcraft College, Livonia, MI; **Geri Pappas**, University of Michigan – Dearborn, Dearborn, MI; **Eleanor Paterson**, Erie Community College, Buffalo, NY; **Sumeeta Patnaik**, Marshall University, Huntington, WV; **Mary Peacock**, Richland College, Dallas, TX; **Kathryn Porter**, University of Houston, Houston, TX; **Eileen Prince**, Prince Language Associates, Newton Highlands, MA; **Marina Ramirez**, Houston Community College, Houston, TX; **Laura Ramm**, Michigan State University, East Lansing, MI; **Chi Rehg**, University of South Florida, Tampa, FL; **Cyndy Reimer**, Douglas College, New Westminster, BC, Canada; **Sydney Rice**, Imperial Valley College, Imperial, CA; **Lynnette Robson**, Mercer University, Macon, GA; **Helen E. Roland**, Miami Dade College, Miami, FL; **Maria Paula Carreira Rolim**, Southeast Missouri State University, Cape Girardeau, MO; **Jill Rolston-Yates**, Texas State University, San Marcos, TX; **David Ross**, Houston Community College, Houston, TX; **Rachel Scheiner**, Seattle Central College, Seattle, WA; **John Schmidt**, Texas Intensive English Program, Austin, TX; **Mariah Schueman**, University of Miami, Coral Gables, FL; **Erika Shadburne**, Austin Community College, Austin, TX; **Mahdi Shamsi**, Houston Community College, Houston, TX; **Osha Sky**, Highline College, Des Moines, WA; **William Slade**, University of Texas, Austin, TX; **Takako Smith**, University of Nebraska – Lincoln, Lincoln, NE; **Barbara Smith-Palinkas**, Hillsborough Community College, Tampa, FL; **Paula Snyder**, University of Missouri, Columbia, MO; **Mary Evelyn Sorrell**, Bilingual Education Institute, Houston, TX; **Kristen Stauffer**, International English Center, Boulder, CO; **Christina Stefanik**, The Language Company, Toledo, OH; **Cory Stewart**, University of Houston, Houston, TX; **Laurie Stusser-McNeill**, Highline College, Des Moines, WA; **Tom Sugawara**, University of Washington, Seattle, WA; **Sara Sulko**, University of Missouri, Columbia, MO; **Mark Sullivan**, University of Colorado Boulder, Boulder, CO; **Olivia Szabo**, Boston University, Boston, MA; **Amber Tallent**, University of Nebraska Omaha, Omaha, NE; **Amy Tate**, Rice University, Houston, TX; **Aya C. Tiacoh**, Bilingual Education Institute, Houston, TX; **Troy Tucker**, Florida SouthWestern State College, Fort Myers, FL; **Anne Tyoan**, Savannah College of Art and Design, Savannah, GA; **Michael Vallee**, International English Center, Boulder, CO; **Andrea Vasquez**, University of Southern Maine, Portland, ME; **Jose Vasquez**, University of Texas Rio Grande Valley, Edinburg, TX; **Maureen Vendeville**, Savannah Technical College, Savannah, GA; **Melissa Vervinck**, Oakland University, Rochester, MI; **Adriana Villarreal**, Universidad Nacional Autonoma de Mexico, San Antonio, TX; **Summer Webb**, International English Center, Boulder, CO; **Mercedes Wilson-Everett**, Houston Community College, Houston, TX; **Lora Yasen**, Tokyo International University of America, Salem, OR; **Dennis Yommer**, Youngstown State University, Youngstown, OH; **Melojeane (Jolene) Zawilinski**, University of Michigan – Flint, Flint, MI.

CREDITS

Photos

Cover, iii KiskaMedia/iStock/Getty Images, **iv** (from top to bottom) Thomas Mangelsen/Minden Pictures, Kenneth Garrett/National Geographic Creative, Ricardo Ribas/Alamy Stock Photo, Anadolu Agency/Getty Images, Sergio Pitamitz/National Geographic Creative, **vi** (from top to bottom) © Monica Serrano, NGM staff; Tony Schicksource: Steven E. Platnick and Claire L. Parkinson, NASA Goddard Space Flight Center, Nick Kaloterakis/National Geographic Creative, David Crigger/Bristol Herald-Courier/AP Images, Gunter Marx/ Alamy Stock Photo, Joel Sartore/National Geographic Creative, **1** Thomas Mangelsen/Minden Pictures, **2** Thomas Marent/Minden Pictures, **5** Michael Nichols/National Geographic Creative, **6** Pressmaster/Shutterstock, **7** hypergurl/Getty Images, **11** Visions of America/Getty Images, **14–15** (t) Michael Fay/National Geographic Creative, **15** (br) Michael Nichols/National Geographic Creative, **16** Michael Poliza/National Geographic Creative, **21** Joel Sartore/National Geographic Creative, **25** Kenneth Garrett/National Geographic Creative, **26** (l) Razvan Ionut Dragomirescu/Shutterstock, **27** (l, tr, c, br) Jason Treat/National Geographic Creative, **29** Kenneth Garrett/National Geographic Creative, **30** Dan Suzio/Getty Images, **31** Kazuhiko Sano/National Geographic Creative, **35** imageBROKER/Alamy Stock Photo, **38–39** Kenneth Garrett/National Geographic Creative, **40** Kenneth Garrett/National Geographic Creative, **49** Ricardo Ribas/Alamy Stock Photo, **50–51** Mike Theiss/National Geographic Creative, **53** Robert Harding/Alamy Stock Photo, **54** Neilson Barnard/Getty Images, **55** John Tomanio/National Geographic, **57** Wangwukong/Getty Images, **58** Cengage Learning, **59** Graeme Robertson/Eyevine/Redux, **62** Michael Loccisano/Getty Images, **63** Rolf Hicker Photography/Alamy Stock Photo, **73** Anadolu Agency/Getty Images, **77** Tom Lynn/Getty Images, **78** © TEAM Network, **79** Glenn Bartley/BIA/Minden Pictures/Getty Images, **81** Joel Sartore/National Geographic Photo Ark/National Geographic Creative, **83** Zachary West/Army National Guard/Getty Images, **86** Rich Reid/National Geographic Creative, **87** Hernan Canellas/National Geographic Image Collection, **88–89** Hernan Canellas/National Geographic Creative, **90** Alejandro Tumas/National Geographic Creative, **92** Hernan Canellas/National Geographic Creative, **99** Sergio Pitamitz/National Geographic Creative, **100–101** Sean Pavone/Alamy Stock Photo, **103** Andrew Bain/Getty Images, **104** (tl) Mark Thiessen/National Geographic Creative, **104–105** Thomas Trutschel/Getty Images, **107** Norman Wharton/Alamy Stock Photo, **109** Jeff Greenberg/Getty Images, **112** Robert Harding Picture Library/National Geographic Creative, **113** © 3 Sisters Adventure, **114** Richard Nowitz/National Geographic Creative, **115** Jason Edwards/National Geographic Creative, **123** © Monica Serrano, NGM Staff; Tony Schick Source: Steven E. Platnick and Claire L. Parkinson, NASA Goddard Space Flight, **124–125** Ignacio Ayestaran/National Geographic Creative, **127** Albert Gea/Reuters, **133** (t) © Jer Thorp, (br) Smith Collection/Gado/Getty Images, **136** Robert Alexander/Getty Images, **137** (tr) Lonely Planet Images/Getty Images, **138** Lam Yik Fei/Bloomberg via Getty Images, **147** Nick Kaloterakis/National Geographic Creative, **151** Brendan McDermid/Reuters, **157** © Day's Edge Productions, **160** Danita Delimont/Alamy Stock Photo, **162** Chris Ratcliffe/Bloomberg via Getty Images, **171** David Crigger/Bristol Herald-Courier/AP Images, **172–173** Lynn Johnson/National Geographic Creative, **172** (bl) Stock Montage/Getty Images, (br) Sebastian Kaulitzki/Science Photo Library/Getty Images, **173** (bl) Kumar Sriskandan/Alamy Stock Photo, (br) Ricardo DeAratanha/Getty Images, **175** Science History Images/Alamy Stock Photo, **176** rosesmith/Shutterstock, **177** DEA/M. Seemuller/Getty Images, **181** © Aydogan Ozcan, **184** Justin Guariglia/XPACIFICA/National Geographic Creative, **185** Shizuka Aoki/National Geographic Creative, **186** Mark Thiessen/National Geographic Creative, **195** Gunter Marx/Alamy Stock Photo, **199** Sandy Huffaker/Getty Images, **201** © United Nations Photo Library, **205** Chris Rainier/Enduring Voices Project/National Geographic Creative, **208** Lynn Johnson/National Geographic Creative, **210** Lynn Johnson/National Geographic Creative, **219** Joel Sartore/National Geographic Creative, **220–221** Juan Velasco/National Geographic Creative, **223** Ralf Dujmovits/National Geographic Creative, **225** Gerlinde Kaltenbrunner/National Geographic Creative, **229** David Doubilet/National Geographic Creative, **232** Arun Sankar/Getty Images, **233** Alison Wright/National Geographic Creative, **234** Alison Wright/National Geographic Creative, **248** Mike Theiss/National Geographic Creative

Texts/Sources

5–7 Adapted from "Office Jungle Mirrors Primate Behavior" by Brian Handwerk: http://news.nationalgeographic.com/news/2005/09/0923_050923_ape_office.html; **14–16** Adapted from "Kings of the Hill?" by Virginia Morrell: NGM November 2002, and "Chimp "Girls" Play With "Dolls" Too—First Wild Evidence" by Brain Handwerk: http://news.nationalgeographic.com/

news/2010/09/101220-chimpanzees-play-nature-nurture-science-animals-evolution/; **29–31** Based on information from "Crime-Fighting Leech Fingers Perp": http://news.nationalgeographic.com/news/2009/10/091020-leech-robber-dna-video-ap.html, "Animal DNA Becoming Crucial CSI Clue": http://news.nationalgeographic.com/news/2006/12/061212-animals-CSI_2.html, and "Iceman Autopsy" by Stephen S. Hall: NGM November 2011; **38–40** Adapted from "King Tut's Family Secrets" by Zahi Hawass: NGM September 2010; **53–55** Adapted from "City Solutions" by Robert Kunzig: NGM December 2011, **62–64** Adapted from "Urban Visionary: One on One" by Keith Bellows: https://www.nationalgeographic.com/travel/traveler-magazine/one-on-one/urban-visionary/; **77–79** Adapted from "Scientists Seek Foolproof Signal to Predict Earthquakes" by Richard A. Lovett: https://news.nationalgeographic.com/news/2013/01/04-earthquakees-defy-prediction-efforts/, and "Birds May Have Sensed Severe Storms Days in Advance" by Carrie Arnold: https://news.nationalgeographic.com/news/2014/12/141218-birds-weather-tornadoes-science-animals-environment/, and additional information from "Wild Animals Can Help 'Predict' Earthquakes, Scientists Say": nbcnews.com, March 24, 2015; **86–90** Adapted from "When Yellowstone Explodes" by Joel Achenbach: NGM August 2009; **103–105** Adapted from "One on One: Jonathan Tourtellot" by Daniel R. Westergren: National Geographic Traveler November 2006; **112–114** Based on information from "3 Sisters Adventure Trekking": http://www.3sistersadventure.com/, and "Australia Through Aboriginal Eyes" by Francis Wilkins: http://news.nationalgeographic.com/news/2004/12/1210_041210_travel_australia.html; **127–129** Adapted from "The 'Rules' of Data Visualization Get an Update" by Geoff McGhee: https://news.nationalgeographic.com/2015/10/151016-data-points-alberto-cairo-interview/, and "A Quick Guide to Spotting Graphics That Lie" by Chiqui Esteban: https://news.nationalgeographic.com/2015/06/150619-data-points-five-ways-to-lie-with-charts/; **136–138** Adapted from "Even Graphics Can Speak With a Foreign Accent" by Chiqui Esteban: https://news.nationalgeographic.com/2015/06/2015626-datapoints-visual-cultures/; **151–153** Adapted from "Leonardo DiCaprio on Interviewing Obama, the Pope": NGM November 2016, and "Seven Things to Know About Climate Change" by Rob Kunzing (Research) and Ryan Williams (NGM Staff): NGM April 2017; **160–162** Adapted from "Nine Ways to Make a Difference": National Geographic EarthPulse State of the Earth 2010; **175–177** Adapted from "Lost History: the Enduring Legacy of Muslim Scientists, Thinkers, and Artists" by Michael Hamilton Morgan: National Geographic Books 2007, pp. 198–199; **184–186** Adapted from "Miracle Grow" by Josie Glausiusz: NGM March 2011, and "Nano's Big Future" by Jennifer Kahn: NGM June 2006; **199–201** Adapted from "English in Decline as a First Language, Study Says," by Stefan Lovgren: http://news.nationalgeographic.com/news/2004/02/0226_040226_language.html; **208–210** Adapted from "Languages Racing to Extinction in 5 Global 'Hotspots'" by Stefan Lovgren: https://news.nationalgeographic.com/news/2007/09/070918-languages-extinct.html, and "Vanishing Voices" by Russ Rymer: NGM July 2012; **223–225** Adapted from "K2: Danger and Desire on the Savage Mountain" by Chip Brown: NGM April 2012; **232–234** Adapted from "Alison Wright: Beating the Impossible": http://adventure.nationalgeographic.com/2008/08/everyday-survival/survivors-text/2

NGM = National Geographic Magazine

Maps and Infographics

26–27 Jason Treat/National Geographic Creative, **51** 5W Infographics, **64** 5W Infographics; source: Urban Observatory, **74–75** National Geographic Creative; source: Münchener Rückversicherungs-Gesellschaft, **100** (bl) 5W Infographics; source: Mastercard Global Destinations Cities Index 2016, **101** (br) 5W Infographics; source: Mastercard Global Destinations Cities Index 2016, **128** Cengage Learning; source: Mann, Bradley & Hughes, *Nature*, 1998, **129** (tl) Cengage Learning; source: Alberto Cairo, (tr) Cengage Learning, **131** (bl, br) Cengage Learning; source: U.S. Bureau of Labor Statistics, **137** (bl) Cengage Learning; source: Monica Serrano/National Geographic Creative, (br) Cengage Learning; source: National Geographic Partners, **142** Cengage Learning; **145** (c, b) Alvaro Valino/National Geographic Creative, **148–149** John Tomanio/National Geographic Magazine/National Geographic Creative, **152** (cr, br) Cengage Learning; sources: NOAA, Carbon Dioxide Information Analysis Center, **153** (tr, cr, br) Cengage Learning; sources: National Snow and Ice Data Center, Munich ReCatSERVICE, Bloomberg New Energy Finance, **161** 5W Infographics; source: National Geographic Maps, **196** (bl) National Geographic Maps, **196–197** National Geographic Maps © 2017, **200** Cengage Learning, **209** National Geographic Maps © 2017

INDEX OF EXAM SKILLS AND TASKS

The activities in *Pathways Reading, Writing, and Critical Thinking* develop **key reading skills** needed for success on standardized tests such as TOEFL® and IELTS. In addition, many of the activities provide useful exam practice because they are similar to **common question types** in these tests.

Key Reading Skills	IELTS	TOEFL®	Page(s)
Recognizing vocabulary from context	✓	✓	4, 9, 13, 18, 28, 42, 52, 66, 76, 81, 92, 116, 131, 140, 164, 188, 202, 227
Identifying main ideas	✓	✓	8, 10, 17, 32, 41, 57, 80, 106, 115, 132, 139, 154, 163, 178, 202, 211, 226, 235
Identifying supporting ideas	✓	✓	9, 10, 17, 18, 56, 57, 92, 107, 130, 139, 187, 202, 211, 235
Scanning for details	✓	✓	17, 32, 41, 42, 65, 80, 130, 139, 163, 164, 179, 202, 204, 211, 212, 228, 235
Making inferences	✓	✓	33, 42, 66, 81, 91, 155, 227
Recognizing pronoun references	✓	✓	82, 188
Understanding charts and infographics	✓		58, 66, 91, 130, 131, 155, 164, 202, 211

Common Question Types	IELTS	TOEFL®	Page(s)
Multiple choice	✓	✓	8, 65, 81, 91, 106, 154, 164, 187, 211, 226, 236
Completion (notes, diagram, chart)	✓		17, 18, 34, 41, 65, 80, 92, 107, 108, 116, 187, 212
Completion (summary)	✓		8, 80, 91, 163, 178, 187, 226
Short answer	✓		9, 33, 56, 66, 80, 91, 92, 107, 116, 131, 139, 140, 154, 163, 164, 179, 202, 203, 211, 235
Matching headings / information	✓		8, 32, 41, 56, 65, 115, 178, 235
Categorizing (Matching features)	✓	✓	8, 18, 32, 66, 106, 115, 139, 155
True / False / Not Given	✓		32, 41, 80, 154
Prose summary		✓	56, 130
Rhetorical purpose		✓	8, 178

Level 3 of *Pathways Reading, Writing, and Critical Thinking* also develops **key writing skills** needed for exam success.

Key Writing Skills	Unit(s)
Writing strong body paragraphs	1, 4, 7, 9, 10
Writing a strong introduction and conclusion	3, 10
Expressing and justifying opinions	6, 7
Giving reasons and examples	1, 5, 6, 7, 8, 9
Paraphrasing / Summarizing	2
Making comparisons	1
Describing problems and solutions	3
Explaining a process	4
Expressing agreement and disagreement	6, 9
Describing a graph or chart	6

Pathways	CEFR	IELTS Band	TOEFL® Score
Level 4	C1	6.5–7.0	81–100
Level 3	**B2**	**5.5–6.0**	**51–80**
Level 2	B1–B2	4.5–5.0	31–50
Level 1	A2–B1	0–4.0	0–30
Foundations	A1–A2		